P9-CJK-848

MANAGER'S NEGOTIATING ANSWER BOOK

GEORGE FULLER

PRENTICE HALL
Englewood Cliffs, New Jersey 07632

Prentice-Hall International (UK) Limited, *London*
Prentice-Hall of Australia Pty. Limited, *Sydney*
Prentice-Hall Canada, Inc., *Toronto*
Prentice-Hall Hispanoamericana, S.A., *Mexico*
Prentice-Hall of India Private Limited, *New Delhi*
Prentice-Hall of Japan, Inc., *Tokyo*
Simon & Schuster Asia Pte. Ltd., *Singapore*
Editora Prentice-Hall do Brasil, Ltda., *Rio de Janeiro*

10 9 8 7 6 5 4 3 2 1

Library of Congress Cataloging-in-Publication Data

Fuller, George
The manager's negotiating answer book / by George Fuller.
p. cm.
Includes index.
ISBN 0-13-155921-4 (case).—ISBN 0-13-155938-9 (pbk.)
1. Negotiation in business. I. Title.
HD58.6.F849 1995
658.4—dc20 95-1458
CIP

ISBN 0-13-155921-4
0-13-155938-9 (pbk.)

PRENTICE HALL
Career & Personal Development
Englewood Cliffs, NJ 07632

A Simon & Schuster Company

Printed in the United States of America

ALSO BY THE AUTHOR

Supervisor's Portable Answer Book, 1990, Prentice Hall
The Negotiator's Handbook, 1991, Prentice Hall
The Supervisor's Big Book of Lists, 1994, Prentice Hall
The First-Time Supervisor's Survival Guide, 1995, Prentice Hall

INTRODUCTION

Few people would deny that negotiating skills are essential for business success. However, for most middle managers and executives, negotiations aren't conducted often enough to learn all the tactics that professional negotiators employ on a daily basis. Furthermore, with a thousand and one other duties to perform, you lack sufficient time to sharpen your skills by reading several books, and perhaps taking a course or two on the subject.

Yet, on those occasions when you're called upon to conduct negotiations, the outcome can be crucial for both your career and your company. So even though the percentage of time you spend negotiating is relatively small, the stakes run disproportionately high. As a result, the ability to negotiate successfully is essential, even though it isn't the prime duty of your position.

On the other hand, it's difficult to justify spending a lot of time learning how to negotiate when it isn't something you do on a daily basis. In fact, reality probably dictates that you spend your time dealing with the crisis of the moment. So along comes the occasion when negotiations are called for, and you're left with little choice but to wing it and hope for the best.

Fortunately, it doesn't have to be that way, since you don't need to know all the gimmicks to be a successful negotiator. And knowing a lot of negotiation theory may enlighten your mind, but it certainly won't lighten your work load. Most negotiations aren't so complex and require only the need to overcome one or two stumbling blocks to reach a successful conclusion. "How do I get this guy to lower his price?" or "How can I get her to accept my offer?" are the sort of one-shot answers you need to solve most negotiation problems.

But even though you don't need to be a negotiation expert to succeed, you do need answers to a few basics. That, in essence, is what the *Manager's Negotiating Answer Book* is all about. It allows you to look up only the one or two answers you need to break a deadlock or to answer the one question you're wondering about before you begin to negotiate. In short, you don't need to spend a lot of time getting the information you need to negotiate successfully. All you have to do is look up the answer to your question in the appropriate section of the *Manager's Negotiating Answer Book*.

You might wonder how all this can be reduced to such simplicity. First, most negotiation problems in business revolve around a relatively limited number of issues. One of the most common examples is the price to be paid. Frankly, how you deal with that issue is basically the same whether you're buying or selling a vacant warehouse or a million dollars worth of inventory. The tactics for asking for and getting a fair price don't vary from one negotiation to the next. What's being negotiated may be different, but the process remains the same. Therefore, the answer to the question of how to get a fair price in negotiations will apply across the board.

The same principle applies to most of the basic elements for successful negotiations. For this reason, the answers in this book will readily solve your own negotiation problems as easily as they resolve the examples given in this book. As a result, you'll quickly and successfully be able to handle your negotiation hassles by simply looking up the answers to problems that are similar to yours.

On the other hand, the scope of the coverage is such that any negotiation problem you might reasonably face is dealt with. The only shortcuts taken were to avoid discussions of theory or long-winded anecdotal examples of successful negotiations. Who cares about that when you're busy trying to settle a negotiation dispute so you can get your other work done.

Beyond any other negotiating you may be called upon to do, there's one topic where negotiating successfully is guaranteed to be of great personal interest, and that's in negotiating the best deal you can when you're job hunting. Since this is a subject of considerable concern, you'll find a separate appendix to this book devoted exclusively to that topic. It is hoped that this career negotiating guide will serve you well in achieving your career goals.

This book was written with the sole purpose of providing an easy way for businesspeople to deal with a complex subject without getting bogged down in a lot of theory or irrelevant detail. Its fundamental goal is to serve as a working tool that will quickly and easily answer any negotiation questions you have. May it serve you well in that regard.

TABLE OF CONTENTS

CHAPTER 1
GETTING THE DEAL DONE QUICKLY AND SMOOTHLY 1

CHAPTER 2
NEGOTIATING DOLLARS AND CENTS 37

CHAPTER 3
OVERCOMING DIFFICULT NEGOTIATION TACTICS 81

CHAPTER 4
LAYING THE GROUNDWORK FOR NEGOTIATION SUCCESS 105

CHAPTER 5
PREPARING FOR PROBLEMS GREAT AND SMALL 133

CHAPTER 6
KEEPING NEGOTIATIONS ON TRACK 165

CHAPTER 7
MASTERING KEY NEGOTIATING SKILLS 189

CHAPTER 8
TRADING BACK AND FORTH TO MAKE THE DEAL 215

CHAPTER 9
DEVELOPING MUTUAL TRUST FOR SMOOTHER NEGOTIATIONS 243

CHAPTER 10
BRINGING NEGOTIATIONS TO A CLOSE 267

APPENDIX
MANAGER'S CAREER NEGOTIATING GUIDE 293

INDEX

CHAPTER 1

GETTING THE DEAL DONE QUICKLY AND SMOOTHLY

No one likes to think about a long and drawn-out negotiation that's loaded with hassles and frustration. On rare occasions, that may be unavoidable. But for the most part, using a few simple tools will allow you to achieve success when you sit down to negotiate with someone. These basics include setting your limits before you start to bargain, structuring your offer to give yourself some flexibility, and knowing the nonhassle ways to negotiate.

None of these things is complicated, but people often enter into negotiations without being adequately prepared. As a result, they negotiate poorly, which often results in a bad deal or no deal at all. And even when they're satisfied with the end result, the headaches of getting the deal done make it seem like it wasn't worth it.

The bottom line is that going into a negotiation session unprepared is like going into battle unarmed. In both cases, the opposition will win an easy victory. So let's look at some ways to win your next negotiation, and a good place to begin is by determining how strong your negotiation position is before you start to bargain.

NEGOTIATING FROM A POSITION OF STRENGTH

You have probably read somewhere that to be successful in negotiations you have to operate from a position of strength. The immediate image formed is to associate this with size. The theory is that a large company, or someone with greater financial resources, will automatically have an advantage when negotiating with smaller, or less financially viable, businesses. However, this is a blind assumption that doesn't necessarily hold true. Here's why.

Q: I've got a ten-person machine shop and I'm about to start negotiations with a much larger business to do some work for them. I'm worried though, since because of their size, I won't be negotiating from a position of strength. As a result, I'll be forced to accept the job at a price that won't give me any profit. Should I do that and hope that I become a valued supplier and then raise my price on the next go-around?

A: The first thing to do is change your attitude. If you are afraid of getting a bad deal before you even start, then you're setting yourself up to fail before you even begin. No one has to accept unfair negotiation terms and conditions. It's a voluntary act, so why would you knowingly accept work where you can't make a profit? Obviously, as you state, you hope to make it up with future business down the road. Is that just a dream—or a reasonable expectation based upon known facts? If it's merely wishful thinking, you should negotiate prices that will give you a profit now.

Q: The buyer says I'm a new supplier and they want to see how we do before giving us any more business. Therefore, don't I have to take the chance that more work will be coming down the road?

A: Of course, tell them that you understand that and that you're willing to take the initial order at a break-even price to prove you're a top-quality producer who can meet their needs. However, in return, insist that an option for additional work be included in the agreement. Include a price for the additional orders that gives you a reasonable profit. If they're leveling with you about future business, a priced option shouldn't be objectionable, since they're under no obligation to exercise the option. On the other hand, if you do a good job, they're more than likely going to exercise the option, since they have a reliable supplier and a price that's already negotiated.

Q: What if they balk at including an option?

A: Then tell them you're taking a big risk by doing the initial work at an unprofitable price, so if they aren't willing to commit to an option for future work, you will have to have a higher price for the initial order.

Q: This is what worries me to start with. If I start talking like that, won't they just go and find someone else? Isn't that why they're operating from a position of strength?

A: They are only operating from a position of strength because you are projecting the attitude of a beggar. You have to act like an equal to be treated like one. If you continually accept unprofitable business on future hopes, and nothing more, you will soon be out of business. That's not to say that such chances shouldn't be taken, but you have to be reasonably certain that future business will be forthcoming. To do this, ask yourself "Why is this company coming to me."

Do you offer them advantages that competitors don't? If not, they can just as likely go to someone else, and they're just doing business with you because they think they can get a bargain. If that's the case, on the next go-around, they will still be trying to stick you with doing work at an unprofitable level.

Q: That sounds good, but how do I put myself on an equal footing with a big company during negotiations?

A: Ask for and expect fair terms, and if you don't get them, be ready and willing to walk away without concluding a deal. If you're going to enter a negotiation expecting to get a bad deal, then you shouldn't be there in the first place. Your position of strength is as good as anyone else's the minute you decide not to accept an unreasonable offer. In fact, if someone wants to walk away from an agreement because you won't accept unfair terms, that's the best thing that could happen to you. Remember, if they're trying to shaft you now, you can't expect they're going to get religion down the road. So either get a fair deal at the start, or forget about the possibility of making a killing on future business.

Q: Are there any general rules for strengthening your negotiation position that I would find helpful?

A: Here are four simple steps you can take no matter what you're negotiating to give yourself a level playing field.

- Determine the maximum price you will pay if you're the buyer, or the minimum price you will accept as the seller before you begin to negotiate.
- Before you start to negotiate, decide what you will do if negotiations fail. In other words, what are your other alternatives?
- Be reasonable during negotiations, but don't give the impression you can be pushed around.
- Be ready to walk away once you are certain that a fair agreement can't be reached.

NOTE: The term "price" is used to describe the need to set the limits you will accept to reach agreement. However, the same principle applies to negotiations where money isn't involved. Whatever the subject matter of the negotiation may be, always decide before you begin how far you will go to reach an agreement. If you do this, you won't get stuck giving away more than you have to or, alternatively, receive less than you expected.

WHAT TO DO WHEN THE OTHER SIDE WON'T BUDGE

A frequent hurdle that has to be overcome in negotiations occurs when the other party simply sticks with a position and refuses to make any concessions to get a deal concluded. This can be a real deal-breaker if it's not handled properly. Yet, there's little to be gained by sitting there and talking yourself blue in the face trying to get the other party to be more flexible. Here are a few alternatives you can try to get the ball rolling again.

Q: I'm trying to conclude a real estate deal for expansion space for my business. The asking price is too high, but the other side won't budge. What should I do?

A: Your basic choices are these:

- Accept their inflated offer. This is exactly what the other side wants you to do, and this approach shouldn't even be considered unless you have unlimited resources and enjoy giving money away.
- Keep talking, trying to convince them to lower their price. If you have both the time and the patience, keeping the dialogue going might work in the long run, especially if the other party is just trying to test your staying power.
- In some situations, offer concessions in some area other than price as an incentive to get the other side to lower their demands. For example, perhaps you could offer to accelerate payment for the property. The specifics of a given situation will dictate what alternatives are available. The important point is to keep this in mind as a way to get a deal moving.
- Offer a compromise price somewhere between what is being asked, and what you have already offered to pay. This is a viable choice if you have room left to maneuver between your previous offer and the maximum amount you are willing to pay for the property. If so, raise your offer enough to be considered significant without going to your limit. If they still won't budge then you should be ready to follow the next alternative, which is:
- Lay your cards on the table, tell them their price is too high, conclude negotiations and tell them to call you if they are willing to accept your offer. Whether you do this before or after making a compromise offer is up to you, and that decision should be based largely on how the negotiations have proceeded up to this point. If the other party hasn't yielded on anything from the beginning, then it's not worth your while to try a compromise offer. If they are just stalling to get you to raise your price, the only way to truly find out is to call their bluff.

Q: It may make sense to say, "Call me when you're ready to be reasonable," but isn't there a good chance that will kill the deal?

A: If you're being asked to pay an unreasonable price, then you're better off if the deal is dead. But if the other party is just bluffing to get you to raise your offer, then they will be in contact with you. In fact, in many situations such as this, once a party makes it clear that they aren't going to agree to unreasonable terms, the other side will start to negotiate seriously.

Q: If I do call a halt to negotiations, I'm left waiting for the other side to get back to me. I need to arrange for additional space for my business, so I can't just sit and wait. How should I handle this?

A: You can do a couple of things. Start right away to consider securing space elsewhere for your business. You may even find a better deal. At some point, if you haven't heard from the other party, you can contact them. Say something such as, "I'm considering another piece of property for my business. I thought I'd give you an opportunity to lower your price before I go ahead." If the other party still won't budge, at least you know the deal is dead unless you want to pay the asking price. On the other hand, if the people you're negotiating with have any intention of lowering the price, they know that this is their last chance.

Q: My job requires me to do quite a bit of negotiating, and I frequently find those I'm doing business with quite unreasonable in terms of being willing to compromise to reach agreement. Am I doing something wrong?

A: You are to the extent that you worry about people being reasonable. What's reasonable to you may be quite unreasonable to someone else. You have to always keep in mind that the other party is looking out for their own interests, just as you are looking out for yours. People will move off their initial negotiation position only if they feel it is both *necessary and reasonable* for them to do so.

It might be reasonable for them to compromise somewhere between what they want and you want, but they aren't going to do so if they don't feel it is necessary. After all, if they think they can reach agreement on their terms, why should they accept anything less? Therefore, in any negotiation where you find the initial position of the other side to be unacceptable, you have to convince them that it's necessary for them to revise their position if they want to reach an agreement with you. On some occasions, this can be done through back-and-forth dialogue. At other times, you have to be ready and willing to show them that you'll take a hike rather than accept their offer.

Q: Why should I have to convince people that it's necessary to be reasonable? I've read that people should negotiate in good faith and that both parties should work together to reach an agreement they're both happy with. Why won't people do that?

A: You can call it good business, or you can call it good negotiating. You can even call it greed, or anything else you want. The fact is that the other party to a negotiation will work with you to reach agreement only to the extent that it serves their interests to do so.

In most business negotiations, the other side is interested in getting the best deal they can. This should also be your objective. The end result is generally something both sides can live with, but it's not a real bargain for either side. How that point is reached is largely irrelevant, but to blindly assume that someone is going to nonchalantly sit down at the negotiating table and say "Let's see what we can do to make us both happy" is naive.

If you want to be a successful negotiator, you had better start by looking out for your own interests, and let the other side worry about theirs. There are, of course, situations where a hang-up of some sort may develop and it's in the interests of both parties to work at coming up with alternatives to get around the hurdle. But even here, the other party isn't doing it because it's the right thing to do but, rather, because it's necessary to reach an agreement.

GETTING THE DEAL DONE QUICKLY

One of the frustrating aspects of conducting negotiations is that it can be a lengthy process of give-and-take before an agreement is finally reached. If you have neither the time, nor the inclination, to participate in the endless jockeying for position that typifies some negotiations, there are ways to make negotiation sessions short and simple.

Q: Usually, when I negotiate, a lot of time is wasted going from start to finish. Why can't people just get to the point and say, "Here's my position, what's yours?" Then they can quickly compromise if there's a variance in the respective positions.

A: There are several reasons why negotiations tend to drag on:

- One or both sides have inexperienced negotiators, and they tend to flounder around instead of getting to the point.
- One or both parties are indecisive and won't bite the bullet.
- One or both negotiators are dragging things out in an attempt to frustrate the other party into making unnecessary concessions.
- One or both sides enter negotiations unprepared and are playing it by ear as they go along.
- In a few instances, the subject matter of the negotiation may be so complex and the issues so involved that it's not possible to come to an agreement quickly.

Q: Most of my negotiations don't involve anything much more complex than establishing the price to be paid. What can I do to get people to wrap things up faster?

A: Right at the start, tell the other party you have no interest in playing negotiation games, and you intend to make your best offer right away. Give them a number that is close to the final figure you're willing to agree to, and ask them to be equally forthright. Even if they come back with a number that's relatively close, you should be able to close the gap without any difficulty. However, if they are way out of line, tell them that, and suggest that they take another look and get back to you. Be sure to set a deadline to convince them that you're serious.

Q: You said to give them a number close to my final figure. Why not just give them my best figure and be done with it?

A: Human nature more than anything. Most people aren't happy unless they believe their shrewd bargaining got you to up the ante. For this reason, no matter how good a first offer may be, it's usually not thought of as the best deal that's attainable. As the thinking goes, a first offer is just someone's starting point, and you have to haggle with them if you want to do better.

For this reason, even though you want to wrap things up in a hurry, leaving yourself a little room to maneuver gives you the flexibility to sweeten the deal a little if they come back and say your figure is a little out of line. Otherwise, you will be putting them in a "take it or leave it" situation, which may make it harder to wrap things up, which was your objective in the first place.

Q: I've tried in the past to lay my cards on the table right away, but the other party still drags things out? What can I do?

A: If you adopt a "Here's the best I can do, let's not play games" posture from the start and the other side isn't cooperative, you have to be ready to end discussions. Politely repeat your position, and tell the party you're negotiating with to contact you when they intend to get serious about reaching agreement. Otherwise, if you continue to engage in extended discussions that are going nowhere, you're just reinforcing the other negotiator's belief that your "serious" offer was just an opening offer. As a result, they may conclude that prolonged negotiations will result in getting you to improve your initial offer. However, once they see you are serious enough to break the discussions off, your point will be made.

Q: How quickly should I try to wrap things up when I enter a negotiation?

A: Once you have made your position known and have heard everything relevant that the other party has to say, the discussions then become more negotiation gamesmanship than anything else. It's at this point that you should bring the discussions to a conclusion. Of course, there are times when the subject matter of the negotiation, and/or the terms and conditions of an agreement, are complex and require lengthy discussions. There's also the opportunity for you to engage in a negotiation contest with the other party in trying to extract a better deal if the circumstances warrant it. However, for many business negotiations there's little to be gained by prolonging things.

NO-HASSLE WAYS TO NEGOTIATE

Many people find negotiations to be intimidating and feel insecure when having to bargain with others. This attitude is partly created by the myth of "supernegotiators" who supposedly get the best of every deal. It's also reinforced by the notion that to be successful at the negotiation table requires the skills of a hassle-creating haggler. The fact is that anyone can negotiate successfully if they enter negotiations adequately prepared, use a little common sense, and refuse to be rattled by the other negotiator's tactics.

Q: I've read a lot about supernegotiators, so why do you call it a myth?

A: There are a lot more "super self-promoters" than there are "supernegotiators." Every so often much is written about some wheeler-dealer who made a fortune in real estate or some other endeavor. The rationale for this success is attributed to the individual's negotiation skills. In reality, the success had nothing to do with the person's skills as a negotiator. They may have had good business judgment in a particular area, which led to a financial windfall. Or perhaps changed economic conditions, or even luck, resulted in someone's success.

Actually, some people who have been touted for their deal-making capabilities have later met with hard times. Did they lose their negotiation skills, or was their initial success the result of other factors that were arbitrarily attributed to their negotiation capabilities? In reality, a good negotiator doesn't seek publicity, since that only serves to make it more difficult to negotiate with others in the future.

Instead, a consistently successful negotiator is more likely to be a low-key individual who is in command of the facts and enters negotiations well prepared to support his or her position. Along with this, good negotiators are able to control their emotions and have the courage to say "No" rather than accept an unsatisfactory offer. These basics are something that you and anyone else can use to negotiate successfully.

Q: That sounds pretty simple, but I regularly negotiate with a guy I call Nick Slick who plays all kinds of games in an attempt to sway me into accepting something less than satisfactory terms. How can I avoid these hassles?

A: Since this happens regularly, you haven't let it be known that you're not willing to engage in endless haggling. When another negotiator tries to use his bag of tricks, you can stop him short by saying something such as, "Look Nick, I've laid my cards on the table, and I'm not going to spend three days trying to nickel-and-dime you to death. So why don't you give me your best offer now, and let's wrap this up." By phrasing it this way, you avoid accusing the other party of being the bottleneck, which will keep them from being defensive when you challenge them.

Most of the time, you will be able to get your point across and be able to conclude negotiations without difficulty. On occasion, negotiators may basically ignore you and go on with their game-playing routine. When this happens, you can let them know you're serious by threatening to end the discussions. If this fails, simply break off negotiations.

Usually, the other negotiator is just as anxious as you are to reach agreement. However, when you get someone who plays negotiation games, you have to be ready to walk away if you expect them to take you seriously.

Q: I've run into people who try to badger me into giving in by belittling what I'm saying, by getting angry, or by employing some other unsavory action. How do I deal with this?

A: By stating you're not going to sit there and take abuse. Threaten to leave, and if necessary say, "I've got to take a break here. When you're ready to calm down and discuss things rationally, let me know." Whatever you do, don't get emotional and take what is being said personally. The other party is hoping you will be badgered into making a careless mistake. As long as you don't lose your temper, that won't happen.

Q: I had a situation last week where the person I was negotiating with got angry, told me I wasn't willing to negotiate, and got up and walked out. The next day the person's boss called me, apologized, and offered to make a deal. Although it wasn't a reasonable offer we did get together and ultimately reached agreement. What happened?

A: You were subjected to a version of the good guy–bad guy tactic where the first negotiator is totally unreasonable and then someone takes over who is more understanding. Those who play this game hope to get a better deal by rattling you. Supposedly, you're so happy to be negotiating with someone who is reasonable that this will convince you to be more generous in the terms that you seek. This is nothing more than a tactic to hoodwink you into making concessions. From a financial standpoint, the second person isn't any better than the first. Just stick with your original position and ignore the role playing.

Q: **My job requires me to do a lot of negotiating with different people and companies. As a result, I don't know what type of tactics I will face when I negotiate with someone new. Are there any specific methods I can use to guarantee that all my negotiations will be hassle-free?**

A: There is no foolproof method that will guarantee you won't run into difficulty during any specific negotiation. The complexity of what's being negotiated can cause negotiations to become long and difficult. Besides this, individuals have good days and bad ones, and if you happen to be negotiating with someone who is in a foul mood, this may affect their attitude at the negotiating table. Other reasons for difficult negotiations include inexperience on the part of the other negotiator or the misfortune of dealing with someone who is by nature indecisive.

Nevertheless, there are some basic measures you can take that will help you conclude most negotiations with a minimum of trouble:

- Prepare your negotiation position before you begin to negotiate, including any concessions you will make to reach agreement.
- Decide if there are any negotiation issues that may cause difficulty. If there are, think about what can be done to resolve them.
- Be professional during negotiations and avoid anger. If you remain calm and businesslike, it will encourage the other party to do likewise.
- Keep the discussion moving toward reaching an agreement. If the discussions wander off course, ask a question or make a statement that will bring them back to the issue at hand.
- Be willing to accept a reasonable offer, rather than striving to squeeze the last nickel out of the deal. Overreaching not only makes it harder to reach agreement, but in extreme cases it can bring about complete failure to conclude an agreement.

HOW TO SET YOUR LIMIT AND MAKE IT STICK

One of the most important parts of your negotiation strategy is to establish the limit on what you will accept to conclude an agreement. In many business transactions this is the highest price you are willing to pay as the buyer or the lowest price you will accept as the seller. If you don't do this before you begin to bargain, you will often end up paying more than you had planned. Of course, deciding your price beforehand doesn't do you any good unless you can subsequently negotiate a deal for that amount. Let's look at how to set your limits and successfully defend them after negotiations begin.

Q: Setting your price sounds real good, but that doesn't work for me. I'm a buyer in a manufacturing company, and most of the items I handle are bought regularly to meet manufacturing schedules. Frequently, I encounter situations where the seller tells me there has been a price increase. This leaves me in a "take it or leave it" situation. So for me, it isn't a question of establishing a price I will accept but, rather, determining if the price offered is reasonable. If the increase is small, I'll accept it without question, which is usually what happens. Is there anything I can do about this, since I feel I'm being nickel and dimed to death?

A: You can try something short term, which may work, but your greatest chance for controlling this sort of situation is to take some long-term measures. This type of buy-sell relationship results when you have been dealing with certain suppliers for a period of time. In these situations, it's much easier for a supplier to raise prices, since it's not easy to just drop a reliable supplier, especially if a price increase is small.

In the short term, you can ask for justification for the price increase. Unfortunately, in many situations the reasons given can't be easily challenged, at least not without spending a lot of time and effort to do so. Furthermore, frequently the price increase is justifiable. For these reasons, most of the time small price increases go unchallenged. Frankly, from a practical standpoint, it's not worth the effort in the short term to try and reduce the price.

For the most part, when you are hit with one of these small price increases, you can argue that it's not justified. Of course, this depends on how badly the supplier wants your business, as well as the availability of alternative sources. If you can convince the supplier that the increase will be detrimental to obtaining future business from you, the supplier may relent. Other than that, unless you're in a position to quickly obtain quotes from other sources, you're stuck with the increase.

Q: What are the long-term measures you mentioned to control this problem?

A: The greatest threat to being stuck with absorbing price increases is when you don't have alternative sources to go to. To prevent yourself from being in this position, it's always wise to have more than one source for any item bought on a regular basis. The more competition there is, the better the deal you will get. Therefore, as a general rule, you should research alternative sources for any item which you buy repetitively. That way, you can buy these items on a competitive bid basis. Even if you still want to deal with one supplier, the fact that you have identified alternative sources will discourage your existing sources from trying to impose arbitrary price increases. This is very basic, but when you have been dealing with the same supplier for an extended period of time, the convenience can cause you to overlook the possibility of seeking alternative sources. It's basically the old "familiarity breeds contempt" argument, and it can lead a supplier into feeling you will readily swallow a price increase without much of an argument.

NOTE: It's worth noting that there are many more considerations in supplier relationships than just getting the best price. Quality and delivery are the most obvious factors that can't be ignored, but there are any number of other technical and administrative elements that can influence a supplier relationship. In fact, if a healthy cooperative relationship has been established, price negotiations will be a secondary consideration.

Q: Assuming that my negotiation position is fair, how can I reach agreement without exceeding the limit I have established.?

A: There are a number of specific techniques for accomplishing this, and they will be discussed at length in later topics. However, the essential key to achieving your objective when you negotiate is a willingness to refuse to accept anything less. This means you have to be willing to walk away without completing a deal if necessary. If the terms you have set for an acceptable agreement are fair, then you need to have the courage to call it quits. More often than not, people fail to do this when they are bargaining, and as a result, they pay more as a buyer or receive less as a seller.

GIVING YOURSELF SOME WIGGLE ROOM

Establishing your acceptable limits for reaching agreement go beyond setting specific terms and leaving it at that. If you enter negotiations with a rigid position, you don't give yourself any room to manuever. This can quickly deadlock a negotiation if the other party offers to make a concession to reach agreement, and in return expects you to do the same thing. If you started off by offering the limit of what you consider to be acceptable, then you have no room to move to reach agreement.

Q: What's wrong with giving someone a firm price as long as you tell them that?

A: If you aren't going to negotiate the price, then there's nothing wrong with stating that. However this should be made clear at the outset. All too often, so-called firm prices aren't really that at all. They are just a negotiation tactic to try and get someone to accept the price without any bargaining.

In any event, someone who takes a firm price position is limiting the number of potential prospects who are willing to accept the price as stated. In addition, if there are other terms and conditions to be agreed upon, the other party is likely to refuse to negotiate. The argument becomes simply, "If you're not willing to discuss price, then I'm not willing to discuss payment terms," or whatever other significant issue remains unresolved. A firm price position can take away the flexibility you need to reach agreement when several issues have to be settled.

Q: Isn't it a waste of time to haggle? Why not save time by giving your best price right at the start?

A: For one thing, leaving yourself a little wiggle room in your price will help you in negotiating other terms and conditions. For example, if you're the seller and you give the prospective buyer a firm price that is the minimum you will accept, the buyer may offer to pay something less. You, of course, have to refuse since you have already given your best price.

Without fail, the buyer will then accuse you of being unwilling to negotiate. In the buyer's mind, you're trying to coerce him into accepting an unreasonable deal. Furthermore, the buyer will inevitably feel he isn't getting a good deal, since he wasn't able to lower your price. This mind-set can exist even when the price is a good one.

There's no mystery about this at all. Whenever you're negotiating, unless the other party finds you willing to compromise, it's a given that your position will be seen as unreasonable. Everyone loves bargains, and unless the other side thinks they're getting one, it's unlikely they will reach agreement with you. Furthermore, the minute you state that the price isn't negotiable, the other party is likely to counter with their own list of nonnegotiables. When this happens, a deadlock is likely to result.

It's much easier in most cases to set your initial price above what you're willing to accept. This will give you the opportunity to trade off lowering your price for other concessions. The same holds true if you're the buyer. Making an initial offer somewhat less than what you're willing to pay will give you added flexibility in reaching agreement.

Q: How far should your initial price be set from the amount you are willing to accept?

A: Leave enough leeway to allow you to make a price concession, but your initial price should be a figure that's believable. There are no hard-and-fast rules, and the differential will largely depend upon the subject matter of the negotiation. For example, if you're selling an off-the-shelf item, your offering price may have to be firm, since it's obvious what the item sells for on the market. However, even here there is often room to maneuver based on the quantities being purchased, payment terms, a variance from the required specifications, or other variables.

For example, if the buyer attempts to get you to lower your price, simply state that the price is standard for the quantity being bought. However, if it's feasible, suggest that the price can be lowered if larger quantities are bought, better payment terms are offered, or whatever else will give you an equivalent or better deal.

Q: In my business, most of my negotiating involves matters other than price, since what the company sells is a standard item. Despite this, I'm always running into buyers who want me to lower my price. Furthermore, there just isn't any leeway to lower the price even if a larger quantity is bought. What's the best way to handle these situations?

A: Briefly explain why the price is firm, but don't waste a lot of effort doing this, especially if you're dealing with someone who should know the price is set. In this type of situation, the buyer is usually just using the firm price as a lever to get you to agree to a better deal on other issues. It's basically a smokescreen being used so the other negotiator can say something such as, "If you expect me to make full payment in thirty days, you should be willing to lower your price."

A good strategy to use in this and similar circumstances is to steer the discussion to the subject being negotiated, which in this case happens to be payment terms. Say something like, "We're discussing payment terms, Harold, not price." Then start talking about possibilities for reaching agreement on payment terms, or whatever else the issue might be.

In fact, whenever anyone wants to tie reaching agreement on one issue with other topics, your position should be that they aren't related. On the other hand, if it's to your advantage to do so, always assert that it's one deal being negotiated, so every term and condition is subject to negotiation.

Q: **Wait a minute. You're telling me that I should negotiate terms separately if it's to my advantage or to lump them together if it's not. That's great, but the other party may look at it the same way. What if they use this approach on me?**

A: If you're dealing with a savvy negotiator, that might happen. If not, you get to do it your way. If the other negotiator is on his or her toes, then you have to be ready to show why the condition you don't want to negotiate isn't related to what remains to be negotiated. Another approach you can take from the start of negotiations is to suggest that each issue be negotiated separately or, for that matter, as a total package, depending upon which strategy is best for you.

If you can get agreement, then you have solved this problem before you even begin to negotiate. The bottom line here is your ability to convince the other side to do it your way. If they agree, then you have a built-in advantage in getting the deal you want. If they don't go along with your suggestion, you may have to work a little harder to come away with a satisfactory deal.

Q: Usually my negotiations involve struggling to get a lower price than is offered. Right now, I have a situation where the price is unbelievably low. Perhaps I'm being paranoid, but I don't feel comfortable about it. Should I just accept it as a stroke of good luck and quit worrying?

A: If you do accept it, the odds are there will be problems down the road. Whenever you're negotiating to buy something and the price the other party offers is unreasonably low, you should exercise caution. Generally, there's a good reason for an exceptionally low price, and a few of the more common ones are the following:

- There's a problem with what you're buying that you don't know about. For example, a piece of land being purchased for business expansion may have drainage problems.
- The other company isn't doing well and needs the business. This might work out all right, but if the company should file for bankruptcy shortly after you sign an agreement, you may never get what you contracted for.
- The other party is deliberately offering a low price to get your business and is hoping to make it up on future work they do for you.
- The opposing negotiator is either careless and has made a mistake or knows the price is too low and plans to try and change the agreement at a later date.

It's all too easy to jump at the chance of getting what looks like a bargain. However, true bargains are hard to find. The more likely situation when something appears to be a bargain is that there are good reasons as to why a price is too low. If you run into one of these situations, it's sensible to chase down an explanation. How you do this will vary in individual cases.

At least initially, try to track the facts down without raising the issue with the other party. After all, you might discover a reason that will lead you to accept the proposed price. Incidentally, never overlook the fact that you may be basing your opinion of the price on information you have that the other party doesn't. For example, perhaps you know there is a major road planned for the area where you're buying land for plant expansion. If this fact is unknown to the other party, then the price is reasonable from their perspective, and you may indeed be getting a bargain.

On the other hand, you may do some checking on the financial viability of the company you're negotiating with and discover its financial situation is so poor the company is having difficulty meeting existing contractual commitments. If this is so, you obviously want to avoid making any commitment—or at least structure the agreement to adequately protect your interests.

EASY WAYS TO WORK AROUND AN IMPASSE

One of the keys to keeping your negotiations from bogging down is learning how to work your way around any impasse that develops. This involves using a little bit of intuition in recognizing when a particular issue may lead to an impasse. If you can spot a potentially troublesome topic early on during negotiations, you may be able to work around it before it becomes a potential deal-breaker. In fact, even before you start to negotiate, you may be aware of terms that are likely to be difficult to resolve. If so, you should consider what alternatives are available for reaching a compromise over the disputed topic.

Q: It seems that whenever I negotiate with a certain executive, an awful lot of time is spent trying to resolve issues that aren't that important. This person has a reputation for not being able to make decisions. How can I keep this bottleneck from making a big deal out of every minor detail we discuss?

A: Negotiations often are deadlocked as much by individual personalities as by actual issues that the negotiating parties can't agree on. Some people think they have to debate every minor point from every conceivable angle. This is particularly true with indecisive individuals. By disputing everything you say, in their minds they hope to justify whatever is agreed to on the basis of having gone to the utmost to negotiate an agreement. In some circumstances, they may hope their stubbornness will bring someone else in to negotiate in their place. If you sense someone is indecisive, say something like, "What do you think we should do here?" when they dispute an inconsequential point. The last thing an indecisive person wants to do is make a decision. If you start taking this approach, they may stop objecting to everything for fear you will ask them how to handle the issue.

In instances where you are negotiating with someone and it appears that their indecision will prevent an agreement from being reached, if it's feasible, you may want to go over their head and negotiate with someone at a higher level. Be sure to assess the practical politics of doing this, since you don't want to alienate the negotiator if you have an ongoing business relationship.

When it comes to personalities who drag negotiations out, don't overlook the fact that you may be dealing with a negotiator who is deliberately doing this. The objective is to cause you to become impatient and, they hope, agree to things you wouldn't do if the discussions were moving along at a more sensible pace. Always keep in mind that patience is not only a virtue, but also a money saver when you're at the negotiating table.

Q: **Is there any way I can head off a potential deadlock before I even start to negotiate?**

A: You can't always know beforehand what issues are most important to the other party. However, if you take some time to plan your negotiation strategy before you begin, you may be able to pinpoint issues that can be potential problems. For those items on which you can anticipate some difficulty in reaching agreement, think about what possible alternatives can be suggested to resolve the issue. Then, if during negotiations you reach a sticking point over one of these topics, raise the alternatives as a way around the issue.

It's sometimes assumed that price is the only major issue that can cause problems in trying to reach agreement. However, there are often many other items that can be equally important to the other party. It may be payment terms, delivery dates, or anything else that for one reason or another is significant enough to cause a deadlock.

Q: **Our company is looking to acquire smaller firms in our field and has been negotiating with the owner of one small business without success. What I can't understand is the reluctance of this individual to agree to our offer, since we're offering far more than the company is worth and the individual admits his business has outgrown his ability to manage it. What are we doing wrong?**

A: Plenty, if you think that money is more important than anything else to everyone who ever started his or her own business. If you had thought the thing through before you started negotiations, one issue that should have come up was the emotional involvement of this person to the business he started. What you probably have to address here is that even though the owner logically knows the business has outgrown him, he has emotional ties to the business that make it difficult for him to sell at any price.

Your solution may be to offer the owner a position where he will still be able to work with the business even though he will no longer own it. If this doesn't move things off dead center, you may be facing a situation where the owner just isn't ready to part with his business. If so, you might as well accept the fact that a deal can't be made at this time. However, if you make an effort to break off negotiations in a cordial manner, you may be able to purchase the business at a later date.

Q: What's the best way to handle an impasse during negotiations?

A: There are a number of measures you can try. The simplest is to suggest that the issue causing difficulty be set aside for further discussion at a later time. Then go on to reach agreement on the other terms of the proposed agreement before going back to the sticking point. This can make it relatively easy to resolve the difficult issue for several reasons. First, with everything else settled, there's more at stake in reaching agreement. Second, agreeing on everything else may in some way have eliminated the major problems that were initially causing the impasse. Third, the intervening period of time may have enabled you or the other party to come up with a creative way to work around the issue.

You may also suggest that negotiations adjourn so that both parties can reassess their positions on the issue that's in dispute. If you're going to do this, be sure to set a time and place for resuming discussions. As an offshoot of this approach, if you are convinced that the other negotiator is being totally unreasonable, you can unilaterally break off negotiations and tell the other party to contact you if they are willing to change their position. Sometimes just the suggestion alone will cause a stubborn negotiator to suddenly become more conciliatory.

Another approach for overcoming a bottleneck is to discuss the issue in detail so you fully understand the problem from the perspective of the other side. After doing this, if the concerns of the other party appear to be legitimate, try working together to brainstorm alternatives for working around the difficulty. Of course, there may be times when an issue is such that agreement can't be reached. If so, then you have to recognize this and end negotiations without an agreement being reached. This is far preferable to making a concession that you know to be unreasonable just for the sake of completing the deal.

HOW TO TELL WHEN "NO" MEANS "MAYBE"

Whenever you're negotiating don't assume that because the other negotiator says "No" to something you propose that this is a definitive answer. Frequently, negotiators do this to get you to accept what they have proposed, or at least force you to offer something that's more acceptable than your previous position. However, if you refuse to take "No" for an answer, the other party may become more flexible about discussing your suggestions. Of course, sometimes "No" means just that, but on other occasions it really means "Maybe." The only way to find the difference between the two is to test the waters. Always keep in mind that if you routinely accept everything you hear at face value at the negotiating table, you're setting yourself up to be taken advantage of. Therefore, an inquisitive mind is a distinct asset when you negotiate.

Q: **If I propose something during negotiations and the other party says it's unacceptable, what can I do?**

A: You can start by asking the other party to explain what's wrong with what you have proposed. This forces people to be specific in their objections to your offer. Often, the initial response will take the form of generalized statements such as, "I can't make a profit at that price" or "Those delivery dates are unreasonable." Don't accept this sort of vague rejection when it's made. Instead, ask questions that force the other person to provide a detailed explanation. Doing this will allow you to test the validity of the objections to your offer. It will also allow you to rebut imprecise and inconclusive answers. This type of approach not only puts the other person on the defensive, but it also allows you to show why your position makes more sense.

Another advantage of doing this is that it may reveal ways you can suggest a compromise that will satisfy the objections to your original proposal. For example, if you offer to buy items at a certain price that the other side refuses to accept, when you probe into the matter, you may discover that by relaxing the specifications for the item, you can get the price you want. There are any number of possibilities for compromise that may arise once you get the other party to expand on his or her reasons for refusing to accept what you propose. This will never become clear if you just accept an initial "No" as the last word on the subject.

Q: If I'm negotiating with someone, and after considerable discussion they still refuse to budge, what should I do?

A: If it's feasible, go on to discuss other matters. If not, just keep talking with the objective of getting the other party to change their mind. However, once you have reached the point where it's obvious they won't give in, you have a decision to make. It's either to offer them something better or break off the negotiations and leave the next move up to them. What you do here will depend upon where you stand in terms of alternatives if the negotiations should fail. If you have acceptable alternatives, then you're in good shape. If not, you have to reassess your position and decide whether you can make a better offer that you can live with.

Q: I'm a midlevel manager who doesn't do any negotiating outside of my company. In fact, it's a decidedly secondary topic with me. Nevertheless, I am concerned with knowing how to negotiate with my boss and others. In particular, how do I deal with my boss when she says "No" to one of my requests, since I obviously can't grill her on why she won't agree with me?

A: Negotiating with a boss requires a little more subtlety than when you're negotiating a business agreement with outsiders. After all, if you value your job, you can't candidly probe into why your request is being turned down. Nevertheless, this doesn't mean you have to tacitly accept the refusal. The trick here is to think through beforehand what arguments you can make to support your position. Then, you have to try and slant these themes in such a way that it's to your boss's advantage to grant your request. The more you can demonstrate that it's good for the boss to give you what you want, the better the chance of your being successful. As for the specific approach to take, it will vary according to the subject matter of your request.

Q: **Well, the hardest task I have is trying to negotiate a decent pay raise for myself. Since I obviously can't quit on the spot, what can I argue about here when she says "No"?**

A: When you present your case to the boss, you should be prepared to show how your efforts have cut costs, increased productivity, or contributed positively to some other definitive measure the boss can relate to. This approach gives your boss something to justify the pay raise. The importance of doing this goes beyond your boss. After all, for the boss to grant your request, she may have to seek approval at higher levels. For this she needs justification. Unfortunately, a busy boss doesn't have a lot of time to sit down and go through this exercise. Therefore, it's far easier to refuse your request, possibly with some bromide such as saying, "Let's look at this again in six months." However, if you supply the facts in your pitch for a raise, then this obstacle is removed.

Even if you don't get immediate agreement, making a solid case now will make it that much easier if you are given a future promise. When the time rolls around, be prepared to trot out your initial figures along with your most recent achievements. A boss may turn down a good pitch the first time around, but if it's repeated at a later date, there's more likelihood it will be acted upon.

Q: **Another major area I have difficulty in negotiating with my boss is trying to get the resources I need to do my job. All I ever hear is, "We're trying to cut costs, Matt, so you'll have to do the best with what you have." How do I work around this argument?**

A: As cleverly as possible. Here, as when you're looking for a pay raise, you have to give your boss plenty of justification. Fortunately, in this area, it's a lot easier to do. For one thing, your arguments become more believable, since your personal gain isn't involved—except to the extent that additional resources will make your job easier.

What you want to do is show the boss the direct benefits of agreeing to your request. For example, if you're looking for additional help, provide facts and figures showing how the additional personnel will increase profits or cut costs for the company. The better you're able to do this, the more successful you will be in getting what you want.

If you're looking for equipment rather than people, you may want to show how the additional equipment will eliminate the need for more employees. In fact, if you can show that the equipment will reduce existing labor requirements, you will probably get approval faster than you dreamed was possible.

SETTING THE STAGE FOR A SWIFT ACCEPTANCE

As was mentioned earlier in this chapter, there are a number of different reasons why negotiations can take longer than necessary to reach agreement. However, whatever the obstacles to a quick agreement, there are a few techniques you can use to help speed things along. Basically, these include the use of deadlines or incentives to motivate the other party to settle with you sooner rather than later.

Q: If I give someone a deadline for accepting my offer, won't they think I am just bluffing to get them to agree to my terms?

A: If you just say something such as, "My offer is good until tomorrow at 5:00 P.M.," then your ultimatum may be viewed as a negotiation tactic and not be taken seriously. However, you can work around this problem by attaching a specific reason to your need for setting a deadline. The reason you give isn't important as long as it's something that is believable. It could be the expiration of a financing deadline by your bank or even something as simple as catching your flight home if you're out of town.

Another good way to encourage a quick settlement is to state that you have another offer waiting in the wings. What you want to do is suggest that if agreement can't be reached by a certain time, then you will have to accept the other offer. Of course, there may even be situations where this is true, but even if it isn't, you can imply that it is. However, unless you have alternate sources to go to, or can otherwise run the risk of the deal falling through, don't fake it with this approach. If you do, and the other party calls your bluff and ignores your ultimatum, you won't have too much credibility if the deadline passes and you continue to negotiate.

Q: Why should I have to resort to tactics such as deadlines to get an agreement finalized? Won't the other party have just as much interest in reaching a speedy conclusion?

A: Most people want to get their business transactions wrapped up without delay.

However, sometimes it may be to the advantage of the other side to prolong the discussions. For example, if you're negotiating with a company whose production lines are operating at 100 percent of capacity to meet demand, there's no immediate imperative to bring new business in. As a result, it's worthwhile for them to take their time and try for a better deal than would be the case if they needed the business right away.

It may also be that the other negotiator senses you're anxious to complete the deal and is just stalling to obtain better terms from you. Anytime the other side knows there's a sense of urgency to complete an agreement, a skilled negotiator may try to take advantage of this opportunity to extract better terms. For this reason, you ordinarily don't want to let the other side know when you're in a hurry to complete a deal. Of course, there may be occasions when this is unavoidable.

Q: My problem is this: I frequently have to negotiate rush deals, and inevitably the people I negotiate with know about it, since I'm always looking for expedited delivery. I'm hesitant to use deadline techniques, as I don't have a good excuse to do so. What can I do to move things along under these circumstances?

A: Your situation appears to be one that is ideal for using incentives to motivate the other party to cooperate in reaching a rapid agreement. What you use as an incentive will vary with the specifics of your situation. It can be favorable payment terms, a commitment for future business, or even a better price.

Be careful though to directly link the incentive with completing a negotiated agreement by a specific time. Otherwise, the other negotiator will assume the more generous terms apply even if the agreement isn't concluded when you wanted it to be. The end result will be the other negotiator expecting to reap the benefits you offered for quick settlement, whether or not your time deadlines were met. This sort of a bind can cause the negotiation process to slow down even further than if you never offered the incentive in the first place. Consequently, if you offer an incentive for quick settlement, be emphatic about taking it back off the table if your conditions aren't met.

WHEN TO PROPOSE TRADE-OFFS TO REACH AGREEMENT

Whenever you negotiate, there will be a disparity between what you want and what the other party to the negotiation seeks to achieve. Otherwise, there wouldn't be anything to bargain about, and negotiations wouldn't even be necessary. Sometimes the only difference will be price, but on many occasions, there will be a number of minor and major issues that you and the other negotiator disagree on.

One of the best ways to move a negotiation along toward conclusion in such a situation is by trading off what you want on one issue against what the other negotiator is seeking on something else. Sometimes this is easy to do, since what may be significant to one party may not matter much to the other person. Your main concern here is to be careful that you don't trade off an item of great value for something meaningless.

Q: When is the appropriate time to propose trade-offs to the other party?

A: Until both parties have discussed their respective positions and the differences in both positions are identified, you don't have any basis for making trade-offs. For this reason, the time to consider making trade-offs is after you know what possibilities exist for doing this. In terms of a specific point in the negotiations, it's generally at the stage where you have several unresolved issues that both sides are pretty adamant about.

Nonetheless, during earlier stages of the negotiations, opportunities may arise for making trade-offs on specific topics. For example, if individual elements of cost are being negotiated and there are differences on a number of items, a handy solution is to trade off acceptance of what you're seeking in one category for the other party's position on another element. You might want to say something such as, "I'll accept your direct labor figures if you'll accept my figures for indirect costs."

Q: When I see the opportunity for a trade-off, should I mention it right away or wait and see what the other side does?

A: Generally speaking, you don't want to start making trade-offs until both negotiation positions have been identified and the entire range of trade-off possibilities is on the table. Otherwise, you could trade something off early on in the negotiations only to later discover that you may have been able to trade your position on that item for a more significant concession by the other party. Nevertheless, if you see an opportunity early on to trade your position on an issue for a concession by the other side that's of real importance to you, take advantage of it. After all, circumstances may be such later in the discussions that you're not able to do as well.

Q: Are there any gimmicks to watch for when making trade-offs?

A: The basic principle when you trade off a concession on a position you have taken in return for a concession on another issue is to get at least equal value. However, concessions aren't always of the nature that they can be quantified, so the exchange value isn't something that can always be converted to hard facts such as dollars and cents. The significant point is to attempt to gauge what you're giving up in return for what you're receiving.

There are a couple of points worth mentioning here. One is to be sure you pin down precisely what's being agreed to when concessions are traded. Otherwise, considerable disagreement can erupt at a later time if the negotiating parties aren't in agreement about prior trade-offs. It also should not be overlooked that the nice thing about trading concessions is when you can concede a point that isn't of major significance to you in return for something that is. This may also be true for the other party to the negotiations. As a result, both parties from their respective viewpoints are giving up virtually nothing for something substantial. It's trade-offs such as this that can make a negotiation a lot easier to complete.

Q: What if there aren't any obvious trade-offs that can be made, even though there are several issues that both parties disagree on?

A: If you get to the point where both sides are pretty well talked out and there are not obvious trade-offs that can be made to close the gap in the respective positions, it's time to think creatively. Since the only other option may be a deadlock that can't be resolved, it's worthwhile to brainstorm with the other party to see what compromises can be made. Often, by working together to jointly resolve differences, a final position can be worked out to which both parties can agree. The only real impediment to doing this is a reluctance to work the problems out together. However, when the alternatives are making hard choices to reach agreement or forgetting the deal entirely, it's time to put any idea of one-upmanship on the backburner.

Frequently negotiations break off without an agreement being reached because neither side was willing to concede anything of substance to reach agreement. Good negotiation requires the ability to compromise when it's necessary to do so. This doesn't mean you have to agree to something unreasonable, but it does require a willingness to be realistic. And a realistic negotiator knows that even though the terms of a deal aren't the best in the world, they are far preferable to no deal at all.

HOW USING CONCESSIONS CAN GET YOU A BETTER DEAL

Making compromises and trading concessions not only expedite reaching agreement, but they also prevent the sort of deadlock that results in negotiations breaking off without any agreement being reached. However, concessions have an added benefit in that you can sometimes use them to get a better deal than would otherwise be possible.

Q: **I don't understand how making concessions can give you a better deal than if you didn't have to make the concessions in the first place? After all, when you make a concession, you're settling for something less than what you originally hoped to get in terms of a deal. Can you enlighten me on this?**

A: First of all, you have to recognize that the original position you start with when you begin to negotiate isn't what you necessarily hope to end up with when negotiations are completed. Instead, your beginning position is the ultimate you would like to achieve. As a buyer you always want the lowest price you can get, while as a seller you're looking for the maximum price someone will pay. Realistically, if you look at it objectively, a deal that's fair to both parties falls somewhere between those two extremes.

This is generally true even when the subject matter of the negotiations doesn't involve money. In brief, no matter what someone is negotiating, they are always looking for the best deal they can get and this is their starting position when negotiating. However, it's not realistic to expect to achieve that goal, and how close you come to it will depend to a large extent on your ability to trade concessions.

For this reason, your original negotiating position when you begin to bargain is much more favorable than what you will eventually end up with under normal circumstances. Of course, there's always the possibility you may successfully negotiate final terms that are precisely those you started out with. The reasons this can happen are varied. Perhaps you do an exceptional job of negotiating, or else your opponent may be an inept bargainer. Maybe there are facts unknown to you that make your original negotiating position quite acceptable to the other side. Whatever the reason, you may get lucky and not have to make any compromises to conclude an agreement.

Nevertheless, the chances of getting a dream deal are remote. It's far more likely you will have to make some concessions at the bargaining table to get a completed agreement. And the crucial point is that if you go about making concessions the right way, you can get a far better deal than if you don't.

Q: How do I go about using concessions to my advantage when I negotiate?

A: First, before negotiations start, decide just how much you're willing to move from your original position to reach agreement. Furthermore, since the subject matter of most negotiations involves a number of issues large and small, take the time to decide which are the ones most important to you. Frequently, as negotiations are proceeding, other issues are raised during discussion which often form the basis for further concessions. In any event, the bottom line in making concessions is to know what you can and can't concede before you start. You should also decide which issues are impossible to compromise on. Let's look at how this can be done.

BACKGROUND

Laura K., a materials manager for a large manufacturer, is planning to negotiate with a supplier for 20,000 gizmos. The item is new so historical cost data are unavailable, but engineering estimates prepared for her indicate the item should cost between $1.00 and $1.25 a unit. She also wants the total quantity delivered in 60 days. However, she can get by with a minimum of 5,000 units by then and an additional 5,000 every 30 days until the full order of 20,000 units has been delivered. Her payment terms will be payment in 30 days with no discount.

CONCESSION POSSIBILITIES

Based on the parameters established for the proposed buy, Laura knows her maximum price will be $1.25 a unit. So she has flexibility to make price concessions between the $1.00 per unit she will initially offer and $1.25. She must have at least 5,000 units in 60 days to go into production, but beyond that she has some flexibility to adjust the delivery schedule. She also has flexibility to vary the payment terms if it becomes necessary to do so.

NONNEGOTIABLES

There are certain concessions Laura can't make:

- She can't pay more than $1.25 per unit.
- She must have 5,000 units delivered within 60 days.
- She has been told the specifications are firm and can't be varied.

Thinking about the proposed procurement before she starts to negotiate has given Laura a firm idea of what is and what isn't negotiable. This will allow her to make any necessary concessions to reach agreement without giving in on any of the items that are firm requirements.

Q: I now know how to decide beforehand what I can and can't concede. What I don't understand is how making a concession can get me a better deal. What does that mean?

A: As negotiations are underway you may find yourself and the other party to the negotiations disagreeing on a number of issues. This gives you the opportunity to try and trade off a point you are willing to concede in exchange for the other negotiator giving in on a point you disagree with. How skillful you are at doing this can influence how good a deal you reach.

In its simplest form, your objective should be to make a concession that doesn't have great significance to you for a substantial concession by the other party. In short, you're giving up very little to get a lot in return.

Q: That sounds great, but why would the other negotiator accept such a deal?

A: For one thing, issues that are in dispute don't necessarily have the same significance for both parties. Let's go back to the example of the gizmos being bought by Laura. She can be pretty flexible about payment provisions, so they're not of great significance to her. On the other hand, the other negotiator may place a high priority on favorable payment terms. Perhaps the negotiator's company doesn't have a great deal of financial liquidity and can't afford to finance the production of the gizmos. With this sort of situation, it's conceivable Laura could negotiate a better unit price in exchange for better payment terms.

When it comes to concessions, it's important to keep in mind that just because something is important to you doesn't mean it carries the same weight with the other party to the negotiations. And, of course, the reverse holds true. It follows that knowing what is important to the other negotiator in terms of priorities can give you a significant advantage when it comes to trading concessions.

Q: It makes sense to make minor concessions in exchange for receiving substantive concessions, but how can I tell what's of top priority to the other negotiator?

A: This will come up during the course of discussions. When you're trying to get the other negotiator to agree to something and you encounter stiff resistance, it's likely this is a substantial sticking point. Once you pinpoint these issues, it's easy enough to think about what you can trade off in the form of a concession in exchange for agreeing with the other party on an item they are adamant about. Negotiators will often give a lot of ground elsewhere to sustain their position on issues they don't have flexibility to bargain on. In fact, frequently you don't even have to probe too much to learn where the other negotiator has problems. Often, you will be told that for one reason or another a certain point isn't negotiable. Actually, there are even instances where you can get a better deal without even making a concession. All you have to do is be patient.

Q: It sounds like pie in the sky to be able to get a better deal without even having to give anything up in exchange. Just how can that be done?

A: It isn't always possible, but there are instances when the other negotiator wants to complete the deal by a certain date. If you know this, you may be able to drive a better bargain in exchange for reaching an early agreement. Typical situations where this occurs are when someone is trying to meet a sales quota or a company wants to book a big order by the end of the fiscal period. No one is foolhardy enough to give away the store to accomplish such a goal, but it makes it easier to get a better deal than you would under normal circumstances. Sometimes the other negotiator will admit to a self-imposed deadline and offer a concession on this basis. On other occasions nothing will be said, even though you're aware of the advantages of a quick deal to the other party. If you exercise a little bit of patience as the deadline approaches, you may be able to get a last-minute concession.

THE PROPER WAY TO CEMENT A DEAL

Sometimes the hardest part of completing a deal is wrapping it up at the end. There are a number of reasons for this. One is that both parties are sometimes reluctant to state that they are making their final offer. This is partly for fear of the other side not accepting the offer, which leaves little recourse other than to break off negotiations. Another reason is the hope, however small it may be, that continuing to negotiate will yield further gains.

It's worthwhile to take the initiative to close a deal when you have received an offer you can accept, and there's little or nothing of value left to discuss. Continuing negotiations beyond this point not only wastes time, but the longer discussions drag on the greater the likelihood that some sticking point will suddenly rear its head.

NOTE: Chapter 10 covers the details of what to do when an agreement is reached. In most business settings, concluding negotiations is only the first step in what has to take place before the agreement is actually signed by both parties. Here, the focus is on how to simply convey the message that it's time to wrap negotiations up.

Q: **I often run into situations where negotiations tend to drag on over relatively minor points at the end. I'm hesitant to try and wrap things up, since I feel I may kill the deal by refusing to continue to discuss some of these petty matters. Can you briefly discuss how to bring a deal to a conclusion?**

A: Sometimes you just have to take the bull by the horns and say something such as, "It looks like we have the workings of a deal. Let's summarize what we have agreed to." Then go on to sum up the points of agreement. More often than not, you won't get an argument from the other party. If the other side still wants to pursue some topic then you have given them an opportunity to say so.

Q: **What if I do this and the other negotiator wants to keep talking about some minor issue?**

A: You have to come right out and say something like, "Look Charlene, we've got everything wrapped up and you continue to nit-pick over a minor detail. If you don't want to agree with the deal we have, just say so and I'll be on my way." Usually this approach will snap someone to her senses, but indecision or some other unknown may cause the negotiator to balk at concluding the agreement. At this point, you are best served by bringing the meeting to an end and telling the other negotiator to call you if she changes her mind about settling the deal. Sometimes it takes something this drastic to demonstrate that you aren't going to change your position on anything else, so it's this deal or nothing. As a result, many times when you do this, you're likely to get a phone call in a day or so agreeing to the deal.

Q: What happens if a few days go by and I don't hear anything. Is the deal dead?

A: Not necessarily, but to confirm whether or not it is, contact the other negotiator and ask if he has changed his mind. He may suggest meeting again, and it's your option as to whether or not you want to do that. On the other hand, perhaps the deal is dead. If so, then go on to your other alternatives.

Although it's rare in most business transactions, there are occasions when negotiations that are apparently settled never result in a firm agreement. Lots of reasons such as intervening events can cause this. In any event, don't fret if this happens to you. You can only go so far toward reaching agreement, and once you have done that, it's better to know that a deal is dead sooner rather than later.

CHAPTER 2

NEGOTIATING DOLLARS AND CENTS

Most negotiations you encounter as a manager involve money either directly or indirectly. Naturally, if you're negotiating to buy or sell goods or services, price is a major factor in the discussions. However, money also becomes a consideration in many internal dealings you have with a boss, corporate staff, and even employees. If you're seeking resources such as new equipment, it's necessary to justify the cost involved. And when you negotiate starting salaries with a new hire or a pay raise with an existing employee, money again is at the heart of the issue. Beyond these matters, you may periodically have to prepare and negotiate budgets for operating your organizational unit.

When it comes to negotiating dollars and cents, one of the most difficult aspects is defending against the overworked challenge that the cost is too high. You have heard it a dozen times in a dozen variations such as, "Your budget is too high" or "That computer system costs too much." The ability to overcome these objections is the key to getting what you're looking for.

There are a number of different aspects to successfully negotiating money matters. First, you have to know how to react when you're challenged on the basis that something is too expensive. If you can prove otherwise, then you're well on your way to getting what you want. Another facet of negotiating money matters is knowing how to compromise to get the most you can out of the situation. A final side of price negotiations that can't be ignored when you're negotiating with buyers or sellers is knowing how to spot, avoid, and/or counter the many price-related tactics and ploys that are used. These issues are discussed in this chapter, and there's no better topic to begin with than knowing why good deals can go down the drain over money issues.

WHY GOOD DEALS TURN SOUR

One of the main reasons negotiations break off without reaching agreement is a failure to agree on price. There are a number of reasons for this:

- An unwillingness to compromise by one or both parties to the negotiation
- An honest, but incorrect, assessment of what constitutes fair value by either party
- An error in judgment by one of the parties that leads them to believe the other party will accept a higher or lower price than is justified
- An undue concentration on price to the exclusion of other aspects of the proposed agreement
- A lack of preparation by one or both parties that leaves them unable to convince the other side of the reasonableness of the price they are willing to buy or sell at

Q: The biggest hassle I find when I'm negotiating is that other people often want more than I'm willing to pay and I'm unable to get them to change their minds. As a result, the negotiations end in failure. This happens to me frequently. Is there something I'm doing wrong?

A: It could be one or a combination of the reasons just mentioned. However, the fact it happens so often indicates that it's likely you are the one causing the problem. First, are you being reasonable in setting the price you're willing to pay? We all know it's great to get a bargain, but the hard fact of life is that bargains are hard to come by. Most of the time, we have to settle for something a little bit less than what we would like. What this means is that as a buyer we may have to pay a little more than we want to. And as a seller, we have to frequently settle for a lower price than we would like to get.

Q: I'm usually the one doing the buying and I'm frankly looking to get a good deal. I figure if the other party realizes I won't pay more than I'm offering, they will lower their price rather than walk away without a deal. After all, something is better than nothing, isn't it?

A: Only a fool will accept an unfair price on the basis that something is better than nothing, and fools in business don't last very long. Although there's nothing wrong with trying to get the best price you can, once you realize the other party isn't going to accept your offer, it's time to do a little compromising.

Q: If that's the situation, how do I know when it's time to be more reasonable in terms of the price I'm willing to pay?

A: Once the discussions get to the point where the other side is about to pack it in rather than give in is a good time to get serious about offering to raise your price a bit. Of course, this depends upon the importance to you of making a deal. If you have readily available alternatives, you can refuse to budge and let the other party walk away. However, this isn't realistic in most business situations.

Q: I just failed to close on what I thought would be the most profitable sale I ever made for my company. It really looked like I had this turkey hooked into paying top dollar. He kept agreeing with my entire pitch. Then, at the last minute he offered to pay a lower price. It still would have been profitable, but since it looked so good up until then, I figured if I refused, he would accept my initial price. As it turns out, I'm the turkey who will probably be stuffed by my boss, since the other party just got up, said I was unreasonable, and walked out the door. I waited a couple of days to see if it was a bluff and then called the prospect on the phone. To sum it up quickly, he said, "The deal was over the minute you refused my counteroffer." What did I do wrong here?

A: Besides trying to be greedy, you also failed to judge the unwillingness of the other party to accept what was essentially too high a price. This is an area that can be a hidden trap if you're trying to extract top dollar and the other party isn't objecting to what you're saying. Not everyone plays games when they negotiate price. Instead some people will only make one counteroffer to a high price. If it's rejected, they call it quits rather than try to negotiate the price down.

This is one of the risks you face if you wait too long to move to a more reasonable position when you're looking for top dollar. Some people enjoy haggling over price, while others will just walk away. This is especially true where the other party has plenty of alternatives to buy what they want. With this sort of situation, it's easy for them to reject your price, since they are fully confident of getting what they want from someone who will be more reasonable.

Q: **My problem concerns price from the vantage point of salary. I asked Ms. P., my boss, for a substantial raise in pay. I thought it was justified, since I had been working long hours for three months on a very important project. The results turned out very well, and Ms. P. praised me long and hard for my accomplishments. As you know, you can't take praise to the bank, so this seemed a good time to make a pitch for a raise. To my surprise, she turned me down explaining that the company wasn't in a position to pay people in my position the salary I was asking. Don't you think she was being unreasonable, or did I just handle it wrong?**

A: Your problem may well have been that you are either misjudging your value to the company or you failed to properly prepare to present your case when you made a pitch for a raise. Of course, as you suggest, your boss may be unreasonable, but from what she said about the company not being able to pay what you're looking for, it seems to indicate your salary demands may have been out of line. This isn't to say you don't do a good job, but only that your price may not represent fair value to your employer.

Perhaps the company isn't in a financial position to pay you more money. Or perhaps you are asking for a higher salary than similar positions pay in the marketplace. These are things you should have found out before you asked for a raise. Whenever you're negotiating, you have to be prepared by knowing as much as possible before you begin to bargain. Otherwise, you're at a great disadvantage, which makes it that much easier to reject your requests.

A more fundamental reason for your request being turned down is that your boss isn't about to establish a precedent for everyone to run into her office and ask for a raise whenever they feel they have done something extraordinary. Doing a good job, even when it requires long hours at work, is a fairly basic expectation of top management. Generally, this will be rewarded over the long haul at regular salary reviews. However, it's the rare occasion when you can successfully plead for a salary increase when it's not even time for your regular review.

This points out another aspect of negotiations, which is proper timing. The timing of negotiations can make for success or failure. Whereas you might have been able to present a strong case for a substantial raise at review time, there wasn't much of a chance when you tried for a raise which fell outside the established procedures for pay reviews. At least this is true for the present. You're best advised to see what happens at your next review. If at that time you can't get an increase that meets your expectations, then test the job market. Even if you can't get what you want elsewhere, at least you will find out that your salary expectations are excessive in the eyes of those who will be paying the bill.

Q: I just completed presenting the budget for my department to my boss. As always we had a sit-down session where we went over everything to establish a final figure. I was shocked to have my boss run his red pencil through one item after another. The result was a reduction of 20% from what I had proposed. I fully expected a 10% cut, but frankly 20% isn't reasonable. I say this because no one else had their budget reduced that much. All I can figure is that I wasn't very convincing, or my boss was not willing to negotiate anything reasonable. What can I do about this?

A: Since no one else's budget was cut to the extent of yours, it's likely you didn't do a very good job of preparing your arguments to support your position. All too often, no matter what the subject matter of the negotiation might be, a failure to prepare your arguments beforehand will put you in peril before you start. On the other hand, if you go into any negotiation well prepared, this alone may get you a better deal than would otherwise be the case.

Q: I recently failed to complete a negotiation where the price I offered was fair, and I pretty much gave in on every other issue, so the end result was a real good deal for the other party. Despite this, the deal fell through, since the other negotiator insisted on a higher price than was justified. I tried to point out all the other concessions I had made, but he wouldn't listen. I finally got fed up and called it quits. Is there anything I could have done better here?

A: That's hard to say, but it does show how negotiations sometimes fail when people become so obsessed with price that they overlook the other terms of the proposed agreement. This is sometimes true even when other concessions have been made that are worth far more than the difference in price the party is squabbling about. In fact, sometimes you can get a better overall deal by giving a little ground on price in exchange for receiving concessions of greater value. For this reason, always avoid keeping your mind on price to the exclusion of all the other aspects of the agreement you're negotiating. It's a total package deal, so if you have several valuable elements to negotiate aside from price, always assess the total offer you're giving or receiving—not the price in and of itself.

SIMPLE ANSWERS TO PRICE OBJECTIONS

Price objections are the norm in many negotiations, and the reasons for this aren't very complicated. The bottom line in business is to make a profit, so generally everyone wants to get the highest price as a seller or the lowest price as a buyer. This brings about almost reflexive objections to any initial price quoted in negotiations. The assumption is that the first price a seller proposes is too high, or the initial offer of a buyer is too low. To counter this, a wide variety of objections are used in an attempt to get a better deal.

Much of this price resistance is easy to deal with, while some of it is harder to overcome. Of course, the simple solution is to avoid giving your best price right at the start of a negotiation. This gives you leeway to adjust your position in response to objections and still get a fair deal. However, there's more to it than that, since by arbitrarily changing your price in response to objections, you send a message that your price isn't firm. As a consequence of doing this, the other party to the negotiations is likely to think you will move even further in price once you've made your initial concession.

Q: No matter how reasonable I try to be in reaching agreement on price, it seems I'm always getting squeezed by buyers to lower it a little bit more. What can I do to avoid this situation?

A: Try turning requests for price reductions to your advantage. Although it can't be done in every instance, if it's feasible, trade off the lower price the person is requesting against changes in the item he's buying from you so that your costs are reduced. For example, if you're selling gizmos of varying complexity for different prices, offer a less expensive variation. Usually, one of two things will happen in this type of situation. The other negotiator will either quit pushing for a price reduction if he wants the exact item that was initially proposed, or else he will accept your suggestion as a workable solution.

Even if you don't have standard items with different specifications at varying prices, you can still use this technique. For instance, perhaps you can reduce costs some other way—by relaxing quality control standards, changing shipping and/or packaging requirements, or some other method. Whatever the change may be, if it allows you to meet the lower price offered and still maintain your profit margin, it's an alternative that can't be overlooked.

Q: That's good for some people, but I'm offering consulting services. Since I'm not offering a product, revising the item being sold to meet a lower price demand won't work.

A: What you can do here is simply change the mix of the number of hours of consulting services being offered to a less senior level. Since your less experienced staff members are at lower rates, this will reduce your overall figure. If you're a one-person firm, or only one person is required on the job, reduce the number of hours, along with a reduction in the specific recommendations you will make. Whether it's a product or a service, with a little bit of thought you can find a way to trade off what you're furnishing in exchange for accepting a lower price. Of course, the main qualifier to consider is whether or not making such an adjustment will make it worthwhile for you to even do the job. If it isn't feasible, avoid making a compromise offer, and if it's suggested by the other side, simply say it's an unacceptable alternative.

Q: I've got a spin-off question in this area. My problem isn't being offered too low a price. Instead, it's the disagreements I have with my boss over my annual salary reviews. She always wants to give me far less than what I'm looking for. How can I wheel and deal on this issue?

A: Even here, you may be able to use a variation of the previous technique. Offer suggestions for expanding your duties as a means of justifying a higher salary. You might find your boss to be receptive, particularly if the boss would like to grant your request, but isn't sure of how it can be justified. If you can show where your duties can be expanded, it will eliminate this problem.

Q: What am I supposed to do once I've made price concessions and tried everything else to reach agreement, only to have the other negotiator say my price is too high?

A: There will be times people aren't willing to pay a reasonable price. The reasons are varied, but in business situations, it frequently happens when buyers think they are in a position to dictate prices to the seller. In general, if your negotiations are usually as a buyer or seller, competition is the best defense against unreasonable demands for price concessions. If there's plenty of competition waiting in the wings, your opposite in the negotiations won't be quite as cocky about pressuring for a more favorable price.

Therefore, always try to keep your options open in terms of other potential buyers or sellers. Besides being good insurance against unreasonable offers, it's also a good psychological boost for yourself when you're negotiating with the knowledge that other possibilities are open if the present deal falls through. However, if the other side won't attempt to reach an agreement you can live with, then you have to accept that, give your best offer, and leave it to the other party to get back to you if they have a change of heart.

KNOWING WHEN TO QUIT ASKING FOR MORE

Logically you want to get the best deal you can when you negotiate. However, there are times you will be better served by not pressing for further concessions. This should always be kept in mind once you have a reasonable deal negotiated, since pressing too hard for further gains can result in no deal at all. Naturally, you won't often be in such an advantageous position, but it can happen enough so you should be on the alert for it.

Q: How can I possibly go wrong by wringing every concession I can out of anyone I'm negotiating with?

A: In more ways than one. For one thing, if you push to the point of being unreasonable when you're negotiating, the other side may just say forget it and leave. As a result, you end up with no deal at all. From another angle, someone may actually accept unreasonable terms and complete an agreement with you. However, the one-sided deal may cause them difficulty in performing the agreement. This can have all sorts of dire consequences, ranging from late delivery or poor quality to an inability to complete the job. When this sort of development takes place, your original good deal may turn into a nightmare. If that happens, let's hope you weren't telling everyone what a great deal you negotiated when the agreement was originally signed. If so, some of these folks may start reminding you about your so-called "great deal" later on when it turns sour.

Q: **I don't want to seem skeptical, but I've never had the good fortune of being in a position to dictate terms to someone else. When does this sort of thing usually happen?**

A: It commonly occurs when one party is more in need of reaching an agreement than the other side. For example, a small business looking to become a regular supplier to a large business can be vulnerable. The large company's negotiator could decide to squeeze every last cent out of the price of what is being bought. The small company looking for regular vendor status might take a losing deal in the hope of being selected for future orders. However, there's nothing to be gained by either party in this sort of situation. The small business will suffer from working at a loss on the transaction, while the large firm runs the risk of not having the deal completed or as a minimum having the vendor come looking for contract relief.

Q: **Because of the nature of my business, I'm often in a position to impose unreasonable terms on others, but I realize it may be detrimental to long-term business relationships. On the other hand, I'm not a mind reader, so how can I tell when the terms I'm trying to negotiate are unfair?**

A: A combination of factors will let you know. First, the other negotiator will likely be howling about how the deal can't be done on such unreasonable terms. Of course, this could be nothing more than a negotiation ploy, so you should seek detailed reasons when this sort of claim is made. Beyond this, when you give someone a "take it or leave it" offer that they are reluctant to accept, you may have made an offer that exceeds the bounds of being reasonable.

Finally, common sense alone may tell you when you cross the line to a one-sided deal. This may be based on factual knowledge, such as knowing the price you're willing to pay is much lower than other suppliers will accept, or maybe you're aware of some reason why the other party will accept an unsatisfactory deal if you force them to. For instance, a prospective supplier may clearly reveal during negotiations the desire to do business with you on a regular basis. Another possibility is knowing the company you're negotiating with is desperate to fill their order books due to a lack of business.

Q: What negotiating I do as a manager is strictly within the company itself. It's mostly on a personal level—with my boss, subordinates, or other managers. Although I'm more interested in knowing how to negotiate to get what I want, are there any situations where I should know when to quit pushing too hard?

A: There are a lot more areas than you would think where you have to know when to call it quits. It isn't always easy to realize this, since a manager's main concern—especially when dealing with a boss—is to avoid being rebuffed rather than worrying about pushing for more than is justified. Here are a few examples where pushing too hard in negotiations can create difficulties:

- Dickering with your superiors for resources. Rather than settling for less than what you request, you continue to pursue your cause. This can be self-defeating if you succeed in angering someone at higher management levels.
- Excessive bargaining with other department heads. This can be troublesome if you succeed in alienating them to the extent that they go out of their way to be uncooperative.
- Bluntly rejecting subordinates who are trying to bargain with you about a wide-ranging number of issues, including pay raises, time off, new equipment, and so forth. As the boss, you're in a position of strength and can pretty much arbitrarily refuse employee demands. However, you can lose out in the long run unless you're

fair, since employees may quit, work slower, or otherwise work less efficiently. You may wish your own boss was more considerate when you're trying to bargain and instead receive rejections, but that doesn't mean you should take it out on those who work for you.

WHY YOU SHOULD ALWAYS LOOK BEYOND THE CURRENT DEAL

It's difficult to think beyond the present when you're negotiating, but frequently future success hinges on how you handle the current situation. For example, if you're looking to establish a long-term customer relationship, the success of the current negotiations may determine whether further agreements result. Therefore, whenever you negotiate, ask yourself what the future implications of the current negotiation might be. This is even true from a personal viewpoint when considering your own career.

Q: I can understand how buyer-seller relationships can be affected in the future, but how can my personal career be impacted this way?

A: One of the most common personal negotiating situations you will be in as a manager is negotiating your compensation package for a new position. Frequently, you may be tempted to accept a lower salary offer rather than risk losing the position by asking for the salary you want. It's easy enough to rationalize by thinking something such as, "I'll make it up in raises once I prove my value to the company." Perhaps you will, but before you blithely make a speculative leap, consider the difference a lower starting salary can make over the years, since future increases are built upon that base.

For example, assume two managers, Sue P. and Bob A., are both offered similar positions at $100,000 a year by the same company. Both are looking for a minimum starting salary of $110,000. Bob A. accepts the employment offer, while Sue P. turns it down and a week later lands a job paying $110,000. Assume they both receive raises of 10 percent per year for the next 10 years. Here's how their earnings would compare over that period.

Year	Bob A.	Sue P.
1	$ 100,000	$ 110,000
2	110,000	121,000
3	121,000	133,100
4	133,100	146,410
5	146,410	161,051
6	161,051	177,156
7	177,156	194,872
8	194,872	214,359
9	214,359	235,795
10	235,795	259,375
Total Earnings	$1,593,743	$1,753,118

As you can see from the numbers, after 10 years, Sue P. is earning almost $24,000 a year more than Bob A. Furthermore, over the 10-year period she has earned over $159,000 more than Bob, or an average of almost $16,000 a year. All from what started out as a $10,000 difference in yearly salary. Of course, this example assumes that both managers get the same percentage raise year after year. It also ignores such factors as promotions, new jobs, and so forth. So it's possible that Bob might come out the winner over the 10-year period. On the other hand, Sue might also do better, which would make her financial advantage over Bob even greater.

It's entirely conceivable that Bob made the right decision in taking the job for $10,000 a year less than he wanted, as long as he took the long-term aspects of what he was negotiating into consideration. Many negotiating situations, both business and personal, have long-term consequences that aren't apparent unless you give it some thought. And although you can't foresee everything that might happen in the future, you can factor some of the more obvious results into your present negotiations.

Q: In terms of buying and selling products and services, what are the types of long-term factors I should be considering?

A: These can vary from one negotiation to the next. Frequently, there may be no future factors to think about. On the other hand, future considerations may weigh heavily on your decision in a current negotiation.

For instance, if a long-term business relationship is under consideration, both negotiating parties should have this foremost in their minds.

Apart from future business relationships, the subject matter of some negotiations may have long-term significance beyond the scope of the current agreement. As an example, if you would need to obtain funding to pay for something you're negotiating, the method of financing might have long-term implications. Such factors as whether or not future cash flow will allow for repayment of any loan may have to be considered. This is true even though how you finance your purchase may not interest the other party to the negotiation—assuming financing terms won't be part of the negotiated agreement. On the other hand, if a large purchase is being paid for out of current earnings, no future considerations may be involved.

Although the type of attention you pay to long-term matters will vary with each negotiation, the key point is to always be sure to consider what if any influence the current negotiation will have, either in terms of your company, yourself, or future relationships with the other party to the transaction.

OVERCOMING THE PERCEPTION OF A HIGH PRICE

One of the hardest negotiating tasks for many people is trying to justify what's perceived to be a high price by the other party. It's sometimes tough even to get a reasonable price, but when you're selling a high-priced product or service, the job becomes even harder. Yet it can be done without too much difficulty if you go about it the right way. The particular tactic you use to do this will vary with the specifics of what you're selling, but the essential point is to be able to prove as best you can that your product or service is worth the price you're asking someone to pay. If you can't do that, then you will have a real problem sustaining your prices in negotiations, unless you don't have any substantive competition.

Q: I'm a sales manager and my company's prices are pretty standard. Unfortunately, even though our products are of higher quality, it's tough on my sales representatives because several of our competitors have lower prices. As a result, prospects are always trying to negotiate price reductions. Are there ways to overcome this problem?

A: If your products are indeed of higher quality than lower-priced competitors, then that is the solution to your problem. However, it goes beyond just saying the quality is better. You have to be able to convince prospects, since you should always be able to get your price as long as you can prove that it's worth what you're asking someone to pay.

What's essentially involved is arming your sales representatives with detailed knowledge supporting the cost involved in providing the higher-quality standards that go into your item. In addition, it would be helpful if you can prove the benefits of this higher quality to your customers. Sometimes in cases such as this it's even possible to show that the higher quality results in cost savings to the customer.

For instance, let's assume that you're selling an item for $12,000, while your competition sells a competitive product for $10,000. However, you have statistics to prove that your product lasts an average of five years versus a lifespan of four years for your competitor's product. Based upon this, the yearly cost of your product is $2,400, while your competitor's is $2,500. In actuality, your machine is less expensive for the customer.

The simple fact is that no matter what it is that's being sold, when there are competitive prices that are lower, you have to be able to show why your prices are the better bargain. Incidentally, when another negotiator makes a claim of competitive prices being lower, don't accept it as fact. Frequently, the other item isn't comparable to your product. So whoever is making the claim is comparing dissimilar items. Once you can prove this to be true, you should be able to sustain your price without difficulty.

Of course, if the buyer doesn't want or need your product and the competitor's product is sufficient for the buyer's needs, you may find that you can't make a deal. Don't fret about this, since you probably ran into a bargain hunter who knew full well you had a superior product, but was trying to purchase it at the same price as a lower-priced competitor's item that still met the buyer's needs.

SELLING VALUE TO JUSTIFY YOUR PRICE

A good way to justify price is to counter the allegation of a high price by demonstrating the value of your product or service to the buyer. Unlike the prior topic where the emphasis was on proving the price was actually less expensive than competing products, here the thrust is to show that there's value in your price even though it can't necessarily be proven on a financial basis. This isn't as hard to do as it may seem, since every day of the week people spend money on items that can't really be justified based upon the price that was paid.

Q: When someone thinks a price is too high, what specifics can I use to overcome this argument?

A: There are a number of general approaches to use depending upon which tactics best suit the product or service you're selling. Let's look at these one by one:

- Tout the excellent customer support you offer. This is especially effective when you're selling a product that is dependent on technical support at the customer's location. In fact, this is a very profitable strategy that can lead to future business if the customer is satisfied with the service you provide. It's also something that the customer can easily relate to as justification for your pricing, since technical support personnel making visits to the customer's facility are a visible reminder of the cost involved. The same procedure applies if you furnish training on the use of your product to a customer's employees.
- Support your product's price by emphasizing the competitive advantage it will give the buyer. There are many ways you can do this, such as showing how your product will increase the customer's productivity, lower costs, or otherwise provide benefits beyond what a competitor's product will offer.
- Defend the higher price in terms of the costs associated with producing a product that has a greater reliability than comparable items sold by competitors. This is especially true where a product's failure will result in substantial costs to the customer.
- Justify a higher price by demonstrating that the initial price is offset by inexpensive upgrades that keep the product's technology current. This works especially well if your competitors lag in leading edge technology, which may be why your price is higher in the first place.
- Play to a customer's ego to support your price. Plant the seed that your product is a cut above the competition. This is relatively easy to do if your company has a long-standing reputation for furnishing

quality products or services. This approach comes in handy if the product is new and consequently has no history of its own in the marketplace. What you're touting is the company's proven record on other products to support your pricing on the current product.

- If you're supplying professional services such as accounting, advertising, public relations, or any form of consulting services, you can use ready availability on short-term notice as justification for your fees. This is especially useful if you're located in the same geographic area as the potential client. The implication is you can be there quickly if you're needed, whereas competitors in more distant locations can't respond as promptly. Conversely, if you're competing against local competitors, the argument for your higher fees can be the wider breadth of expertise available within your firm.

Naturally, there are any number of other tactics to use that can effectively support a higher price. The only real limitation is your ingenuity at coming up with sound reasons to support your position. However, if you can't do that, then you better lower your prices or be prepared to accept rejection by savvy negotiators.

Q: Our company has one really stiff competitor, and buyers continually reject our arguments that we have a superior product that justifies our higher price. That doesn't make sense because we have a gut feel our product is the better one. What can we do to convince people?

A: Your comment about having a gut feel that your product is superior is the answer to your problem. That implies you really don't have any detailed knowledge about your competitor's product. If you want to be able to defend your price against all comers, you better know what they're offering up as competition. Find out everything you can about the other product and compare its attributes to your item. When the evaluation is complete, be honest as to whether or not your product is really superior. If it isn't, you need another hook to justify your higher price.

Q: I've been given the assignment of planning a four-day corporate meeting for senior executives at an off-site facility. I don't know why I was given this duty, since I'm a human resources manager with the company, not a meeting planner. We're located in Minnesota, and the CEO wants the meeting to be held in Florida in early March. I've gotten preliminary information from several potential facilities. I don't know how to compare costs since there are so many variables involved. How am I ever going to justify which is the best value in terms of price?

A: Before you worry about justifying the price, you better concentrate on making a firm commitment somewhere. Otherwise, you may be literally left out in the cold next March if the top brass don't get their Florida meeting. Actually, your question demonstrates two important points. One is that every now and then a price, be it high or low, isn't really a serious consideration. If price was really that important here, the meeting could be held a lot closer to the company's location.

The second point is that sometimes whether or not a price is high is a matter of perception. The price you pay for the meeting site you ultimately select will be judged as reasonable or unreasonable by the senior executives attending the meeting. The criteria will be very subjective, specifically how well they enjoyed their four-day stay. In fact, if they enjoy themselves, you may find yourself with this assignment again.

Many products and services justify high prices because of the perception of the buyer that they're worth it. This isn't because of any hard facts that will sustain the price, but rather factors such as image, ego, personal enjoyment, and so forth. Therefore, a price that appears to be high if viewed from a cost analysis viewpoint isn't expensive at all in the eyes of the buyer. For this reason, don't go about trying to justify a high price unless and until it's challenged on that basis. And even then, the person may not really be questioning the price, but rather using that argument as an excuse for not going through with a purchase.

Q: **I'm in commercial real estate, and it seems that everyone is looking for a bargain when it comes to leasing office space. What can I do to avoid offering all sorts of concessions to sign up tenants?**

A: First, do your utmost to convince potential tenants of the advantages of signing up for space in your building. Do this from the perspective of the tenant's business. For example, the location of your building may be better suited for the prospect's business than comparable properties. And don't overlook such factors as parking and/or public transportation. Also specify precisely what services will be provided in such areas as maintenance, heating, ventilating, and air conditioning.

In short, the key is to be able to show how your building meets the tenant's needs, either as is or with potential improvements. If you express an understanding of the prospects' business needs and a willingness to work with them to meet their requirements, you're well on your way to getting your price per square foot without making a lot of concessions. This isn't a guarantee you'll always be successful, since occupancy rates and other factors will obviously play a role. However, the more you do to convince prospects of your ability to foresee their needs, the more likely they will see added value in negotiating a higher rent with you.

THE PROS AND CONS OF SPLITTING THE DIFFERENCE

When there are monetary differences between the positions of two parties to a negotiation, sooner or later one or the other will recommend splitting the difference between the two positions. This may seem like a prudent way to resolve a disagreement on price, and it is under certain conditions, particularly where the difference is small and the final figure is one that both parties can live with. At other times, this technique is misused, and it can create problems in trying to reach a final agreement.

Q: I recently had a negotiation where there was a wide variance in price between the positions of the two parties. The other negotiator suggested we split the difference and wrap the deal up. That was impossible for me to do since I would have been paying much more than what I was buying was worth. As a result, I insisted that we discuss why there was such a sharp difference in our respective positions. As it turned out, the other negotiator refused to do that, and we broke negotiations off without reaching agreement. Is it unusual for there to be such discrepancies in the price positions of each of the negotiating parties?

A: This usually happens when one of the parties starts off by making an initial offer that is way out of line. The other party is likely to counter with a more reasonable figure. Then, hoping to make a windfall, the negotiator making the first offer will suggest splitting the difference. Of course, if that is done, the negotiator who made the reasonable counteroffer is going to get burned.

Let's look at a simple example where a reasonable price for an item is roughly $100,000. Joe M. makes an initial offer to sell for $140,000. Jodi C. comes back with an offer to buy at a price of $90,000. Joe M. then suggests splitting the difference between his price of $140,000 and Jodi's offer of $90,000. The midpoint of the $50,000 difference in the two positions would be $115,000. If Jodi accepted, she would be paying about $15,000 more than is reasonable.

What frequently happens when someone refuses to split the difference is for the other negotiator to accuse the party of being unwilling to negotiate. The sensible negotiator is then put on the defensive instead of the person who made the ridiculous offer. This type of tactic, rather than serving to speed up the negotiation process, can slow it down considerably. For one thing, the credibility of the party attempting this ploy is destroyed, which makes it harder for the other party to place any reliance on anything the person says.

Q: What should I do when someone wants to split the difference between reasonable and unreasonable offers?

A: The minute you get an offer to buy or sell that is way out of line, instead of countering with a reasonable offer of your own, tell the other negotiator the offer is out of line and ask for justification. Keep the focus on the unreasonable offer rather than ignoring it and making a reasonable counteroffer. However, if the discussion heads nowhere and the other party says something such as, "Well what are you willing to pay?" then counter with an equally unreasonable offer on your part. Once you do that, you probably won't hear anything further about splitting the difference, but if you do then you will end up with a fair price. Let's go back to the example where a reasonable price was about $100,000 and Joe made his unreasonable offer of $140,000. If at that point Jodi came back with a counteroffer of $60,000, rather than the $90,000 she offered, splitting the difference between $140,000 and $60,000 would result in agreement at $100,000.

Q: When is it useful to split the difference between two positions?

A: When negotiations have gotten to the point where there are minor differences between the two parties and both price positions are within a reasonable range, there's little to be gained by a lot of quibbling since both negotiators will feel their price is justified. At this stage, splitting the difference is a convenient means of resolving the dispute.

Q: Why do some negotiators almost always try to split the difference in the offers that separate the two parties?

A: There are several reasons why this is done. The first, as has already been discussed, is when it's used as a technique to try and reap a windfall profit. However, even here most negotiators don't expect this to happen very often. Instead, what they are hoping for is to haggle back and forth on price without getting into the details behind the respective offers. This is done to avoid discussing the merits of the price being proposed. So when you have someone starting off with a split-the-difference proposal, the odds are they can't substantively withstand close scrutiny of their offer. In other instances, beginning negotiators use this technique when they're not properly prepared to discuss the issues on their merits. Therefore, to avoid doing this, they make a split-the-difference offer.

Q: What specifics should I be looking at when someone offers to split the difference?

A: There are a number of factors to consider. First, at what stage of the negotiations does this offer take place? If it's right at the beginning of negotiations, it may indicate that the other party, for one reason or another, doesn't want to get involved in detailed discussions of the pros and cons of the subject matter of the negotiation. On the other hand, if it takes place after a fair amount of discussion, along with concessions and trade-offs by both parties, it is probably just an attempt to close the final gap without getting deadlocked over insignificant differences in price.

Don't overlook the possibility of gaining other concessions in exchange for splitting the difference in price. Even though you might not accept the price that would result from splitting the difference, it can be advantageous to do so if you can get other concessions as part of the bargain. For example, if accepting a split-the-difference offer would mean paying $5,000 more than you want to, see if you can make this up with favorable payment terms, revised product specifications, or some other item. If so, this will facilitate reaching agreement, and you will still get a deal you can accept.

Finally, always try to close the gap between the respective positions on price before entertaining any offer to split the difference. The exception would be if the other negotiator makes an offer to split the difference that is within a range you consider to be acceptable.

Q: I recently completed a negotiation where the other party made an offer that was within 2% of my price. It was acceptable to me and I agreed to it. Should I have tried to split the difference with such a small amount of money at stake?

A: It's always amazing the way people act when they're dealing with the company's money rather than their own. Would you be happier with a pay raise of 5% or 7%? Sounds like a foolish question, but it's only 2% as in the negotiation. Furthermore, 2% of what? If it's $1,000,000, we're talking about $20,000, whereas if it's $10,000, it's $200. But even assuming it is the lower amount, would you refuse a gift of $200? Business negotiations are generally conducted with a lot less care than if the money were the negotiator's own funds. However, even individuals sometimes get carried away when they're making large personal expenditures.They will spend a few thousand more on a house or an automobile than they originally intended, simply because they decide it's a small part of the total cost of the item and worth paying to get what they want.

To specifically answer the question, why not offer to split the difference? No matter what the dollar figure, it's money you have saved. Naturally, if the other party strenuously objects, you can say something like, "All right, Sam, I'll accept your offer so we can wrap the deal up." The closer people come to reaching agreement during negotiations, the more careless they tend to become. Always strive to be as precise as possible, even if the sum involved isn't large in the total scheme of things. On the other hand, use common sense in assessing the situation, since you don't want to toss away a complex agreement over small sums. So if the discussions have been long and involved, trying to split the difference at the last minute may not be the wisest choice to make.

HOW TO PROVE ANY PRICE IS A BARGAIN

If there's one thing you can be sure of it's that you will always find people with price objections. Even when by any objective standard a price is reasonable, someone you're negotiating with will want to argue otherwise. The biggest problem you have to overcome in this area may be your own defensiveness on this issue. Let's be realistic. If you consider your price to be too high, you won't be able to do that good of a job in defending it in negotiations. In fact, if you don't think your price is reasonable, you're probably better off letting someone else do the negotiating. So the first person you have to convince that your price isn't high is yourself. If you can do that successfully, you ought to be able to persuade those you negotiate with. After all, you know more than they do about what you're selling.

Does this mean that everyone will always agree with you? Of course not. Some people wouldn't know a bargain if it was staring them in the face. Others may silently agree with you, but just not be able to afford what you're asking them to pay. But by and large, most of the people you negotiate with will come around to your viewpoint once you satisfy them that your price is reasonable. One good way to do this is to break down the price into components so it doesn't look so intimidating.

Q: **If you're asking someone to pay a certain amount, let's say $4,000 for something, the bottom line is they are still going to look at it as $4,000, no matter how much you break the figure down. How can doing that lead someone to see your price as reasonable if he initially thought $4,000 was too much to pay?**

A: The same reasons that lead people to pay more than they originally intended to for things all the time. Did you ever go out to buy something personally and come home happy with a purchase even though you spent more than the figure you had in mind when you left your house? Let's say it was an automobile. Why did you pay more? Perhaps it was the leather seats, or the bigger engine, or a larger-capacity fuel tank. Who knows? It might have just been the color of the car you saw that had a few options you didn't really want, but you couldn't get that color in a car without the options. The bottom line is that you sometimes spend more than you originally intended for reasons that make sense to you alone. And although people aren't always willing to admit it, more often than not, the salesperson is the one who convinced them to spend the additional money. All of which means that when you're negotiating and someone challenges your price as being too high, you have to put on your selling hat.

Q: I can't disagree that people don't sometimes spend more than they had originally planned, but how does that relate to quoting a price and then breaking it down to components? Usually it's a case of starting with a lower price and adding things on.

A: It can be done either way. However, that would depend upon what you're selling. Many business or industrial products aren't susceptible to being sold with various models and options as an automobile is. Therefore, you have a set price to start with. However, you can take that price and break it down into its components to show the party you're negotiating with that the overall price isn't high at all once you look at what it's comprised of.

For example, show how much is spent on things such as design engineering, quality control, and whatever else goes into making your product superior. Let the other negotiator know that it's this extra attention to detail that differentiates both your product and its price from competitors. Of course, the factors you talk about will vary with what you're selling, but the principle remains the same. Don't stop there though.

Get the other negotiator involved by asking questions that require a positive response such as, "You don't want to buy something you have to worry about breaking down and halting your production line do you?" or "You don't want a machine that requires expensive maintenance do you?" Whatever your questions, the thrust of them should be to get the buyer thinking of the advantages of your product, not its price. Once you have the buyer thinking of all the wonderful qualities of your product, and silently worrying about the problems that might develop with lower-priced competitive products, you're in good shape to negotiate a sale.

Incidentally, it's always helpful during negotiations to listen carefully to anything the other party says that indicates particular qualities or features the buyer is looking for. If it isn't fairly obvious from the discussions, try to ask questions that will reveal the product characteristics the buyer is most interested in. This will let you concentrate on pitching those angles of your product that meet the buyer's needs. For example, if a buyer has revealed real concern about reliability, concentrate on showing how your product meets these needs.

Q: I'm looking at price from the vantage point of a buyer instead of a seller. One of the sales pitches I continually hear is someone had to

raise his price because of increases in his supplier's costs. How should I deal with this?

A: If the increase is valid, unless you have other sources that use alternative materials not affected by a price increase, then you may be stuck with it. However, whenever someone makes this assertion, ask her to prove it to you, since there are a couple of gimmicks sometimes used by sellers. One is to increase a price to compensate for higher supplier prices when the material in question will come out of inventory bought at a lower price. The second is to increase the price by a higher percentage than the amount of the supplier price increase. All of which gives the seller a windfall profit if you accept their assertion unchallenged.

With many items, prices are pretty volatile based on supply and demand factors. This is especially true of commodity prices, and increases are passed quickly down the chain of distribution. What occasionally is overlooked is that these prices can go *up or down*, and while every seller will hastily raise prices, it's not always the same when prices should be reduced. For this reason, if you are regularly buying products subject to price swings of this nature, you should be independently tracking material prices so you can benefit from any price reductions.

Incidentally, if you're a seller of products that are subject to regular price increases due to supplier costs, you can use this factor to justify a price that someone is challenging as being too high. Say something such as, "Now's the time to make the deal, Pete, since prices will be going higher in a few weeks."

USING CONCESSIONS TO GET BETTER TERMS

When negotiations start, there is a difference in the positions of the two parties that may be minor or substantial and involve either a single topic such as price or a large number of different issues. The negotiation process will encompass give-and-take until the gaps in the respective positions are closed and an agreement is reached or the parties conclude individually or jointly that a satisfactory resolution of differences isn't possible.

Closing the gap between the two negotiation positions requires the parties to make concessions to reach agreement. How effective you are at granting or obtaining concessions will to a large extent determine whether the negotiation succeeds—for both you and the other party. This is so, since if you can't convince the other party to make the concessions necessary to give you a deal you can accept, then you won't be able to make the deal, and both sides will lose out. It must be hoped that the other negotiator realizes this and is just as concerned with reaching agreement.

Although price concessions aren't always an issue in negotiations, they frequently cause the most difficulty, since they involve something everyone can relate to, namely, money. They are also an area where you can benefit by bargaining wisely, so let's look at how this can be done.

Q: I don't like to waste time negotiating, since my other duties as a manager keep me busy enough. Therefore, when I do negotiate, I simply figure out the minimum terms I will accept and then make an offer on that basis. In other words, I don't have any wiggle room, so I'm making a "take it or leave it" offer. Unfortunately, this doesn't seem to save me much time at all since I'm inevitably dragged into extended discussions that always seem to end up with me being accused of refusing to negotiate. Is there any way around this?

A: It would make sense if both parties come right out and give the other side their best offer right at the start. Unfortunately, it rarely works that way, so you have to leave yourself some leeway to make concessions when you negotiate. Otherwise, the other negotiator will think you're unreasonable, unwilling to negotiate, and trying to make a windfall profit at his or her expense.

Q: That seems like a terrible waste of time. If both parties started with the bottom line they would accept, wouldn't it be much quicker getting things done?

A: Maybe it would in some situations, but in others it might not make any difference at all. Generally, there will always be a spread between what each party feels is acceptable to them. If both parties make their best offer at the beginning of negotiations, there will still be a gap to be closed. However, since each party has started at pretty much what they consider to be reasonable, a lot of time may be consumed for each side to agree to terms that close that gap. This is so since the going gets tough when negotiators have to make substantive concessions to complete an agreement. As a result, you may have both negotiators at loggerheads with each other right at the start of negotiations.

On the other hand, if each party gives themselves some leeway in their opening position, it's easier to make some initial concessions at the beginning. This will make the start of negotiations a lot easier for both sides. Then, by the time it gets down to the final gaps to be closed, both negotiators will have developed a rapport that may help them overcome the tough spots that remain. Therefore, if both sides have left themselves room, they may find it easier to cover the final hurdles than when they go at it right from the beginning.

Furthermore, sometimes when room to maneuver is left in a negotiation position, agreement can be reached without ever whittling the argument down to two positions that are only narrowly apart but both quite reasonable. This happens when the negotiators agree to terms in one fell swoop, which not only cover the fat in both positions, but also compromise whatever the differences in their hard-core positions may have been. In other words, sometimes the more room you have to negotiate, the easier it is to complete agreement.

Q: To allow myself some room to negotiate, what should my position be when I start negotiations?

A: You want to establish a position that is essentially the best deal you hope to get. Nevertheless, you have to be sensible in doing this, while at the same time giving yourself some bargaining room. If you start with what is a totally unrealistic offer, the other party may become much harder to deal with, and in some instances may conclude right away that you aren't even trying to negotiate seriously.

Q: How do you go about deciding what you can concede when you establish your negotiating position?

A: In terms of price, it's easy enough to decide that your initial position will be some figure, say, 10 to 15% below what you are ultimately willing to pay as a buyer or above what you will accept as a seller. The extent of flexibility you leave yourself on price depends somewhat on what is being negotiated. The key is to set a figure that will give you enough room to maneuver during negotiations, but appears reasonable enough to be believable as an opening offer.

As far as other possible concessions, although you can look at the possibilities before negotiations start, the back-and-forth dialogue during negotiations will dictate the specifics of what you're willing to concede. For instance, before negotiations begin you may establish a specific delivery date for items you're buying. However, during negotiations you may be offered more favorable payment terms in exchange for a different delivery schedule, which may be to your benefit to accept. Therefore, before negotiations begin, you can't identify every area where you would be willing to make concessions, since that depends upon what you are offered in return for making the concession.

What you can and should do is to pinpoint areas where you aren't willing to make concessions. By doing this you give yourself the flexibility to make trade-offs in virtually anything else. At the same time, you have identified nonnegotiables so as to prevent them from being inadvertently considered as concession areas during negotiations. It's also important to try and prioritize any areas where you may potentially make concessions when negotiations start. By doing this, you know which concessions are of the greatest value to you.

Q: What are the fundamental procedures for making concessions?

A: Follow a good basic procedure:

- Establish what your overall position will be before negotiations begin. This will consist of what you will accept if necessary to complete a deal as well as an opening position that will give you some leeway to bargain.
- If the negotiations involve agreeing on price, decide the highest price you're willing to pay if you're the buyer or the lowest price you will accept as a seller. Then, decide how much price flexibility to add to your opening offer.
- Decide what issues are nonnegotiable and cannot be varied during the negotiations. Be realistic when doing this, since the more rigid your position, the harder it will be to reach an agreement.
- Give some thought to areas for possible concessions, keeping in mind that the circumstances may change as negotiations proceed.
- Try to assign priorities in terms of the areas you may be willing to make concessions in.

- When negotiations begin, try to avoid being the one to make the first offer to compromise.
- Don't be in a hurry to make concessions. Once you make a concession, it's gone, and once you trade away all your possible concessions, you are left with nothing to bargain with.
- Always try to trade your lowest-priority concessions for high-priority concessions from the other negotiator.
- Always be ready to terminate discussions when concessions have been made by both sides and your final concession/offer isn't accepted.

Q: One of the procedures listed for making concessions is to avoid making the first offer to compromise. Why is that?

A: It gives you a chance to see how far the other person is willing to move off his or her position before you have to respond. If you're the one making an offer to compromise, you have to decide how far to go from your initial position. This can cause difficulty. Perhaps you will compromise too much and have the other party come back and offer to move only minimally from their position. Having the ability to react to an offer of compromise is preferable to being the one who has to make the offer.

Q: It was also mentioned that low-priority concessions should be traded for high-priority concessions. What does this mean, and how is it done?

A: The less you have to give away in concessions, the better the deal you will end up with. Therefore, the more often you can get the other negotiator to trade something of importance to you for a minor concession in return, the better off you will be.

Q: That sounds great, but what negotiator is foolish enough to trade major concessions for minor ones?

A: Never assume the value of any concession you make to the other party. Just because it may be relatively insignificant to you doesn't mean it isn't of major importance to the other negotiator. For example, you may not consider making a concession on payment terms very important to you, but a company with cash flow problems might consider that to be a major concession.

Incidentally, when negotiations start, look for clues from the other side as to areas of greater importance, since this will alert you to the kinds of concessions the other negotiator will be looking for. Whatever the specifics may be, don't assume your low-priority concession isn't a high-priority item with the other negotiator. For this reason, always treat every concession you make as a major one. This gives you credibility in expecting a significant concession in return.

Q: The subject of concessions is interesting, but I don't know how it would apply to me since my position doesn't require me to do any buying or selling. The biggest negotiation problems I face are trying to get the resources I need to do my job, and my boss and other senior managers aren't willing to bargain, much less make any concessions. For example, we have several makes of older computers, and the three managers who report to me are always hounding me about getting new computers to improve productivity. Whenever I bring this subject up with my boss, all I hear is that it's too expensive.

A: Your failure to get your computers may be partly due to not looking at the possibility of getting a concession from your boss. If you have given your boss evidence that the computers will enhance productivity, the objection is probably based on the significant cost associated with replacing a large number of computers at once. Why not try to get your boss to make a concession to buy a few at a time. Then you can go back later and prove the productivity gains made with the new computers justify buying more. Since the initial expenditure will be a lot less, your boss will likely go along with this. If so, you have effectively made a concession of your need to replace all the computers at once in exchange for getting a limited number.

It's meaningful to look at matters such as these from a negotiation perspective, since there's a tendency to think there's nothing to bargain about. However, there usually are trade-offs that can be bargained for in this and many similar managerial situations that aren't thought of as such. What you have here is something you're offering your boss (increased productivity) in exchange for something you want (new computers). How do you negotiate to get what you want? First, as you did, you make a proposal showing how productivity will be increased by replacing the outdated computers. Your boss refuses your offer since at the moment saving the money is a higher priority. However, with your negotiation hat on, you offer a compromise that may be considered acceptable. The moral is simply to remember that a lot of things are negotiable if you put them in that context.

HOW TO AVOID PENNY-ANTE PLOYS

Fortunately, most business negotiators tend to be pretty forthright. However, on occasion you will run into someone who thinks negotiating skills are measured by the number of tricks and tactics that are used in negotiations. When that happens, you have to work around the nonsense as best you can. Let's look at some of the various schemes you may encounter and what you can do to cope.

Q: I'm a little bit frustrated by a couple of people I negotiate with on a regular basis. They are generally loud and abusive and try to get their way by bullying tactics. Although it's distressing to me, because of circumstances, I have to continue to deal with them. Is there anything I can do to counter these actions?

A: The best approach is to ignore people who try to intimidate you to get what they want. It's not easy to do, but everyone except the worst offenders will tone their rhetoric down once they see it doesn't bother you. If you find this impossible to do, or their behavior doesn't stop, you might want to calmly say, "We're here to negotiate, not to argue. If we can't discuss things in a reasonable manner I intend to leave." If the behavior continues then say, "Call me when you calm down," and get up and leave the room. It's especially effective if you can do this at a time when you know the offending party has a deadline to meet. When this happens, they will be around to see you shortly in a more subdued manner.

Q: What do people think they're gaining by getting angry when they negotiate? It just makes me mad.

A: In a few cases it's the personality of the individual. Although that doesn't make it any easier to tolerate, at least it's understandable. In other instances, inexperienced negotiators may become angry out of frustration over their own inability to be as convincing as they would like to be. On other occasions you may run into a negotiator who uses anger as a tactic to obscure the fact that his or her negotiating position is weak. And, finally, there are those who hope to upset you to the extent that you will make careless mistakes.

Incidentally, whatever the reason for the anger, always try to remain calm and concentrate on the facts of the negotiation. It may even work to your benefit, since if someone gets hotheaded, they're not thinking clearly, and when that happens, it can be to your advantage.

Q: Every time I negotiate with a person I'll call Joanne S., she threatens to take her business somewhere else if I don't lower my prices. I think she's just bluffing, but I'm not certain enough to call her bluff. Therefore, I usually give her a price reduction. I'm still making a small profit on doing business with this company, but I don't get the prices I do elsewhere. Is there any way to combat this short of telling her to take her business elsewhere?

A: There are a wide variety of intimidation tricks used in negotiations ranging from strike threats made by unions to threats to hire replacement workers by companies. On a smaller scale are coercive tactics ranging from faked deadlines to threats not to do business with you unless you yield to the demands being made.

No matter in what form the threat may be, the solution to not being intimidated is to refuse to cave in to the pressure. The reason you're continually pressured to lower your prices is because you didn't stand your ground the first time around. About all you can do the next time Joanne threatens to take her business elsewhere is to say, "We've done business together for a long while, Joanne, and I hope we can continue to do so. However, I am unable to lower my prices." It's now her move, but it's unlikely she will make good on her threat. First, she would have to find another source for the same product at the same price. If she was unhappy with doing business with you, she would have gone somewhere else a long time ago. So she's not going to leave now, even though she can no longer get you to agree to a bargain-basement price.

Q: It seems that every time I negotiate with someone I find a different tactic being used. Can you summarize some of the common ploys used in negotiations and how to cope with them?

A: Intimidation has just been discussed. Other tactics you may encounter are

- **Stonewalling.** This is where someone essentially refuses to budge from their negotiation position. To cope with this, you can either start to stonewall yourself, or you can break off the negotiations with a suggestion to the other party to contact you if they seriously want to negotiate.
- **Good-bad negotiator tactics.** This tactic is known by various names, such as the good cop–bad cop ploy. In this case, one negotiator adopts an entirely unreasonable position, and then a second negotiator takes over and acts much more cooperative and willing to negotiate. The gimmick's intent is have the one party so relieved to be dealing with the second negotiator that they are more willing to reach an agreement that favors the other party. Ignore the personalities and stick to your position, since neither negotiator is trying to do you a favor.
- **Evasion tactics.** A certain amount of evasion is to be expected when you negotiate, since the other party isn't about to help you do your job. However, you may find yourself becoming frustrated by negotiators who refuse to support their claims with documentation, respond in generalities, and are consistently evasive. A pattern of evasion indicates either the negotiator is using this as a tactic or, even worse, is hiding facts that would reveal something substantive that you should know before making a commitment. If you're convinced that the other negotiator is deliberately evasive, ask probing questions to get the facts you need. If you're unsuccessful, state that you can't reach agreement without getting the information you seek. Assuming that you're not satisfied with the answers you get, you have to decide whether or not you want to proceed toward negotiating an agreement. If you do, be sure to include in the written agreement any provisions you feel are necessary to protect your interests.

- **Stalling tactics.** Occasionally you will find someone who appears to be deliberately slowing the negotiation process down. Assuming that it isn't a person who is just indecisive, it may be a tactic to extract a better deal from you. This is especially true if you have a deadline to meet and the other party is aware of it. Prevention is the key to success here. Unless it's unavoidable, never let it be known you're facing a deadline. Of course, in some situations there's no way to keep the other party from knowing you face time constraints. In this event, if it's possible, give the impression that your deadline is sooner than it really is. That way if someone tries to put deadline pressures on you, once your phony date has passed it will be assumed it didn't matter to you. Then the negotiations should move along as expected.

- **Deadline pressures.** The flip side of a party stalling when you face deadlines is their use as a threat to get you to accept unreasonable demands. The other negotiator will make an unreasonable offer and then give you until a specific time to accept it. You can handle this situation by making your own offer and say something such as, "Since you have a deadline and can't discuss the issues, I've given you my best offer. Let me know by your deadline if it's acceptable." This effectively transfers the deadline to them and puts them in the position of having to contact you.

- **Taking you out of the loop.** Occasionally a negotiator may decide you're doing such a good job that he or she would prefer to deal with someone else. This can take a couple of different forms. One tactic is to tell you how unreasonable you are and to request that your boss get involved. Don't give in to this demand but, instead, respond by saying something such as, "If you no longer wish to negotiate with me, that's your option. As far as I'm concerned, if you break off negotiations, all talks are ended. Therefore, I'm not getting anyone else involved." This puts the other side on the spot, since they know they may still have to deal with you. As a result they will probably grumble and continue to negotiate. The other approach is to go over your head without even mentioning it to you. In either event, if your boss or another senior manager is contacted, he or she should take a firm stand. It's appropriate in this situation for a boss to state that you are conducting the negotiations and she does not intend to interfere.

NOTE: These are among the most common tactics you may encounter across the negotiation table. There are others that will be discussed elsewhere in this book. Beyond that, you may run into almost any sort of negotiation ploy, since a wily negotiator is limited only by his or her imagination.

WHERE TO START—AND FINISH—WHEN YOU'RE TALKING MONEY

One of the thorniest points in negotiations is deciding the best approach for initiating discussions about price. Frequently the initial price offer is contained in a proposal by the buyer or seller before negotiations even begin. Under these circumstances, the initial opening offer is established. On other occasions it may not be raised until the negotiating parties sit down to bargain. This adds the additional wrinkle of who will make the initial price offer. Then, as negotiations proceed, there are the inevitable questions about offers, counteroffers, and final offers, which incidentally are seldom as final as they seem when they're made. In essence, the entire process of moving from an initial price to a final agreed-upon price may be as simple as an offer and an acceptance, or a long, complicated process. How you handle it will determine how satisfied you are with the end result. Let's look at some of the possibilities that may arise along the way.

Q: I recently had a negotiation where I made a one-shot offer right at the beginning to wrap the deal up quick. I said, "Look, Carla, the best I can do is $74,000. Let's settle it for that and wrap this up. She then said she couldn't sell for less than $95,000. I had a long and frustrating negotiation session since from then on she kept insisting we split the difference between the two figures. That was ridiculous since I would have wound up paying $84,500. As it was, after some hard bargaining we ended up settling at $80,000, which was still about $6,000 more than I hoped to pay. I obviously screwed up by making a quick offer to settle at a reasonable price, since she countered with a high figure and then tried to con me into splitting the difference. Isn't it possible to make a reasonable initial offer and get a settlement without someone trying to take advantage of you?

A: Often people will deal realistically when you give them a reasonable offer; however, you can't always count on it, so it presents some pitfalls. For many business transactions there won't be much of a price variance to start with. This is especially true for commodity-type or off-the-shelf items that are bought and sold on a regular basis. In these circumstances, most of your negotiation efforts will be geared toward reaching agreement on items such as delivery schedules, payment terms, and other nonprice-related issues. With these items there's no reason you can't make an initial offer and have it readily accepted.

Other business transactions will present greater difficulty in negotiating a fair price, largely because it's harder to agree on what a fair price should be. A good example is real estate. Although factors such as location, selling prices for similar properties, and condition of the property can establish rough parameters, there's still an element of guesswork involved. Furthermore, it can be even trickier with some types of commercial real estate, since there aren't always going to be similar properties available for price comparisons. Then, there are topics such as research and development where the subject matter is only roughly defined, which makes establishing a price largely guesswork.

To answer your question directly, making an opening offer designed to reach agreement quickly will largely be influenced by the subject matter of the negotiation. If it's a readily available product with several potential sources, there's no reason for price negotiations to be difficult. On the other hand, if you're negotiating something of complexity or scarcity, then you may have to spend a considerable amount of time on price negotiations. In these cases, you're better off making an opening offer that will give you some flexibility, rather than getting yourself in a bind by leading with your best price.

Q: **My greatest difficulty in negotiations is when the price positions are fairly close in terms of dollars and cents. At this point, I don't want to budge because it's getting into the area of the amount of profitability on a project. Naturally, this is true for the other party, so we spend a lot of time trying to reach agreement on what isn't an awful lot of money. Are there any ways to avoid this last-minute haggling over peanuts?**

A: If it was peanuts, you wouldn't be haggling about it. As you said it isn't a large amount, but it may represent the difference between a profit or a loss, which is why the going gets tough when price negotiations are nearing their end. It's at this time that negotiators often think, "Why doesn't she give in. We're not talking much money?" Needless to say, the other negotiator feels the same way about you. This attitude often leads negotiators into a contest of wills, in which neither party is willing to bend. There are two practical ways to get around this problem.

The first approach is to split the difference, since arguably both parties have a price position that is fairly reasonable. Splitting the difference won't give anyone a great deal, but it will give both sides a doable deal. To do this, say something such as, "Carol, since we're so close to wrapping this up, why don't we just split the difference since it's not a lot of money. Otherwise, we will never get this deal done." Most of the time this technique will work, unless the other negotiator wants to try and squeeze further. If that happens, threaten to call the deal off, and if necessary, leave with a message for the other party to call you if there is a change of heart.

The second way to go about this is to see what you can get in terms of concessions in exchange for giving in on the money issue. Often this can turn out to be a good deal for you, especially if the other side is so focused on price that it obscures their thinking on other issues. You always have to keep in mind that gaining concessions on other terms of the proposed agreement can yield cost savings far in excess of what you make by concentrating on price alone. Relaxed product specifications, method of packaging and shipment, and numerous other areas are fertile ground for offsetting concessions which can vastly improve the deal you get.

Q: When I get a counteroffer, I'm always unsure of whether I should question the counteroffer or make a corresponding counteroffer of my own. Any suggestions?

A: Whenever you receive a counteroffer, this shifts the burden to you to make the next move. Don't immediately make a counteroffer since you may be unnecessarily giving away money. Instead, ask for an explanation of the counteroffer. If the answer indicates that it's made based on some form of reevaluation of the other negotiator's cost position, then consider it on the merits. Then, at that time, you might want to make a counteroffer of your own.

If, on the other hand, the negotiator says something to the effect of, "I just made this offer to try and get the deal done," then you may want to respond with your own counteroffer. If so, preface it by saying something such as, "Since you made a counteroffer to try and get this thing done, Joe, I'm going to give you a new figure we can settle on right now, but it's the best I can do." This sends the message that you're making an offer that is your best one and that you hope it will inspire acceptance. Needless to say, you should still have left yourself a little flexibility to adjust your price further, since the other negotiator may come back with yet another offer. Sometimes there can be a whole series of offers and counteroffers each of which brings the parties a little closer to reaching final agreement.

Q: I just completed an agreement with someone who four times during the negotiations gave me a "final" offer. Each time I just said it was unacceptable and kept on negotiating. How can I tell when an offer is truly "final" and will be the last offer I receive?

A: You handled the situation as you should have when you receive a so-called "final" offer, since the best approach is to keep right on negotiating. You will know when an offer is really final when someone walks out the door after you refuse to accept it. All too often, people pull the final offer trigger when the gun isn't even loaded. If you make a final offer, to make it stick you have to be ready to break off negotiations when the offer is rejected. Otherwise, your credibility is destroyed. Furthermore, subsequent offers won't be taken seriously, so in the end you will have to refuse to negotiate further anyway. So if you do make a final offer, do it once, and hope you can make it stick.

Q: What happens if I make a final offer and it's refused? Isn't that the end of the road for the proposed agreement being negotiated?

A: Not necessarily. If you should make a final offer and it's refused, break off negotiations. If you don't hear from the other party within a reasonable period of time, contact them. Even if they still refuse your offer, if you desire you can sweeten your offer at this point. That alone may be the clincher to seal a deal. If not, and you aren't willing to make further concessions, this may be one of those negotiations that just aren't going to end with an agreement.

TIP: When it comes to making offers, don't characterize them as final offers unless they truly are. Otherwise, you won't be able to convince people of the finality of your position. As a result, they will be looking for further concessions, even when you have gone beyond the point of having any remaining concessions to make. This can cause greater difficulty in reaching an agreement than if you never represented an offer as final in the first place. The point of a final offer is to signify you are offering your best terms for reaching agreement which leaves nothing further to negotiate. It may inspire the other party to accept your offer.

Q: What if I make a "final" offer and the other party then comes back with a counteroffer that is very close to my offer?

A: If it meets your criteria for acceptance, then by all means agree to the deal. Just because final offers shouldn't be frivolous doesn't mean you can't continue to negotiate after one has been rejected. However, it may not be wise to quibble over a minor difference in a counteroffer given in response to your final offer. Negotiations sometimes get to the point where someone has to bite the bullet and agree to the last offer. When you make a legitimate final offer and receive a counterproposal that comes close, this indicates that the other party has taken your final offer seriously. For this reason, if you don't accept the counteroffer, there's a possibility that the other party may feel you're being unreasonable and decide to call the negotiations off. This is especially true if there are other alternatives in terms of obtaining the goods or services elsewhere. That may not happen, but why risk it when you have an offer you can live with?

PITFALLS TO AVOID WHEN YOU'RE TALKING PRICE

There are a number of price-related issues that can cause problems for you if you're not careful. These include being defensive about the price you're asking as a seller or are willing to pay as a buyer. If you don't display confidence that you consider your price to be reasonable, then the signs of this lack of conviction will be quickly picked up by a savvy negotiator. Not only will this make it more difficult to get the price you want, but it may also serve to prolong negotiations.

In fact, there are times when price shouldn't even be a major consideration in your discussions. Often too much emphasis is placed on the monetary aspects of a negotiation to the exclusion of more important items. Therefore, in some cases while the other negotiator is busy trying to get a better price, you can capitalize on this by gaining valuable concessions in other areas.

One area of negotiation that has several snares you have to anticipate is negotiating salary when you are looking for a new job. All too often, managers who excel at negotiations when representing their employer on business get downright reticent about asking for money when bargaining for their own personal interests. Let's look at a couple of areas where this can cause problems.

Q: **I'm about to embark on what I consider to be the most important price negotiations I'll ever conduct, which is my pay and benefits package with a company that's interviewing me next week. What pitfalls should I try to avoid when I talk with them about salary?**

A: There are a few points you should keep in mind when you're talking about negotiating your salary. The first is to avoid being defensive about the salary figure you're asking for. When people are going to be discussing salary, there's an inclination to worry about being priced out of the market by asking for too high a salary. This is self-defeating. Unless you're asking for an amount that is completely out of range for the managerial position you're seeking, it won't disqualify you. In fact, if you ask for too low a salary, it may raise questions in the interviewer's mind about your self-confidence or whether your actual qualifications are as strong as shown on your resume. For this reason, always ask for what you think you're worth. If it's considered too high, the interviewer will let you know about it in a diplomatic way.

The second point is to sidestep mentioning what you want in terms of salary as long as you can. It's to your advantage if the company makes the first offer, since they may make an offer above what you were anticipating. You will never know how high that might have been if you're the one to give the first salary figure. In terms of how to carry this off, generally the interviewer will ask what sort of salary you're looking for. You can respond by saying something such as, "I'm willing to entertain a reasonable offer in line with my background and qualifications. What do you have in mind?" If you get lucky, the interviewer will quote you a figure, or perhaps a salary range. This gives you a starting point for responding.

If the interviewer doesn't take the bait and tosses the ball back to you, you have to give an answer. But even then, you can quote a range that meets your salary goals. This works well as long as the bottom figure in your range is acceptable to you. The advantage of doing this is that the company is more than likely going to make an offer somewhat above the minimum figure in the range you give them. The reason for this sign of generosity is to give you the impression the company isn't cheap. Employers often like to impress prospective job candidates with how generous they are to employees, although you may find out differently after you're on the payroll.

A final point that bears mentioning is not to concentrate on salary to the detriment of your benefits package—or relocation expenses if you're moving from a distant location. Frequently, you can obtain concessions in other parts of your compensation package that can turn a marginally acceptable salary into an overall attractive offer. Always remember, if you don't ask, you will never know what the answer will be. Therefore, there's nothing to be gained by being shy when you're negotiating your own future.

NOTE: The three points on salary negotiations just discussed apply equally when you're negotiating the price for goods or services. First, don't be defensive about the price. Second, whenever possible let the other party make the first price offer. And third, don't concentrate on price to the exclusion of other terms.

Q: **I'm looking to relocate from Arizona to New England and have interviews scheduled with a couple of prospective employers. I'm concerned my relocation expenses may exclude me from final consideration for these and other job possibilities. Should I tell employers I will pay my own relocation costs?**

A: As a general rule, most companies pay relocation costs when they fill management vacancies with candidates who live outside the immediate area. Although it can be a significant expense, it's part of the cost of doing business if a company wants to hire the best managers it can get. Therefore, in top management positions these costs won't affect the selection process. However, at middle management levels in specialties where there may be a significant number of local candidates, relocation expenses could be a factor in the hiring decision for some employers.

In direct response to the question, whether or not you should tell employers you will pay your own relocation expenses will partly be determined by the type of position you're seeking. If a company contacts you in response to a solicitation, they are aware of the fact that you will have to relocate, so they probably won't have a problem with paying relocation expenses. Where you could be losing out is from prospective employers not contacting you when they see you live outside of the immediate geographic area. If it's a problem for them, they won't even consider you for an interview.

If you're getting plenty of nibbles, however, don't worry about relocation costs. On the other hand, if you're not getting much response, and your expertise is in a particularly competitive career area, then you might want to consider letting potential employers know you are willing to forgo relocation expenses. Of course, there's also a practical side to this. If you're single and have little in the way of household goods to move, the financial impact of not getting relocation expenses will be minimal. Conversely, if you have a large quantity of household goods and a family to move, then it isn't feasible to offer to forgo relocation expenses under any but the most dire circumstances.

Incidentally, if you receive a job offer, be sure to pin down the specific relocation expenses that will be paid by your new employer. This is because when negotiations are drawing to a close, the sweet scent of victory sometimes overwhelms the sour scent of potential problems down the road. Guard against future disappointment by getting all the facts before you accept an offer.

TWO-BIT MONEY TACTICS YOU SHOULD WATCH OUT FOR

From time to time you may run across a negotiator who will try every trick in the book to squeeze another dollar out of the proposed agreement. Needless to say, this can be frustrating when you're trying to reach an understanding. However, no matter how close the deal is to being done, you always have to remain alert. In fact, toward the end of negotiations is when you may be most vulnerable to someone trying to slip something by you.

At the other extreme you may begin a negotiation by experiencing the pleasant surprise of someone making an offer that is extremely favorable to you. Here, too, what appears to be a good deal may not turn out to be so, since an offer that's unrealistically favorable can also pose potential problems. These cases often represent someone trying to make money in the long term by buying in cheaply in the current negotiation. But whether it's at the start or near the end of negotiations it always pays to be prepared for someone trying to make money at your expense. Here are a few ways they go about trying to do this.

Q: I'm puzzled about something. I have received an offer for work to be performed for our company that is substantially lower than competitors. In looking into it, it's a reputable outfit and they're known for doing a good job. Nevertheless, I'm suspicious about the low price. Should I forget about it and celebrate my good fortune?

A: Probably not, unless you want to celebrate now and regret it later. Any offer that's substantially lower than it should be presents the potential for causing problems at a later date. Sometimes people are so happy about getting what they perceive to be a bargain that they forget about the problems that can be caused if the other party can't furnish what they promised.

Q: Why would someone bid lower than what is reasonable to do a job?

A: One reason is that they don't know what they're doing and have underestimated what it takes to do the job. In a case such as this, it makes sense for you to carefully point out the performance requirements of the job to make certain the bidder understands them. If they insist they do, question any cost estimates they give you a lot more closely than you would under normal circumstances. Assuming that someone still doesn't recognize the error of their ways, you may be wise to avoid doing business with them, unless you can negotiate sufficient performance guarantees and include them in any agreement.

A second reason a party may bid lower than expected is with the hope of making up the difference on future business. What the party is doing is taking a risk that the low bid will get them the job, which will lead to their becoming a long-term supplier for you. As long as you're sure this is the reason behind their low bid, then there's usually little risk involved for you since someone with this kind of motive will strive to give you the best performance possible. What you should guard against, however, is the possibility that the company doesn't have the capabilities to perform the work you're contracting for. On occasion, a company may seek new business that is beyond their ability to perform.

Q: I'm having difficulty working with a company we have under contract. We initially made an agreement with them to do some work for $750,000. Now they're proposing changes to the specifications in the agreement that they say will improve the performance of the machinery we're buying. This will cost an additional $300,000, and they say the machinery we're buying won't work effectively unless we add the additional requirements. They're very adamant about this and assert they won't guarantee performance of the equipment without the changes. I don't want to get stuck with something I can't use. On the other hand, I don't want to spend another $300,000. It seems to me they should have known about this when they signed the original contract. Are they trying to pull a fast one? What are my alternatives?

A: Of course, you have legal remedies if the current agreement isn't performed according to its terms. However, legal recourse won't solve the practical problem about what to do about the proposed changes, since you want a machine that meets your requirements, not a lawsuit. It looks as if you're in a situation in which a company gives you an unreasonably low bid with the hope of making more money on the current work by asking for changes in the agreement as the work proceeds. This is done by proposing changes to the work that supposedly weren't foreseen when the agreement was negotiated.

The best solution for these situations is to avoid them by not making contractual agreements where bidders are offering unreasonably low prices and changes to the specifications can be easily justified. This is often true with contracts involving the use of new or constantly changing technology. Of course, once you're in this bind, the choice boils down to either insisting on performance in accordance with the contract terms or accepting the changes and paying for them. Get your lawyers involved early in these situations, since if you insist on performance as originally negotiated, there may be problems with the finished product. (The supplier may not be making a profit because of the original low bid and may cut corners trying to finish the job.)

Try to jawbone the supplier into completing the agreement that was signed, and during the remaining performance period keep a close watch on the job's progress. As for the future, avoid getting yourself in this position by not blindly accepting a price that appears to be too low. Always investigate fully rather than assuming you're getting a bargain, because the chances are you're not.

Q: One irritating aspect of negotiating with people is running into someone who tries to nickel and dime you to death. I deal with one person who when we just about have things wrapped up always says something such as, "If you add another $100, we have a deal." This, mind you, is when we're talking overall prices that are $50,000 or $60,000. It's not the lousy $100 that bothers me, but that the person insists on arguing about peanuts. What can I do to put a halt to this nonsense?

A: This is a negotiating tactic that some people call "picking up the loose change." Admittedly, it can be annoying, but it's easy enough to put to a halt. You can do this in one of two ways. The simplest approach is to say "No" the next time this stunt is pulled. The other party isn't going to walk away from a deal over $100. Unfortunately, those who play this game don't quit easily, so your rejection is likely to trigger a response such as, "Well, if you won't give me the $100, I'll settle for $50, but that's it." All of which means you're going to have to turn the person down again so the message sinks in.

An alternative approach to handling this hassle is to maneuver yourself into a position to be the one to make the $50 or $100 pitch at the end. If you do this with a confirmed nickel and dimer, you'll have to restrain yourself from laughing when you see how fast they turn you down.

CHAPTER 3

OVERCOMING DIFFICULT NEGOTIATION TACTICS

One of the least pleasant aspects of negotiating occurs when you're dealing with a negotiator who employs every tactic and trick in the book to obtain a better deal than is otherwise justified. If you don't know how to counter these techniques, not only will it be a frustrating experience, but it could also be a costly one. The topics in this chapter cover how to handle some of the more common ploys used by some negotiators, and how to avoid being frustrated by them.

Besides those who play gamesmanship to the hilt, there are other barriers you may have to conquer to negotiate with a minimum of fuss. You may encounter people who are indecisive or by their nature are stubborn. In addition, you may encounter last-minute obstacles or phony issues that present a roadblock to reaching agreement. Knowing how to overcome these impediments can increase your chances of reaching a satisfactory agreement.

HOW TO WORK AROUND A STUBBORN NEGOTIATOR

Stubborn people are never easy to deal with, but until you have been forced to face such a person across the negotiating table, you won't know how frustrating it can be when they refuse to concede even minor points. When you're up against a stubborn—and totally irresponsible—negotiator, you have to avoid being rattled. Some people may be stubborn by nature, while others may adopt this attitude as a negotiation technique. Whether it's one or the other or a combination of the two doesn't really matter in terms of its tendency to slow negotiations down. However, it can make a difference in how you deal with the situation, since someone who is being stubborn to gain a negotiation advantage will come around once he sees that you're not going to tolerate this kind of nonsense. On the other hand, if it's a personality trait, you have to recognize it as such and work around it, since there's little you can say or do that will change the person's attitude.

Q: I've had about six negotiation meetings over the past three weeks trying to agree on price for some orders we're placing with a large manufacturer. No matter what I do or say, the other negotiator refuses to budge one inch. I'm essentially right where I was when I started negotiating. I have to wrap this up, but I don't intend to give in to this negotiator's demands. My problem is that this company is our sole source supplier, so I can't take our business elsewhere. What can I do to get this guy to be more cooperative?

A: Obviously, the other negotiator sees no compelling reason to do anything other than stick with his position. This may be because he is naturally stubborn, which is more likely if he has done little or no negotiating in the past, since some negotiators with little or no bargaining experience feel the way to get the best deal is to refuse to budge. On the other hand, if you know this person negotiates on a regular basis, then it's just a tactic to get you to give in to the person's demands. Whichever the case may be, you have to force some action or continue to be frustrated, since it's obvious the negotiator doesn't see where it's in his interests to move things along.

Q: Just what sort of action should I take?

A: There are a couple of possibilities. One is to make a final offer and leave it up to the other person to contact you. In fact, if it's feasible, put it in writing, and send a copy both to your boss and to the other negotiator's superior. By doing this, you avoid the negotiator later denying you made such an offer. This can be important if you ultimately get the negotiator's boss involved to resolve the deadlock. Furthermore, if the negotiator has been diddling for no apparent reason, his boss may put the pressure on him to move things along.

Alternatively, you can accuse the negotiator of refusing to bargain and go right around him to someone higher in his organization. Once you have established that other people in the negotiator's company are aware of the situation, you will either get some action or will at least know it's a company negotiating position, and not simply the stubbornness of the negotiator. Of course, frequently when this happens, the negotiator's boss may get involved but choose to deal directly with your boss. For this reason, always keep you own boss closely apprised of the situation as it develops.

In any event, once you let it be known that you are no longer going to tolerate someone stonewalling, the issue should be resolved. Incidentally, when only one source is available to do business with, as in this example, it isn't always easy to get a decent deal. Therefore, whenever possible, it's important to have alternative sources when you run into a negotiator who is going to take advantage of being a sole source supplier.

Q: I'm heading out to Seattle next week from our company headquarters in Cincinnati to negotiate a contract with a supplier. I'm concerned about what to do if I can't get the negotiations completed in the two days I will be there. On one occasion in the past I had to reschedule a flight three times because of difficulties in wrapping a deal up.

A: There's always the possibility that negotiating an agreement will take longer than anticipated. For this reason, it pays to be flexible in your scheduling when you are on a business trip for negotiating purposes. In fact, if someone knows you are anxious to catch a flight, they may deliberately let things drag down to the wire hoping you will make a last-minute concession to wrap things up. You can avoid this problem by not showing any indication of impatience to meet scheduled travel arrangements. Otherwise, you may find a trip to be far more costly than it should have been if you strike a hasty deal just to catch a flight.

Q: I negotiate quite frequently with a woman who is pretty reasonable to deal with, except on one issue. All she says about this one topic is that's it's not negotiable and refuses to budge from her terms. How can I counter this stubbornness on her part?

A: This probably has nothing to do with being stubborn at all. She, like you, has certain items that she doesn't consider to be negotiable.

Assuming that the issue is not a deal breaker, recognize it and work around it. However, when you run into a situation where something is allegedly nonnegotiable, try to get offsetting concessions elsewhere in exchange for accepting the nonnegotiable item. Say something such as, "I'll go along with your position on that if you will . . . ," and then ask for a concession on something of importance to you. This is the easiest and simplest way around sticking points in negotiations.

WHAT TO DO WHEN THE OTHER PARTY IS INDECISIVE

It's probably a matter of preference as to who you would least prefer to deal with: someone who is stubborn or someone who is indecisive. Whereas one refuses to make a decision, the other is incapable of making one. In either case, your patience is sure to be tested. However, with indecisive individuals you can work around the problem by looking for a way to get the decision made for them. Let's look at how to do that.

Q: I'm dealing with someone right now who is about to drive me up a wall. He neither agrees nor disagrees with anything I suggest. It's always, "We'll see" or "Let me think about that." I'm getting nowhere fast. How can I get this guy to make a decision?

A: One way is to force the individual to make a decision. For example, try saying something such as, "I've given you my offer. The decision is now yours. Otherwise, we might as well call the whole thing off." What you're doing here is forcing the negotiator to accept your offer, come back with an alternative that you can negotiate, or let the deal fall through. Either way, a decision has to be made, even if it's to let the deal fall through. Since that's the least desirable choice of all, the person will likely accept your offer or at least propose some modifications to it.

In situations such as this, an indecisive negotiator will be inclined to take your offer to his or her boss for a decision. In fact, you may well find the person's boss doing the final negotiating. Sometimes in these circumstances you may even want to suggest that the person's boss be brought in. However, try to do so in such a manner that it doesn't upset the other person. Look for a way to suggest it that is nonthreatening. For example, you could say something such as, "I can see where you aren't certain about that

Tom. Why don't we see what Mr. Blanchard (his boss) thinks. I certainly don't want *us* agreeing to anything that your company can't live with. After all, we'll be working together on this project."

Notice the way the suggestion is phrased so that it emphasizes cooperation rather than implying any need to get the boss involved for decision-making purposes. It's very important not to alienate someone who is by nature indecisive. It's difficult enough to get them to render a decision, without giving them additional reasons to procrastinate.

Q: I've got three days to get an agreement negotiated and the person I'm dealing with is so indecisive that seems impossible. What can I do?

A: Lay your cards on the table. Say, "Look, if we don't wrap this deal up by tomorrow, there won't be any deal. Here's my offer. If you need to talk it over within your organization, let's break off the talks for now and you can get back to me tomorrow." Assuming the person doesn't respond, then go right over their head to their boss. When you're stuck in a deadline situation, there's no point in worrying about whose sensitivities might be offended.

Q: I'm negotiating with several people from a company I do business with. The technical people are very cooperative, but the negotiator won't make a decision. How can I work around him?

A: Having a number of other people involved in a negotiation works to your advantage when you have an indecisive individual. You can seek the agreement of the technical personnel, since their opinions will provide reassurance for an indecisive negotiator. Although the negotiator will be the one making the final decision, if his negotiation team members make strong recommendations, he will likely go along with what they suggest. Therefore, in situations such as this, focus your energies on convincing the negotiation team members and let them, in turn, convince the negotiator.

Q: Is there any one key factor to focus on when you're negotiating with people who are indecisive?

A: What you want to do is give them as few options as possible on which to make a decision. The fewer choices they have, the fewer decisions they have to make. For this reason, try to negotiate in such a way that you aren't proposing a lot of alternative solutions for the issues being negotiated. Incidentally, as a last resort when you have an indecisive person holding things up, make the decision for him. In fact, you might want to go so far as to give them a written agreement setting forth all of the proposed terms. This sort of approach gives them only one decision to make rather than a lot of little decisions that go into the back-and-forth bargaining of a typical negotiation meeting.

A FEW INTIMIDATION TRICKS AND HOW TO BLUNT THEM

Most business negotiations are conducted in a fairly straightforward manner. Nevertheless, you may from time-to-time run into a negotiator or two who thinks the route to negotiation success is based on the ability to intimidate people. Some of these attempts will be easy to ignore, while others may have to be openly challenged. Whatever the case, let's look at a few of the more common intimidation ploys you may encounter.

Q: I've had a couple of negotiations where the other party threatened to do business with my competition if I didn't accept the terms that were being offered. Although I refused, I have to admit that the deals I struck weren't as good as they might have been if I didn't have that threat hanging over my head. Is there a good way to counter this tactic?

A: The only way to counter a threat to do business with the competition is simply to ignore it. Someone wouldn't be dealing with you in the first place if they weren't convinced of the need to do so. These are generally idle threats made simply to induce you into offering a better deal.

Of course, on occasion, you may find someone trying to play one competitor against another to obtain better terms. This is certainly reasonable if you know from the start you're engaged in a competitive negotiation situation. Under these conditions, make your best offer and be done with it. All too often, people panic and let themselves get squeezed into a deal they wouldn't ordinarily accept because of the competitive nature of the negotiations. This can be foolhardy in the long run. Rather than agree to unacceptable terms to keep a competitor from getting the business, over the long haul you may be better served by backing off. Let the competitor be the one who loses money. Naturally, there are a number of variables involved in circumstances such as this, but for the most part, it just doesn't make sense to accept money-losing deals.

Q: What can I do if someone makes an offer I don't like and gives me a deadline for accepting it?

A: The best approach is to proceed as if a deadline didn't exist. Keep on negotiating, and sometimes you will find the alleged deadline come and go with the other negotiator not even mentioning the fact. Even if the other negotiator calls a halt to negotiations when the deadline is reached, it probably is still a bluff. Negotiations may break off, but in a day or so, when the other side realizes the intimidation tactic didn't work, they will likely call you to resume discussions.

Anytime there is a valid deadline, you're going to know about it from the start of negotiations. Furthermore, it isn't hard to determine if the reason for the deadline is valid. Therefore, when you get last-minute deadline ultimatums, they're often just idle threats that are being made to inspire you to accept less than reasonable terms.

Q: I deal with someone who pure and simple tries to bully his way to getting what he wants by putting down everything I say and otherwise being obnoxious. What can be done about this?

A: If at all possible, ignore these tactics. Nothing gets under the skin of someone who operates this way any better than seeing their behavior ignored. However, if you just don't feel up to dealing with this nonsense, tell them in a calm tone of voice to knock it off. If they persist—which they probably will—just get up and leave. Tell them to call you when they want to negotiate in a dignified manner. This is a good approach if you expect to be negotiating with this person in the future. It's easy enough to put up with this nonsense on a one-time deal, but if you're going to be dealing with a jerk over a period of time, it's better to curb this behavior at the start.

Q: I hate to admit it, but I have a short fuse and I'm inclined to lose my temper when someone starts to give me a hard time. Is there any disadvantage to responding to bullying with a little intimidating of your own?

A: It's essential to keep your emotions under control, since when you lose your temper, you also lose your concentration on the task at hand, which is to negotiate the best deal you can. For this reason, getting flustered can cause you to make careless mistakes. This is, in fact, one of the main reasons some negotiators try to get you angry. It distracts you from your main goal. So if you do have a tendency to lose your temper, call a short recess whenever you know you're about to lose your composure.

TIPS FOR OVERCOMING STALLING TACTICS

As a negotiation moves along, you may start to suspect that the other negotiator is stalling rather than attempting to wrap things up. Although this isn't necessarily fatal in terms of completing a deal, it's a warning signal that you should pay attention to, since it could indicate a lack of intention to reach agreement with you. There are a number of reasons someone might deliberately use stalling tactics:

- You have a deadline to meet.
- They're trying to wear you down in the hopes you will accept terms out of frustration.
- They're negotiating simultaneously with someone else.

Q: I'm a little confused about something. What's the difference between a negotiator being stubborn, as opposed to someone being indecisive, or someone who is just stalling?

A: First, the one similarity in all three of these predicaments is that the negotiations are slowed down. However, there are different ways to deal with each of these situations, which is why they are separate topics in this chapter. Nevertheless, it may not always be easy to distinguish one from the other, so don't worry about it. The important point to recognize is that the other party to the negotiation isn't being cooperative. So whether or not you can identify the reason, you have to take some action to conclude the negotiations.

A stubborn negotiator refuses to budge on any issue, while indecisive negotiators aren't deliberately uncooperative, but are inherently incapable of making decisions. Stalling tactics are when a negotiator, who is otherwise willing to negotiate, hesitates in reaching a final agreement for the reasons just noted. It's a negotiation tactic pure and simple, and it has nothing to do with the personality of the individual.

Q: What's the best way to handle it when someone appears to be stalling?

A: There are basically two things you can do. One is to break off negotiations; the other is to give the other side an incentive for settling quickly by sweetening your offer. Of course, if you're in no hurry to settle yourself, and have an abundance of patience, you can just keep right on talking to see if you can outlast the other negotiator. However, that plays into the other parties' hands if their purpose for slowing things down is because they are simultaneously negotiating with someone else. So for the most part, you have to bring things to a head.

If you don't feel it's justified to increase your offer, tell the other negotiator you will have to leave if an agreement can't be reached. When someone is just stalling to try and get a better deal, this usually jars them into action.

However, if you have some flexibility in your negotiating position, you can try making an offer that is contingent upon immediate acceptance. Just be sure your sweetened offer is accepted without delay. Otherwise, you will make the concession and the negotiator will continue to stall. Of course, that could happen anyway, but if it does, just get up and leave.

Q: How should I phrase an offer designed to get immediate acceptance?

A: You could say, "We've covered everything that has to be covered, Victoria, so there's no point in prolonging these discussions any further. In the interests of settling right now, I'm going to add $3,000 to my offer. It makes no sense on my part to do it, but if you really want to reach agreement, you'll accept it since it's too good a deal to pass up. However, that means we settle right here and now. I won't settle for this higher figure at a later date, so it's now or never. What do you say?"

Naturally, the specifics will vary, but the point is to emphasize that you are raising the stakes to get agreement. Should the negotiator not settle immediately, but call you in a day or two, you have the option of refusing to agree to the higher figure.

Q: I'm in the middle of a lengthy negotiation for some commercial property our company is buying. Last night, I inadvertently learned through a friend who is reliable that the people I'm dealing with are also negotiating with another company. To put it mildly, I'm not a happy camper, and I feel like going into the negotiation meeting this morning and telling the sellers what they can do with their property. Even though we would like to buy it, it's not essential and we have other options. How would you recommend handling this situation?

A: Calm down and play it for all it's worth. Since it's not a deal you have to make, why not lowball your offer and go for getting a bargain. The other party is stringing you along, so why get mad when you can get even? Of course, you have to play this just right. If you let your final offer be known right away, since it is low, the chances are the other potential buyer may offer a better deal.

What you want to do is to stall in making your final offer until you're reasonably certain the other potential buyer is no longer interested. The chances are this will become evident the minute the other negotiator becomes serious about wrapping the deal up. When that happens say something such as, "In thinking this whole thing through, it appears the property isn't worth as much as we originally thought. Therefore, we can only offer you $ . . . ." This may work if the other possibility to sell has fallen through, but even if it doesn't, it's worth a try. After all, the other negotiator was using you while trying to get a better deal elsewhere, so it's only fair you should go for the good deal yourself.

Q: What happens if I know someone else is bidding on something, but I don't have any other viable options?

A: Try making your best offer contingent upon quick acceptance. This forces the other side to risk losing your offer if they can't get a better price elsewhere. Otherwise, the negotiator will get you in the middle of a bidding war, and if this happens, you're bound to pay more than what you want to spend.

SEVERAL EASY WAYS TO COUNTER VAGUE ANSWERS AND EVASIVE TACTICS

Even though it may not be part of your basic nature, you may have to press hard to get the information you need from the party you're negotiating with. Most people won't deliberately misrepresent something, but a shrewd negotiator isn't about to point out the problems with something. Therefore, it's up to you to ferret out the facts. Otherwise, the deal you make may not turn out to be the bargain you thought it was going to be. So unless you want to run the risk of getting burned, you had better pin down someone who is being vague or evasive.

Q: When I ask questions about the technical details of some equipment I'm buying, I get vague answers. What can I do to get the specifics I require to make an intelligent buying decision?

A: Vague answers may be deliberate if the other negotiator doesn't want to reveal certain information to you. On the other hand, an imprecise answer may be unintentional. This can happen when the person doesn't have the knowledge to answer the question or the question itself was vague. Therefore, before you assume that the negotiator is deliberately trying to conceal something, try asking your question differently to be certain it's understood.

If the information you seek still isn't forthcoming, tell the negotiator you need these facts to make a decision. Assuming there is no deliberate intent to deceive, the person will likely offer to get you the information. However, if you get an argument about the need for the information, or some other inexact reply, see if you can get some indication of why the other person is trying to intentionally avoid answering your query. Keep pressing your case until you either get what you want or are satisfied as to why it can't be furnished. If necessary, and the information is vital enough to justify it, threaten to halt the negotiations until you get what you need.

Q: I think I'm about to set a world record for dealing with the dumbest negotiator there is. He apparently knows nothing, since I haven't yet gotten one solid answer to a question. How this guy could survive 15 years with the same company is beyond me. What should I do here?

A: You might want to start by reevaluating your assessment of the negotiator's intelligence. Just because you're not getting the answers you want doesn't mean the other negotiator doesn't know what he's doing. In fact, as your question indicates, he's been doing this job for a long time. This alone should tell you that it's not that he doesn't know the answers, but rather that he chooses not to furnish them to you.

Unfortunately, it appears that your failure to recognize this may be due to the fact you're angry and frustrated. As mentioned before, there's no room for letting your emotions cloud your judgment when you're negotiating. So to start with, relax, assume the person is in full command of the facts, and decide how you're going to obtain what you need to know.

To be successful here, state calmly but emphatically that you expect answers to questions you raise if an agreement is to be reached. Ask the other negotiator if he's going to cooperate. The odds are that if you do this, the reply will be in some form of denial that the person is being evasive. In fact, you will probably be accused of not asking clear and accurate questions. However, the odds are your future questions will be responded to in more detail.

Q: How should I phrase my challenge to the other party?

A: Although the circumstances may justify a slightly different approach, here's a good general way to handle this.

You: "Stacey, you keep avoiding answering my questions. Unless I get answers, we aren't going to be able to reach agreement. If you're not willing to cooperate, let me know and we can call it quits right now."

Stacey: "What's with you? I'm answering the questions. Perhaps you just don't understand the technicalities."

You: "Knock it off. There's nothing technical about asking how many hours of labor are required to produce one unit."

Stacey: "You never asked that question. Is that what you want to know?"

You: "That's only one of the questions I have. There are others."

Stacey: "Well let's have them. I can't answer questions if you don't ask them."

You: "Let's answer the first question before we go on to anything else. How many hours of direct labor are required to produce one unit?"

Stacey: "I'll have to get those figures from our cost accounting department."

You: "Great. How long will that take?"

Stacey: "A couple of hours. In the meantime, let's go on to your next question."

You: "It's almost lunch time anyway. Let's break for lunch and be back in two hours. That will give you time to get the data from cost accounting."

NOTE: There are a couple of points to mention about this exchange. First, since the other negotiator hasn't furnished any information yet, it's better to see what sort of response is forthcoming to the first question before going on to any others. Sometimes a negotiator will start to promise all kinds of information, but then continue the discussion in the hope that what was asked for is forgotten as negotiations proceed.

Of course, it's not absolutely necessary to wait if you don't need the information to go on to other matters. But if it's feasible, it's worth doing, since it sends a signal you're not going to continue until you get your answer. This will help set the stage for timely responses as the negotiations continue. It's also important to state the question precisely as was done here. Otherwise, this provides an opening for someone to give you information that doesn't directly answer your question. When you challenge the data, the reply will likely be, "Oh, I thought that was what you asked for."

Q: **When someone doesn't answer questions, that's relatively easy to challenge. What I'm dealing with is a negotiator who answers everything, but tends to be evasive in doing so. I'm not sure whether it's me or the negotiator. What are some things to look for that would indicate someone is trying to hide something?**

A: There are all sorts of ways people can be evasive during negotiations. Some of the more common things to look for are

- The responses to questions are phrased in generalities, rather than specifics.

- Answers are given to questions other than what you asked about.
- There's a great deal of stalling in answering your questions.
- Support documentation you ask for isn't furnished.
- The other party states they don't have the information you seek.
- Attempts are made to shift the discussion from the subject you're pursuing.

Q: I've tried everything possible, but I can't seem to get enough information to make an informed judgment. I have a gut feeling that the other negotiator is concealing material facts. What can I do about this?

A: In a situation such as this, there are two approaches you can take. One is to forget the whole thing. When you're unable to get the data you need to make an informed opinion, it's foolhardy to conclude an agreement. Obviously, what you don't know and haven't been told isn't beneficial to you. On the other hand, in certain cases, if you can put sufficient safeguards in a written agreement to protect yourself, then there's nothing to prevent you from going ahead. However, be extremely cautious about doing this, and be certain you're adequately protected.

Q: I'm in the process of changing jobs and I want to be prepared for interviews. In the past, it always seems I got vague answers when I asked questions about salary. The interviewer always seemed to try and put the burden on me by asking what salary I was looking for. I'd rather have them make an offer without knowing what I wanted. Once I give them a figure, they certainly aren't going to pay me more than that. Is there a way to pin down interviewers in terms of compensation packages.

A: Here's a situation where you have to be vague yourself. When the interviewer asks what sort of salary you're looking for, give a generalized answer such as, "I'm open to a reasonable offer that is in line with my experience." The interviewer is likely to then ask you what you think that is. Instead of giving a figure you can say, "I hesitate to be specific since the salary is part of a total compensation package. Therefore, you're in a more informed position than I am to make the call." It's doubtful you will be pushed any further on the issue, but if the interviewer insists, give a figure that is on the high side, but cover yourself by saying, "This is roughly where I want to be, but then again, fringe benefits and other factors come into play, so I want you to know this isn't cast in concrete." An alternative approach would be to give the negotiator a range you would accept. But make the low end the minimum you would take the job for in case they come back and offer you the bottom figure on the range you give. However, it's likely they will offer you something higher than that in an attempt to avoid appearing to be cheap.

HOW TO HANDLE ANY ULTIMATUM

One negotiation tactic you may have to deal with is some form of an ultimatum. Of course, depending upon the specifics of the negotiation, ultimatums can be made in various ways. However, in most business negotiations these typically take one of two forms: a deadline to accept an offer or an assertion that the offer is on a "take it or leave it" basis. Nevertheless, no matter what sort of an ultimatum may be made, there are effective ways to deal with them. The three most obvious approaches to dealing with any ultimatum are to

- Essentially ignore the threat.
- Respond with your own ultimatum.
- Recognize the ultimatum and accommodate it.

Q: Why would you want to risk ignoring an ultimatum when it's made?

A: The purpose of an ultimatum is to force you to agree to terms or conditions you don't want to accept. Generally, the ultimatum is being used as a negotiation ploy to try and panic you into accepting the other negotiator's offer or else risk not completing a deal at all. By doing this, the other negotiator has control of the situation. He either gets what he wants if you accept his terms, or he has the option of breaking off the negotiations. In essence, he has the possibility for gain if you accept the offer, with virtually nothing to lose, since even if you refuse he can continue to negotiate.

You, on the other hand, are in a much riskier position. If you accept the terms offered, you have a lousy deal, and if you refuse, there's the threat of no deal at all. Since you're not about to agree to a bad deal in the first place, there's little to be lost by ignoring the threat. Even if the other negotiator calls it quits, the only deal you're losing at this stage is one you don't want in the first place.

Furthermore, by ignoring the ultimatum you're displaying a cavalier attitude toward the threat, which has to leave the other negotiator thinking it doesn't matter to you whether a deal is made or not. At a minimum, it sends a very clear signal that you aren't going to accept an agreement based upon the terms that are being offered. Therefore, if negotiations continue, you have gained a tactical advantage in getting a better deal than is currently on the table.

Q: When someone gives you an ultimatum, how should you go about countering it with an ultimatum of your own?

A: Of the approaches you can take, one is to escalate your demands to compensate for the unreasonable terms you're being offered. A simple example is if the other negotiator gives you a "take it or leave it" selling price of, say, $150,000, respond with a "take it or leave it" offer to buy for $100,000, even though you consider somewhere around $135,000 to be acceptable.

Q: It seems to me that doing something like that is almost suicidal in terms of getting a deal done. Won't it make it that much more likely that the other party will just walk away and forget the whole thing?

A: You have to keep in mind that you were offered an ultimatum to accept an unreasonable deal. If the other negotiator was serious when such an offer was made, then there's no deal to be made anyway, unless you accept the unreasonable terms being offered. On the other hand, if the negotiator just issued the ultimatum as a ploy to get a better deal, he will quickly see that his game playing is making an agreement even more difficult. He will also recognize that he's not dealing with a fool who will accept anything just to get the deal done. As a result, it's likely the other negotiator will respond to your counterattack with language such as, "That's not even a reasonable price you're offering. Aren't you serious about negotiating?" You can then respond in kind. Whatever the verbal back-and-forth might be, the end result will be a more reasonable approach to reaching a negotiated agreement.

Q: In my management position, I don't have to do a lot of negotiating so I really don't want to get into this sort of gamesmanship. What are my other alternatives for dealing with an ultimatum?

A: That's understandable, and if you want to be straightforward in your response, let's look at a couple of representative replies you can give to an ultimatum and some probable reactions from the other negotiator.

Action: "Look, Carol, I'd like to get an agreement signed off, but I'm not going to accept those terms."

Reaction: "Well, it's these terms or no terms."

Your options: Here you can either accept the unreasonable conditions or just call it quits. Of course, the other party could subsequently contact you and attempt to resume discussions. If that happens, you haven't lost anything, assuming you're still interested in reaching an agreement with this person.

Action: "Jack, I don't want to spend all day arguing about this. What you're offering is unacceptable. If you can't do any better than that, we won't be able to reach agreement."

Reaction: "That's the best I can do, but in the interests of getting this settled, I'll lower my figure 10%."

Your options: Sometimes, a negotiator will come back with a slightly sweeter offer, but one that is still unacceptable. This gives you the option of trying some back-and-forth negotiating with a number of repetitive offers and counteroffers. Alternatively, you can call it quits at this point. How you handle these situations is a matter of choice, but unless you want to accept unreasonable terms, you ultimately have to refuse to be intimidated by the ultimatum.

Q: One of the options mentioned was to accept the terms offered by the ultimatum. Why would anyone do that?

A: It may be that the offer upon which the ultimatum was based isn't the best deal in the world, but is nevertheless one that you can live with. If this is the case, it may be preferable to accept the offer rather than run the risk of not reaching an agreement. Whether or not a marginally reasonable offer should be accepted is contingent upon the alternatives available if negotiations should fail. The better your alternatives to a negotiated agreement, the less need there is to accept anything other than favorable terms.

TECHNIQUES FOR GETTING DEADLOCKS OFF DEAD-CENTER

Although it's not inevitable, many times negotiations get bogged down over one or more issues with neither party willing to yield in their position. However, despite the reluctance of either side to budge, it's necessary to find common ground, since the alternative is no agreement at all. Therefore, although this is a point where the two parties may be unhappy with each other's unyielding position, it's also the point in time where it's most necessary for the two sides to work together to get their differences resolved.

Q: I've encountered a deadlock in negotiations I'm conducting with another manager in the company. It concerns the preparation of reports done by my department. The other manager supplies input for these reports, and she claims she can't furnish the data by the time I need it to meet the report distribution date. She's offered to furnish summary figures by my deadline, but I don't find that to be a satisfactory solution.

What it boils down to is that the departments working for her would have to work overtime to furnish the data I need, while one of the departments reporting to me would have to work overtime if the data were delivered on the schedule she wants. It's a budget problem for one of us whichever way you slice it.

The director of operations, to whom we both report, initially told us to work out the details. However, I don't think he assumed there would be additional labor costs involved. How can this deadlock be resolved?

A: Your first choice should be to explore alternatives in terms of the data required or the report schedules. Assuming this has been done, the solution here is for the two of you to jointly discuss the situation with the operations manager. Explain that all other alternatives have been looked at, and none of them are satisfactory. This is a situation where the director of operations should be the decision maker, since one of the groups will be incurring additional labor costs. From a negotiation standpoint, this is the sort of deadlock that in more formal negotiations would call for a mediator or arbitrator to settle the dispute. This is just one of the many internal situations where managers are negotiating on a daily basis without actually thinking of it as such.

Q: One of the sales representatives who works for me has dumped a problem in my lap. There's a deadlock in reaching agreement with a customer over a large order. The problem isn't price, which is the usual issue, but rather delivery dates. The dates the customer wants can't be met. However, the customer is insistent on those dates or nothing at all. This isn't an account we can afford to lose. How can I resolve this deadlock and still keep this customer?

A: Often the solution to a deadlock during negotiations is for one of the parties to solve the problem internally within their own organization. Here, it would appear your best bet is to talk to the manager in charge of production and see what can be done about filling the order by the requested delivery dates. Perhaps quantities can be shifted or production can be increased. If you encounter resistance from the production manager, take this problem to a higher level, since the importance of retaining this customer may require a higher level directive to override any resistance you get from the production department. Incidentally, if substantial costs for overtime pay will be necessary to meet the delivery dates, this should be discussed with the customer by the person doing the direct negotiations. It's one thing to please a customer, but it's something else to lose money to do so.

Q: I've run into a deadlock in negotiations, and there's no apparent reason for it other than the unwillingness of the other side to show any movement in their negotiating position. What can I do about this?

A: This isn't unusual, and it doesn't result from a deadlock over a particular issue, but rather results from one party holding firm in their position in the hopes of getting the other side to accept their terms. When this happens, let the other party know you have no intention of agreeing with their settlement terms.You might want to suggest a recess so they can take another look at their position. If you get a negative response, your choices boil down to keeping the discussions going in an attempt to get the other party off dead center or breaking off negotiations with an invitation to call you if they change their mind.

Q: **There's a snag in our negotiations, which had been going smoothly right down to the end where we were trying to agree on a final price. Although the difference isn't substantial, the other negotiator refuses any alternative to close the gap. I even suggested we split the difference, and when that was refused, offered to absorb two-thirds of the difference to get the thing settled. When that wasn't accepted, I called for a recess, which is where I'm at right now. Why is this person being so unreasonable?**

A: There's no way to be sure of why the other negotiator feels so strongly about the issue without doing a little bit of probing to find out what the reason is. However, this may be a situation where the negotiator has been given a price edict by a higher authority and therefore is refusing to budge. If you can find this out, then there are a couple of ways to handle it. First, try suggesting that the negotiator's boss get involved. Failing that, make it clear that the offer is unacceptable. That way, the negotiator can relay this information back to his or her boss.

Sometimes, this sort of predicament can be resolved by looking for some alternative to trade off that will give you equal value for what you're conceding. This approach has the benefit of allowing the other negotiator to win on the sticking point. Often, with a little creativity you can do well with making this sort of trade-off, since the problem issue is so significant to the other side that there may be a willingness to make substantive concessions in unrelated areas.

Q: **We've just started negotiating to purchase some assets from a small company that's going out of business; however, we're already having difficulty resolving one issue. At this pace these negotiations could go on forever. Any suggestions on how to speed things up?**

A: Whenever one issue threatens to deadlock negotiations, set it aside if possible and go on to discuss other terms and conditions. This not only keeps the negotiations from stalling, but it may make it easier to resolve the deadlocked item later on. Sometimes settling most of the terms and conditions makes the negotiating parties more amenable to seeking a satisfactory solution to what otherwise would have been a significant hang-up.

Q: **I'm stuck at my bottom price limit which the party I'm negotiating with finds to be a little too high. We've gone back and forth on this; it's obvious they won't budge, and I can't lower my price anymore. Is there any other option besides throwing in the towel and calling the deal off?**

A: If it's feasible, try sweetening your offer to compensate for the other side accepting your price. The specifics will vary with what you're selling, but there are all sorts of possibilities for almost any situation. A higher-quality item, accelerated delivery, and more favorable payment terms are just a few of the candidates you should consider.

WAYS TO DEFUSE PHONY ISSUES

All sorts of bogus issues may be raised during a negotiation meeting by the other negotiator. Whatever the supposed justification for raising the phony claim may appear to be, the ultimate objective is usually to obtain a better deal for the other side. This isn't always the motive, however, since it's possible to use some form of excuse for any number of reasons, including just not wanting to go through with the current deal. Regardless of the intention, you must recognize and counter these excuses as quickly as possible.

Q: **We're negotiating to buy a small chain of stores to give us entry into another regional market. However, the negotiations aren't getting anywhere, since the owner of the stores keeps dragging his feet whenever the deal appears to be wrapped up. At first we thought it was price, but we upped our bid a couple of times and still can't get the deal signed. Now he keeps bringing up petty issues, and every time we resolve one, up comes another. Is there any way to pin this deal down?**

A: There may not be. This could well be a case of phony issues being raised to disguise the real reason, which may be that the owner really doesn't want to sell the business. On occasion, people conduct business negotiations without any intention of following through to a final agreement. As here, it may be a case of a business owner unwilling to relinquish control of his business. In other situations, it may be a desire to test the market to see what value the market places on a company or piece of real property. Whatever the reason, once you see that the discussions aren't heading toward agreement, pin the other party down to a yes or no in terms of negotiating a settlement so you're not spinning your wheels indefinitely.

Q: One of the most annoying things I encounter when negotiating are people who say they have to check my offer out with a boss or some other authority figure before they can accept it. Invariably, they come back and state that the offer was refused. Frequently, I'm given another figure that I'm told is acceptable. Am I being suckered, and if so, how do I deal with this sort of hassle?

A: This is a standard gimmick used to extract a better deal near the end of a negotiation. This "authority figure" ploy is probably the most common of the phony issues you will run into. It's easy enough to recognize once you realize this is what is taking place. Here's what happens:

You reach an agreement with the other negotiator who qualifies it by saying he has to clear it with his superiors. After a brief recess, the negotiator returns and states that his boss wouldn't buy the deal. He'll then likely offer terms that are allegedly acceptable to his boss. These terms are, of course, less favorable to you than what had been originally agreed upon with the negotiator.

You can handle this situation in a couple of ways. The first is to insist that you will accept only what you and the negotiator had agreed to. This forces the other negotiator to make the next move. Often, after some discussion, the negotiator will go back to his superiors and then come back and agree to your terms. Alternatively, one of his bosses may show up to argue the issue. In any event, standing your ground is the key to success here.

As another alternative, you can state that you will have to check out their offer with your own bosses. Call for a short recess during which time you can either discuss the matter with your boss or, if you have complete authority to do what you want, simply do nothing. Then go back into negotiations and state that your superiors won't accept anything other than what you and the negotiator had agreed upon.

Incidentally, you can avoid this kind of ploy by asking at the beginning of negotiations if the person negotiating has authority to agree to terms. Of course, business procedure being what it is, many large transactions require various approvals before they can be finalized. This is understandable. What you want to preclude is the gimmick of trying to extract a little better deal at the last moment, so by talking about negotiation authority right at the start, you send a clear message that you don't expect a penny-ante ploy to be pulled at the end.

HOW TO SLICE AND DICE LAST-MINUTE OBSTACLES

As much as you do to try and avoid it, you will often experience last-minute obstacles that threaten to derail the agreement you have worked so hard to negotiate. Frequently, these complications seem overwhelming, but many of them can be overcome by attacking them piecemeal. Whatever the bottleneck may be, if you and the other negotiator work together to solve the problem, the difficulty can often be overcome without too much effort.

Q: After lengthy negotiations to settle a large number of technical issues, we're finally down to establishing an agreed-upon price. However, the other negotiator and I are having trouble agreeing on the elements of cost involved in the work to be done. Is there any way to avoid getting bogged down in disagreements on individual cost issues?

A: The simplest thing to do is to reach agreement on a total price and ignore the cost elements that comprise it. What's important is the price to be paid, not what it's comprised of. The cost of labor, overhead, profit, and so forth don't matter as long as you are satisfied with the total price to be paid. This approach can save a lot of headaches. For example, when prices are established on an element-by-element basis, there's bound to be disagreement as to what's reasonable. This is especially true when people talk about profit. If you're getting a lower price than elsewhere, what difference does it make if the lowest-price supplier is making a higher profit than competitors?

Q: Final negotiations have come to a standstill on a project I'm working on. What happened is that I thought that we had agreed on something early on in the negotiations, while the other negotiator thinks otherwise. As a result, we are having trouble finalizing the agreement. Can anything be done to prevent this sort of misunderstanding?

A: When complex negotiations requiring agreement on a large number of terms and conditions is required, carelessness can lead to misinterpretation of what was said previously when it comes time to pull everything together for a final agreement. For this reason, whenever an agreement is reached on an issue, the agreement should be written down if possible for later reference. That way, at a later point in the negotiations it will be easy to refresh memories as to what was agreed to. Otherwise, meaningless disputes can break out that scuttle a negotiation because of a failure to adequately document agreements made early on in the negotiation process.

Q: **I've just completed negotiations on a contract for work to be done for our company. Before the contract can be signed, I have to get a number of internal approvals, My problem is that one division head is threatening not to sign off. He won't admit it, but his real objection is that he wanted the work to be done internally. How can I get around this hurdle?**

A: A negotiator is often second-guessed within a company, but the problem you have goes beyond that. It's basically a political issue, and you have little choice but to bring management pressure to bear to get this agreement approved. You shouldn't have any trouble doing this, since it will be pretty obvious to everyone that the refusal is based upon a case of sour grapes. Incidentally, whenever you have to negotiate anything that may have internal opposition, try to neutralize it beforehand. This will prevent problems later on.

CHAPTER 4

LAYING THE GROUNDWORK FOR NEGOTIATION SUCCESS

As with a lot of other things in life, paying attention to the minor details involved in negotiations can pay dividends, while failing to do so can lead to failure. For example, it might not seem particularly important as to who you designate to assist you in negotiating a deal. Unfortunately, it may be only when it's too late that you realize the wrong person on your negotiating team can do more to scuttle a deal than the opposing negotiator.

It's also easy to overlook the advantages of researching the opposition before you negotiate. This is commonly neglected, especially in view of the heavy work loads of most managers. In fact, unless the negotiation is of major proportions, it's impossible to spend any extensive period of time in preparation.

However, there are details overlooked that don't involve a great deal of time in preparing. These include selecting the right time and place to negotiate, what documentation you will furnish or receive, and what if any experts you will use. One of the most neglected items that can have a significant impact is knowing how to structure a negotiated agreement to encourage performance. After all, the best deal in the world is worthless if what you negotiated for isn't what you eventually get. All these elements for negotiation success are covered in the following topics.

STRATEGIES FOR PICKING NEGOTIATION TEAM PARTICIPANTS

Most routine negotiating situations won't involve the participation of anyone other than yourself and the other negotiator. In other instances, the technical nature of the subject matter may dictate that you have someone with the necessary technical expertise with you for assistance. And where the negotiations are large and complex, there may be a number of people participating as members of your negotiating team. In any event, there are a number of factors to consider in choosing anyone who will participate.

Q: Since I will be the one making the decisions, what difference does it make who I select to assist me?

A: First, on a practical level, the sheer number of people who participate in negotiations can cause problems. The more people there are, the longer the negotiations are likely to take. It also becomes harder to exercise control over the issues being discussed. This can lead to the discussions going off on tangents or an excessive amount of time being spent on relatively minor issues. This is particularly true if technical participants get involved in lengthy deliberations with their counterparts representing the other side. In addition, there's always the danger of someone on your team revealing information you prefer to keep from the other negotiator.

Beyond this is the simple problem of logistics. The more people you have participating, the larger the facility that will be required for the talks. This problem will be compounded, since as you bring people with specific skills in to discuss certain areas, the other negotiator will probably want his own experts sitting in on the discussions. An even more important logistical consideration comes up if you will be conducting the negotiations at an out-of-town location. Here, travel and lodging costs are an influencing factor in limiting the size of your negotiation team.

Aside from the number of participants, the attributes of individuals can't be ignored. Someone who is particularly talkative may monopolize the discussions so you have a great deal of difficulty getting anything done. Not to mention the fact that this sort of person can have you holding your breath in fear of the person saying the wrong thing.

Q: I have a complex negotiation coming up that because of its technical nature and substantial dollar value will require the participation of several people as part of my negotiation team. What measures can I take to limit the number of people on my team?

A: Try to limit your team to those with a wide breadth of knowledge in the particular area they will furnish guidance on; this will preclude the necessity of having several people from any one discipline on your team. Furthermore, rather than having everyone sit through every negotiation session, keep your experts "on call" to be used as needed. It's a lot easier to control matters when you have the expertise available for use without actually having them in the meeting when they're not needed.

Q: I have an engineer who has worked with me on prior negotiations who has caused me problems by shooting off his mouth when he shouldn't. At the last negotiation he participated in, he and his counterpart at the other company got together and recommended substantial changes in the technical work statement, which would have cost considerably more money. In fact, on more than one occasion I've had technical types wanting to make changes to add bells and whistles of one sort or another. I've told this guy a dozen times not to do this, but he refuses to listen. It's not that he's being deliberately malicious, but rather that he gets so wrapped up in the technical aspects of things, he neglects to consider the costs involved. How can I control this?

A: Limit his participation as much as possible. In short, have him on call to answer technical questions, but don't let him sit through the entire process. Second, interrupt him the minute he starts going off on a tangent by saying something such as, "We'll talk about that later, Jim. Right now, we have other issues to discuss." These are, of course, stopgap measures that you may already have tried. However, there's another possibility that could solve the problem.

Many times the person with the most expertise in an area is chosen as a negotiation team member, with little or no thought given to their personality and demeanor. You may find yourself better off by selecting someone who may not be quite as competent technically, but is less likely to cause problems during negotiations. This is a trade-off that's worth considering in any given situation.

Q: What are the overall criteria I should look for in picking negotiation team members?

A: Before you do anything else, decide if, in fact, you need any assistance. Many business negotiations are routine and can be handled on a one-on-one basis. Incidentally, don't arbitrarily decide to add members to your negotiating team just because the other negotiator has assistance. If there is no valid reason to have anyone else present, let the other negotiator run the risk of having a team member foul up by saying the wrong thing.

On the other hand, if both you and the other negotiator plan to have other people in attendance, try to reach an agreement on how many people each of you will have. This, of course, isn't always possible, but if it's feasible, it helps to limit the number of attendees.

As far as the individual traits you're looking for when you select team members, you obviously want to pick people with the requisite skills needed to assist you, whether they be financial, legal, or technical. However, if you have several people who possess the necessary skills, select the one who follows directions best and is least likely to say anything out of turn.

Q: I've been assigned the responsibility of negotiating an agreement with a consulting firm to do some work for us. I've selected people from two technical areas that will work closely with the consultants, and I need someone from a third area. My problem is that the person I would logically pick was opposed to having consultants do this work for us. Yet this is the person most knowledgeable about this area. Am I looking for trouble if I select her for my team?

A: Not necessarily. Making this person part of your negotiating team will give her a vested interest in the results. Furthermore, by letting her contribute in selecting a consulting firm, she will be part of the solution. If she isn't on the team, she will be in a position to sit back and criticize everything that takes place on the project. Naturally, you may feel she might cause problems during negotiations, but if anything out of line comes up, you can always remove her from the team. And if she simply confines her actions to asking hard but fair questions, then you will have gained a valued asset.

USING TIME AND LOCATION OF MEETINGS TO YOUR ADVANTAGE

Negotiations are stressful enough as it is without undue pressures being added. Therefore, the comfort factor alone is a good enough reason to schedule negotiations at a time and place most favorable to you. However, beyond this very basic desire, there are a number of other things to consider when you're dealing with the logistics of setting up a negotiation meeting. Some of these are fundamental, such as having the meeting in a room with ample space for the participants, at a location that will be free from interruptions and other distractions. Other considerations such as whether to hold the meeting at your place of business or the other party's premises can have significant meaning from a negotiating standpoint.

Q: I've read where it's important to hold negotiation meetings at your place of business to give yourself a "home court" advantage. Is this true?

A: There are advantages to conducting negotiations at your location. However, sometimes there are compelling reasons for having the negotiations elsewhere. Benefits of meeting at your place of business include

- You can select the meeting room, seating arrangements, and other logistical details.
- Your stress is lower when you don't have to endure the fatigue-related problems of travel.
- You have no deadline pressures imposed if you have no return travel to book.
- You have ready access to anyone you need to call upon to answer questions that come up during negotiations.
- You can show the other party the capabilities of your company such as production or research facilities.
- You get a psychological boost from being on familiar turf.

Q: You mentioned there are times when it's beneficial to negotiate at the location of the party you're doing business with. When would this be preferred to negotiating at your home base?

A: There are a couple of reasons why hitting the road may be to your benefit. For one thing, it puts you in a position to ask for documentation and other support data during discussions. Since you're at the other party's facility, they can't use the excuse that it's not available. This is a common response used when people are away from their place of business. When someone asks for something the response is typically, "We didn't bring that information with us." You avoid this type of brush-off when you are on-site.

Holding negotiations away from home also gives you the opportunity to view any facilities that may be involved in the work to be done under the agreement being negotiated. This won't apply in every situation, but when it does, it's something to take into account in deciding where negotiations will be held.

Incidentally, when you are on the road, besides any necessary experts that accompany you, always make arrangements for people you may have to contact to be available when needed. This can avoid the frustration of trying to track someone down in a hurry.

Q: What does timing have to do with negotiation meetings?

A: Although it isn't always true, there are occasions when proper timing can be crucial to negotiation success. For example, if you're on the buying side of a negotiation situation, it's a lot easier to get a good deal if you're negotiating with a company during a slack period in their business. Whatever you are negotiating, whenever you have the option as to when to negotiate, it's generally better to do so when the other side faces circumstances that make it more likely they will be motivated to reach agreement on a deal.

There's another aspect of timing that is relevant when the specifics of timing will have no direct impact on the negotiations. It just involves courtesy in scheduling a meeting to accommodate the other party. This won't make or break a deal one way or the other, but not being rigid about the day or time of a meeting will help get things off on the right foot. And being helpful in this regard can establish good rapport that can carry over into the negotiations themselves. Sometimes it's a combination of little things rather than any grand strategy that works best in any business environment.

THE ABCs OF NEGOTIATION MEETINGS

As with any other meeting you conduct as a manager, a negotiation meeting will be worthwhile if you plan it properly. However, unlike other meetings that you have exclusive control over, the other party to the negotiation will influence the outcome of any negotiation session. Therefore, maintaining control of the meeting so you keep it on the right course is a lot trickier when you're negotiating.

Most business negotiation meetings are pretty informal and often consist of a one-on-one meeting with your counterpart. This, of course, depends upon the nature of the transaction, and negotiations involving complex matters can result in large meetings and the involvement of a significant number of people. But whether a negotiation meeting is large or small, there are a number of fundamentals to follow that will improve your chances for having a successful negotiation session. These include preparing a formal or informal agenda, briefing anyone who will be participating in the negotiations, as well as tactics for keeping the meeting running smoothly.

Q: Since meetings are so time consuming, wouldn't it be preferable to conduct negotiations using the phone, fax, and computer-based communications?

A: These are all useful adjuncts to any negotiation, and simple transactions involving minimal negotiation can be conducted in this fashion. However, any negotiation requiring back-and-forth exchange to resolve substantive differences are best handled in a face-to-face meeting. First, telecommunications are impersonal and don't provide for using your personality in convincing the other party to accept your point of view. They can, in fact, make it even harder to reach agreement, since it's a lot easier to reject an offer over the phone than it is when the person is sitting across the table. Fax and on-line computer transmissions also pose potential security problems for sensitive company information. So except for routine transactions, meeting in person is the best approach for most negotiations.

Q: I've never bothered to prepare an agenda beforehand for a negotiation meeting, since it's just too time consuming a detail considering how seldom I negotiate anything and the scope of my other managerial duties. Isn't a prepared agenda a waste of time anyway, since negotiations never seem to follow any preconceived pattern?

A: Contrary to your belief that preparing an agenda will be time consuming, it actually can be a time-saver. Just jotting down a list of topics you want to cover will avoid having to make follow-up calls or additional meetings to cover items that were forgotten in the initial meeting. In addition, preparing an agenda forces you to think about the negotiation beforehand. This planning can not only save time by keeping the negotiation meeting on course, but it can also save money by avoiding costly blunders that result from carelessness.

Whenever an agenda is mentioned, it conjures up an image of a long and detailed document, which is wrong. An agenda can consist of little more than a few handwritten notes or a brief outline in your personal planner. Don't view a negotiation meeting agenda as some sort of formal document that requires the i's to be dotted and the t's to be crossed. If you have a relatively simple negotiation to conduct, a brief list of things you want to cover during negotiations will suffice.

Q: What sort of items should be included in a negotiation agenda?

A: Specialized topics to be included in your agenda will hinge upon what is being negotiated. The general items to be included consist of basics such as time, date, and location of the meeting and a list of attendees. Negotiation-specific items in your agenda should include potential questions the other side may be expected to ask as well as questions you want to raise. You may also want to outline your negotiation position and possible concessions you are willing to make if it becomes necessary to do so. Incidentally, if other people from your company will be assisting you, identify their responsibilities during the negotiation meeting.

Q: Who should you distribute the agenda to?

A: The segment with basic facts on time, date, location, and attendees can be given to participants who will be assisting you, but it's not necessary to do this. The information on possible concessions and your negotiation objective should be kept confidential. Although it isn't likely someone assisting you would leak the contents to the other side, a careless copy left lying around could cause trouble. Furthermore, there's no need to distribute this information since before the negotiation meeting begins, a prenegotiation meeting should be held if you will have other people on your negotiation team.

Q: What's the purpose of having a prenegotiation meeting?

A: A prenegotiation meeting will allow you to go over your game plan with negotiation team members. Make sure everyone understands their responsibilities. Be particularly careful to identify who will respond to questions in a particular area. You don't want team members in a meeting to be contradicting one another or offering information that's better kept private.

Q: This sounds pretty basic, but I've never done any negotiating before, and I'd like to have my first assignment in this area go well. What I want to know is the best way to get a negotiation meeting started.

A: First things first. The best way to start a negotiation meeting has nothing at all to do with the subject matter. The initial moments should serve as an ice-breaker. Any negotiation will go smoother if the participants are relaxed and informal. It's a business deal that's being transacted not a war of wills. Therefore, start the meeting off with idle chit-chat. If the meeting is at your location, you may want to offer coffee or soft drinks to the opposing negotiator.

It's worth mentioning that a negotiation session requires you to be alert and well rested. Therefore, get a good night's sleep the night before the meeting, and arise early enough so you won't be stressed out from rushing in the morning. Sometimes people work late into the night preparing for a complex negotiation when they would be better served by getting their rest.

Q: Are there any basic guidelines for conducting a negotiation meeting?

A: A negotiation can take many twists and turns that were totally unpredictable when you first sat down to begin. However, within this framework there are some basics you want to follow. Always strive to keep the meeting focused on the task at hand. Otherwise, people will go off on tangents that are not only time consuming, but also may cause confusion in determining what was already discussed and resolved and what remains to be agreed upon. To guard against this, and for practical purposes, take notes of agreements so you can recap at the end of the meeting.

Let the other party do as much talking as they want, since the more they talk, the more you are likely to learn. Even if you have questions on something that was said, hold them until the other side has finished presenting their position. If you're asked an unexpected question, don't volunteer a hasty answer. If necessary, promise to get the answer later. This will give you time to formulate a reply to a tricky question.

At the end of the negotiation session, summarize what has been agreed to. If the meetings are to continue, agree with the other negotiator on what will be covered next. Finally, at the end of the negotiations, go over all the points of agreement. You should also offer to be the one to prepare the final document if it's feasible to do this. That way, you will be able to control the language that goes into it.

Q: I know from experience that it's important to be the one who controls the meeting. How can you do this successfully when you have the other negotiator to deal with?

A: Of course, having control of the meeting lets you concentrate on what you want to talk about rather than be placed upon the defensive. Nevertheless, you can't bulldoze the other party into submission, so you have to be discreet. You will gain subtle control if you take the initiative at the beginning of the meeting. Also, be the one who suggests breaks for coffee and lunch. Actions such as these will make you the dominant player in the meeting without overtly offending anyone.

HOW TO SIZE UP YOUR OPPOSITION

You obviously know what you hope to achieve when you set out to negotiate with someone else. What isn't always so apparent is what the objectives of the other party are. Naturally, most of the time the basic goal of the other party is evident. This is particularly true in a negotiation to buy or sell a product or service, where the most favorable price that can be secured is an obvious goal. Nonetheless, there may be secondary motives even here that aren't apparent on the surface. For example, a company can have a number of reasons for accepting a lower price than competitors might offer. Perhaps it needs the business, or maybe it is looking to establish a long-term business relationship with a prospective customer. Being able to assess any underlying objectives before negotiations start will give you a leg up on getting the best deal you can.

On another level, knowing as much as you can about the company or individual you're dealing with can influence how you negotiate with them, or in extreme cases whether you negotiate at all. For instance, should you discover that a company has a track record of not delivering on time, you may decide to forgo dealing with them. Therefore, for these reasons, it pays to do some preliminary research before you begin to negotiate with another party.

Q: How should you go about researching a company you plan to negotiate with?

A: How deeply you delve into a competitor's track record will depend first and foremost upon the size and complexity of the transaction to be negotiated. If it's significant, then such factors as credit reports, database research, and discreet inquiries with contacts who have dealt with the company are in order. If the negotiation isn't of a magnitude to warrant this then even here you should perform at least a cursory analysis of readily available information.

In terms of a general assessment of the other party to the negotiations, a few questions need to be answered:

- What kind of track record does the company have in this type of work?
- Do they deliver on schedule?
- Have they experienced quality problems?
- Have they failed to satisfactorily complete other projects?
- Are their prices comparable with competitors?
- What is the overall impact of what will be negotiated on the company?
- Do they have the resources to do the job?

- If they don't, are additional resources readily available?
- Will the company's size influence the attention they give to your job?
- Is the company financially stable?
- Will they be asking for special payment terms?
- What is the financial impact of this project on the company?

These are just a few of the questions you want to consider in assessing a company you will be negotiating with, particularly if the project is of some significance. What you want to do beforehand is assure yourself of the credibility of the other party as well as their capability to perform the work.

Q: My problem is a little different. I don't negotiate with outsiders. The only bargaining I do is internally with my boss and others in the course of handling my management duties. However, I don't seem to do so well at convincing others to see things my way. An associate of mine at work who is very good at sizing up people she deals with says I should concentrate more on looking at the way I deal with different people. I'd certainly like to succeed in this area, since associates and particularly my boss tend to brush me aside when I ask for anything. What can I do to cure this problem?

A: This question has application to gauging the reaction of those you negotiate with formally as well as the bargaining that takes place in the day-to-day conduct of business. What you want to do is learn to watch people's reactions to various situations. A scowl, frown, or even hand gestures can indicate the person's reaction to what was said. You should also pay close attention to what people say, as you can learn a lot more by listening than by talking.

In terms of the specifics of what to look for when you're bargaining, start with the overall attitude of the person you're dealing with. Is the person relaxed and friendly, or is there an indication that the person is impatient and anxious to end the discussion. For example, if a manager is trying to get a boss to hire more people and the boss is sympathetic when refusing the request, it carries a different connotation than when a boss dismisses such a request out of hand by saying additional help isn't needed.

Someone's tone of voice can also be instructive in assessing your chances of success if you continue to pursue the topic under discussion. An abrupt reply can signal that there's no point in going further in the conversation, while a pleasant and hesitant rejection might indicate a little more convincing will turn the tide in your favor. Of course, you can't read too much into any of these individual nuances, but if you deal with the same people on a regular basis, you should be able to detect subtle signs of their intentions by their behavior.

It takes time to learn how to gauge what people's reactions will be. You will never be able to do so with 100% certainty, but by watching how others successfully interact to get what they want, you will pick up some pointers to improve your own chances. Of course, there's a lot more that goes into bargaining successfully than the ability to size people up, but it's a start in the right direction.

WHY REMAINING CALM WILL SERVE YOU WELL

As a manager you have undoubtedly had your patience tested time and time again in various situations. And on more than one occasion, you may have exploded in anger, even when it wasn't in you best interests to do so. In the hectic pace of the business world, this isn't an unusual reaction, and there probably weren't any negative consequences. However, when you're bargaining with someone, losing your patience can directly result in failing to accomplish your negotiation goals. Therefore, even more than in your other management duties, there's a significant incentive to keep your cool during negotiations.

Q: **I frequently have the misfortune to negotiate with someone who really gets under my skin. This individual is always making snide remarks or demeaning the worth of the work we do for his company. In the past, I've always succeeded in biting my tongue, but I'm wondering whether it might be better to tell him off. Do you think that would succeed in changing his attitude during negotiations?**

A: The individual you mention may just have an unpleasant personality. It's more likely, though, that this is the other negotiator's perception of what a tough negotiator is supposed to act like. Nevertheless, whatever accounts for the person's bluster, nothing can be gained by you reacting in anger. Actually, this will only give the individual satisfaction by getting under your skin. And if it's a personality trait you're dealing with, an emotional response on your part isn't going to cure it.

On the other hand, if the negotiator is adopting this posture as a negotiating tactic, seeing you respond in anger will just convince him that the tactic is working. Therefore, here, too, you can expect the nasty demeanor to continue unabated. As a result, there's nothing to be gained by telling the person off. In fact, there's potentially more to be lost than to be gained. Once you lose control of your emotions, it will hinder your ability to concentrate on achieving your negotiation goals. Once you decide to respond to negative behavior at the bargaining table, you're shifting your position to responding to the other person's tactics, rather than concentrating on achieving your objective. And that, precisely, is what the other negotiator wants you to do.

Q: It seems to me that many of the managers I do any negotiating with tend to see the image of a good negotiator and a tough negotiator as being synonymous. As a result, I run into a lot of people who aren't very pleasant when they do any bargaining. Why do they act like that? Should I be doing the same thing?

A: Part of the problem is perception. You often see successful negotiators described as tough, hard-nosed, or unyielding. This is interpreted to mean their behavior, when it's actually the inner strength to be unemotional and logical that is being described. This is unfortunate, since the attitudes of both parties to a negotiation go a long way toward making any negotiation a success. For your part, being able to maintain control of your emotions will help prevent careless mistakes and allow you to do the clear-headed thinking necessary to bargain successfully. Sometimes you will even find that a negotiator who starts out being belligerent will shift to a more reasonable posture once it's obvious you're not a table-pounding hothead.

Q: If being nasty isn't a desirable negotiating trait, why is it practiced?

A: It's generally done by those who aren't so confident of their persuasive skills, so they hope to succeed by bullying tactics.

Q: I know someone who does pretty well by being what I'll politely call pushy at the negotiating table.

A: As with any other type of bullying, it sometimes meets with limited success with people who succumb to these tactics. However, as with any other type of bully, they generally pay for their tactics when they run into someone who refuses to be bullied. And at the negotiating table, these types often have their pockets picked without even realizing it as they sit there blustering and boasting.

WHEN AND HOW TO GIVE DOCUMENTATION

What someone says at the negotiation table is one thing, while what they can prove is something else again. So no matter how persuasive you may be in your arguments to support your position, it's reasonable to expect the other party to want proof to back up your assertions. In other circumstances, you may want to volunteer data even when it isn't asked for if it adds credibility to your negotiating position. Most of the time this involves paperwork of one form or another. In fact, many negotiations start off with a written proposal. In any event, whether you have given someone a written proposal and additional information is requested, or you are supporting verbal claims, the judicious use of documentation is an invaluable aid.

Q: I was recently asked for some cost data to support a proposal I was negotiating. Unfortunately, the data weren't readily available, and as a result our company didn't get the contract we were seeking. Are there ways to prevent this from happening?

A: It's always important to be ready to supply backup data in support of your negotiating position. Usually the information is available, but what sometimes happens is that the request wasn't anticipated and someone has to go digging it up. This can present problems during negotiations. For one thing it can raise the suspicion that the figures you furnished were cobbled together without any real justification behind them. It also projects an image of inefficiency. Finally, the faster you're able to provide information in response to a request, the quicker the other negotiator's questions will be answered. Not only will this move the process along faster, but it also discourages the other party from probing even further.

For these reasons, it pays to plan as much as possible to have the documentation you need available when called for. Of course, everything can't be anticipated beforehand, but you should be prepared to have the proper people in your organization ready to respond quickly. This means as a minimum they should be put on notice that they may be called upon to supply information you need.

Q: My problem isn't so much furnishing documentation, but being asked to defend facts and figures I've supplied with my proposal. Are there any recommended ways to support information you have already furnished?

A: Sometimes additional data can be used to support your position. Some of the forms of justification you can use are the following:

- Bills of material, engineering estimates, and subcontractor quotations are all useful in supporting your position when costs are questioned.
- If a particular provision is objected to, if it's feasible, show that it is a standard industry requirement. Failing that, offer proof that it's readily accepted by everyone else you do business with.
- Prove that a requirement is necessary to comply with government regulations or some other third-party requirement.

Q: How can I justify provisions in a proposed agreement when they can't be backed up with documentation?

A: When you don't have any form of written evidence to support your position, there are other methods you can use to bolster your case. For example, if a particular provision is challenged, perhaps you can assert that it's a requirement imposed corporatewide that you don't have the authority to waive. If the other party is insistent it be removed, say that to seek a waiver will require a substantial period of time. This is sometimes effective when the other party is anxious to reach agreement.

Another tactic is to state that the offensive provision is standard legal boilerplate required by company counsel. Sometimes if the objection isn't significant, this argument will work because the other negotiator doesn't want to go through the hassle of getting his legal counsel involved with yours, which in effect will delay any agreement until the issue is resolved.

A less likely strategy, but one that will work in certain circumstances, is to prove to the other party that the provision is as much in his interest as it is in yours. In some areas, such as quality provisions, this isn't too hard to do, but for the most part it isn't easy to convince someone who objects to something that it's in their best interests. However, it provides a good test of your persuasion skills, and even if you aren't successful you haven't lost anything by trying.

Q: **Fortunately any negotiating I do as a manager is mostly in my own behalf such as getting my budgets approved and the like. However, I'm lobbying my boss now to upgrade my position to give me management responsibility for an additional department in our company. In what ways would documentation support my position?**

A: What someone says is often viewed as self-serving, especially as here where you're promoting your own cause. This perception can be offset by furnishing written documentation that supports your position. To be successful in this case, you want to show the advantages to the company in general and your boss in particular to be gained by giving you the additional duties. One obvious way is to show how it will provide better leadership for the additional department you will manage. Perhaps you can also show where it will obviate the need to hire another manager to oversee the department, which will result in costs savings to the company.

SAVVY WAYS TO GET VALUABLE INFORMATION

Aside from the need to furnish documentation to support your position, you will often be looking for information for your own negotiating purposes. This will fall into two general categories. One is generalized data on the company you are dealing with, while the second type is that pertaining to the subject matter of the negotiation.

Some of it will be relatively easy to obtain, while other information will be hard to come by. In any event, if you require information and the other party expresses a reluctance to furnish it, proceed with caution. There may be a valid reason for not supplying the data, but, the refusal may be because it will be damaging to the other person's negotiating stance.

Q: My negotiating counterpart is refusing to supply me with certain data on the basis that it's proprietary. How should this refusal be dealt with?

A: That depends in large part on the circumstances. As a minimum, ask for proof that what you want is in fact proprietary. Sometimes this is just used as an excuse to avoid giving you data necessary to properly evaluate someone's offer. If it is indeed proprietary, and you are satisfied it is such, then look for nonproprietary information that will substantially answer your questions. Of course, if that isn't possible, then you have to decide if the lack of information is critical enough to prevent going ahead with negotiations. If it is, tell the other party, which leaves the decision with them as to what information they will provide to satisfactorily answer your questions.

Q: I'm negotiating with someone who always provides data when I ask for it, but it's either incomplete or furnished in such bulk that it takes forever to dig through it to get the information needed to properly evaluate the other company's proposal. Is there anything that can be done about this?

A: Often, requests for information are met with a deliberate intent to minimally comply. Sometimes it's in the form of incomplete data, while at other times the tactic is to shower you with paper and let you search to find what you need. You first want to jawbone the other negotiator about the inadequacy of the information being furnished. You might want to encourage compliance by intimating that if the data is indicative of the company's lack of efficiency, you may not want to do business with them. A second approach is to state in writing precisely what you are looking for. This eliminates the argument that someone didn't understand what you wanted. However, this isn't always something you can do, since it's not always that easy to pinpoint with precision what you want to see.

Q: I've had a shouting match with the people I'm negotiating with. I don't think I'm getting everything I need, while they claim they are providing everything I ask for. It's pretty hard to pinpoint, since they insist on knowing precisely what I want, when I'm actually on a bit of a fishing expedition. How can I convince them to be more helpful in giving me what I need?

A: You certainly aren't going to do it by getting angry with them. Furthermore, they don't appear to be entirely to blame since you stated you were on a fishing expedition, in effect looking for something, but not really knowing what you were looking for. Successful negotiations are a two-way street, and if there are data you genuinely need, let them know why you need it in a reasonable manner. That way, you may have some success in getting some useful information.

Q: There's some information I'm seeking on one particular topic, but I don't want to ask for it directly, since that will put the negotiator on notice that I'm looking into a particular area. Any suggestions on how to get what I want without tipping my hand?

A: There are a couple of ways you could go about this. One is to ask for a large quantity of information in a number of areas at once. This way the information you're looking for will be lumped with other topics and may not stand out by itself. In fact the very volume of data you're looking for will lead the other negotiator to believe you're not zeroing in on anything specific. Another approach if it fits your circumstances is to have one of your technical or accounting people ask for the data as part of their review if they are dealing directly with their counterparts. This way you may get your hands on what you need without the other negotiator even realizing it.

DEALING WITH EXPERTS—YOURS AND THEIRS

Some negotiations involve the contributions of people with a special expertise in a subject area. These people may be participants in one phase of the negotiations, or in some situations may participate from beginning to end. This is particularly true in negotiations involving highly technical matters that require the ongoing presence of experts. Most of the people you use in the negotiations will be employees of your company, but on occasion you may have a specialized situation that requires the contributions of outside experts. This poses the added burden of hiring the experts as well as controlling their use during the negotiation process. Along with your own experts, you may have to contend with those used by the other negotiator. So although experts can be useful during negotiations, they also present potential problems if their contributions aren't properly managed.

Q: **When should experts be used to assist in the negotiation process? The only people I ever have help me are employees from various departments of my company such as accounting or engineering.**

A: The use of the word *experts* includes company employees whom you have participate in negotiations, as well as outside experts. This is true since if someone isn't in a meeting to contribute their knowledge in a particular area, they shouldn't be there in the first place. Therefore, your own accountants and engineers should be there to contribute expertise in their specialty. If not, they shouldn't be in the meetings at all. You don't want to bring people to negotiation meetings on the possibility they may be needed, since it only presents the opportunity for them to do more damage than good by inadvertently saying the wrong thing. It also gives the other negotiator the opportunity to ask them questions that wouldn't be raised if they weren't there. So in terms of your own employees, don't have them in attendance if they're not needed.

As for planning the use of either internal or outside expertise, for the most part this should be done before you begin to negotiate. The very subject matter of some negotiations will dictate the need to have an ongoing presence in certain technical areas, while other negotiations may call for bringing in experts on an as-needed basis. Of course, as negotiations proceed, questions may be raised that necessitate calling upon someone with the capabilities to provide the answer.

Naturally, when you anticipate the need to use outside experts in the negotiation process, the planning has to be done in advance, since you have to make both financial and logistical arrangements for their presence. So for the most part, consultants and others will be hired in the planning stages of the negotiation process.

Q: **In general terms, what can experts contribute to your negotiation position?**

A: They provide credibility to support areas of your proposal that may be challenged. This is particularly true with outside experts, whose statements will carry much more weight than those of your own employees, even though you're paying the freight for their supposedly objective advice. In other situations, outside experts may be proposed as subcontractors to do some of the work on the project being negotiated. Your own internal experts' primary function will be to answer questions within their area of expertise that are raised by the other negotiator.

Q: I'm a senior manager responsible for a large contract for support services we will be providing to another company. Although I'm not directly involved in the negotiations, a problem has been brought to my attention by a manager who reports to me and supervises the people doing the negotiating. It seems that a representative of one of the subcontractors who will be working with us has been participating in the negotiations. Unfortunately, he has been making suggestions during negotiations that the scope of his company's efforts be expanded. The company we are negotiating with has picked up on this and is looking at it favorably. The bad news is that they don't want to add money to the deal for this, but want instead to cut back on our share of the pie to pay for the additional work of the subcontractor. I'm being asked what should be done about this. Any suggestions?

A: This points out a prime reason why outsiders shouldn't be randomly allowed to participate in negotiations. When they are absolutely necessary, it's crucial to brief them beforehand about what should and should not be discussed. Furthermore, they should participate only in those parts of the discussion where their contribution is essential, after which they should be excused from attendance.

In terms of the specific situation, the subcontractor should be removed as a participant. Have your people talk to him and let him know that his ad hoc remarks are creating problems. Suggest that if the problem can't be resolved, he will have to requote his segment of the work to absorb the additional costs of the added work. That should send a message to not foul up the works.

Have your negotiators tell the company people you're negotiating with that the structure of the work to be performed won't permit cutting your segment of the effort down. Suggest that if they consider additional subcontractor effort to be worthwhile, they will have to pay extra for it.

If that doesn't solve the problem and the contractor is still insistent, then suggest that it may be necessary to seek out another subcontractor who can do the work cheaper. That way, perhaps the additional effort could be accommodated within the available funds. If the other side insists that this is the way they want to go, then ask for quotes for the revised effort from a number of possible subcontractors, including the one you were originally proposing to use. Finally, if you get someone cheaper than your original subcontractor, give them the work and teach the culprit that talking out of turn cost him participation in your project.

Incidentally, after you give this advice to your subordinates, you might also suggest to the manager in charge of negotiations that a policy should be prepared on when and how to use outsiders in negotiation sessions.

Q: **During negotiations with another company, the other side suggested we bring a certain consultant on board as part of our team to do work for this company. What are the pros and cons of doing this?**

A: If the consultant will unquestionably add value to your effort, it's a real positive to agree to this request, since it also increases your chances of getting a contract to do the work. Even if the consultant isn't needed, you can't ignore the fact it was requested by the company you hope to do business with. Therefore, unless the costs would be out of line, you may want to hire the consultant as a goodwill gesture.

Q: **Speaking of costs, outside experts don't come cheap. What factors should be considered when negotiating agreements with them?**

A: Whenever you negotiate to hire consultants the first thing to look for is to make sure you're going to get what you pay for. Sometimes the expert you think you're getting isn't going to be the person who is assigned to do the work. This is significant in two ways. First, you may be paying for top talent and getting lesser paid associates. Second, the people assigned may not have the expertise you were expecting to get. Therefore, make sure any agreement contains provisions identifying who will be doing the work. Furthermore, always limit the number of hours to be billed, since an open-ended agreement is an invitation to run up charges.

Q: During a recent negotiation I had the other negotiator bring in an expert who supported the position the negotiator was taking. I'm not altogether convinced of what he was saying, but because of deadline pressures, I essentially accepted the facts as confirmed by the expert. It's not that they were incorrect, but simply that I would have felt better about having some expertise on my side to verify this. How can I prevent this from happening during negotiations, and if I can't, what can I do to counter expert advice?

A: First, just because someone wheels in a so-called expert to support their position doesn't mean you have to accept what is said. As far as countering expert advice, the starting point is to try and anticipate its use by the other side before negotiations begin. If you know beforehand—or are at least reasonably certain—that experts will be used by the opposition, have your own experts ready to rebut what is said. Of course, it's not always possible or practical to do that, so there are other ways to downplay someone's use of an expert.

First, protest when the other negotiator is about to call on an expert. Say something such as, "I don't have anyone available who can relate to what your expert will discuss, so there's no point in calling upon him." This may not prevent the expert from appearing, but if so, simply ignore what was said in subsequent discussions.

Another approach you can take is to question the expert's credentials as to their relationship to the subject matter being negotiated. This isn't always as hard as it seems, since some experts tend to project expertise in a limited area across a broad spectrum.

HOW TO STRUCTURE AGREEMENTS TO ENCOURAGE PERFORMANCE

It's hard enough to negotiate an agreement, but it can be even more frustrating to discover at a later date that your hard-won agreement isn't working out as planned. All too often, problems with performance can turn what originally looked like a good deal into a nightmare. Of course, sometimes these performance problems are inevitable, and indeed they may result from changing economic conditions or other factors that couldn't be foreseen. Nevertheless, to guard against performance failures, it's important to build as many safeguards into the agreement as are feasible. Actually, some of these measures are pretty basic, and the only danger is not to overlook them when you're negotiating.

Q: Why not leave any provisions to ensure satisfactory performance until you are writing up the agreement?

A: By the time you get to formalizing an agreement, everything should be pretty well negotiated. Otherwise, it will seriously extend the time required to reach agreement if you're still trying to negotiate items when you're at the stage of putting your agreement in writing. Furthermore, some of the constraints you want to build in to encourage performance can impact cost and performance parameters. As a result, they should be negotiated when these topics are covered during negotiations.

Q: As the division manager responsible for signing contracts, I'm reviewing an agreement we're about to sign with a small business who will supply us with some items we use in our production process. I'm a little leery about it since it appears to be priced too low. I don't want to rock the boat, and it's certainly hard to be critical of my people for doing a good negotiating job. On the other hand, the items being supplied are critical, and I can't risk having the contractor fail to perform. Is there anything that can be done here to safeguard performance?

A: Your concern is certainly justified, and it points out the potential danger in putting the squeeze on someone in negotiations to the extent they accept an unreasonable deal. Naturally, that's their responsibility, not yours. Nevertheless, in many situations suppliers can be pressured to accept terms that may be almost impossible to meet. Sure they should refuse, but if a substantial part of their business is tied to one company, they will take undue risks to keep the business relationship going. As a result, they may put themselves in a financially precarious position, or else cut corners to save money, resulting in an inferior product

As far as the contract under review is concerned, have your people include provisions to protect against a failure to perform. This could be in the form of restrictive payment provisions, some form of performance bond, or liquidated damages. However, where you have a new supplier the company hasn't worked with before, the best guarantee of successful completion is to have your people closely monitor the work as it goes along so that action can be taken the minute a problem appears.

Q: Is it practical to place incentives in a contract to encourage superior performance?

A: It is, but for most run-of-the-mill business transactions they're not practical. They are most likely to be used in research and development efforts where you want to motivate the contractor to exceed agreed-to performance parameters.

Q: What safeguards can I take when I'm negotiating agreements with suppliers to encourage performance?

A: The most important thing to look at from a negotiating perspective is to ensure that you're satisfied that the other party can do what they promise. It helps in this regard if you don't try to impose goals that can't be met, such as unrealistic delivery dates or too stringent quality provisions. Another factor often overlooked is to establish a cooperative atmosphere where the supplier is encouraged to work closely with your people to solve problems that arise. This is especially important in situations where the supplier will be working with your company on a long-term basis.

HOW AND WHEN TO USE STONEWALLING TACTICS

No matter how reasonable you try to be in reaching an agreement, on occasion another negotiator will persist in trying to get you to make further concessions. When this happens you have to be persistent in sticking to your position. Doing this involves being able to successfully defend your negotiation position, while simultaneously pointing out the flaws in the opposition's arguments.

Q: I've been trying to reach an agreement with someone for over a week, but they keep insisting that my position is invalid. I keep pointing out why it's their position, not mine, that's unreasonable. How long can this go on?

A: Until one of you accepts the other's viewpoint, either of you offers some compromise position, or an intermediary steps in to make the decision. Obviously, there is no rush to reach agreement, since deadlines of one sort or another are always a strong motivator when two parties are deadlocked. Consequently, as long as there's nothing significant at stake, keep holding out until the other person realizes you won't be swayed.

Q: It seems to me that stonewalling runs the risk of someone deciding that since you won't budge from your position, then they might as well not even try to reach agreement. Isn't it likely then that stonewalling can result in the other party ending the negotiations?

A: This is always a possibility. However, you don't want to adopt an inflexible position unless you have negotiated to the point where you have made your most reasonable offer and the other side is still looking for further concessions. At this stage, the options are basically to hold your ground and try to convince the other party to see things your way, or run the risk of not getting a deal at all. And since no deal is better than a lousy deal, it doesn't matter much if the other party stalks off.

Q: It sounds like stonewalling is the equivalent of a "take it or leave it" offer. Is this true?

A: No it isn't and here is why. A "take it or leave it" offer implies that an offer is made and someone is given the option of accepting it or nothing. Here, what we are talking about is negotiating in good faith to the point where you have made your best offer. Then you should refuse to alter your position any further. However, you still should continue to discuss the merits of both positions in the hopes of eventually convincing the other party to see things your way. Stonewalling comes into the picture when you refuse to grant further concessions.

Q: One of the managers I deal with at work is habitually giving me excuses as to why certain reports can't be finished by my due date. It seems I'm forever giving him time extensions. What happens is we wind up bargaining back and forth as to the date the reports will be delivered. Should I insist on the reports as due and no longer bargain with him about extension dates?

A: This is more like a charitable exercise on your part than it is a negotiation exercise. There's nothing for you to gain by bargaining over when the reports will be furnished. The other person has no incentive to meet your due date, since you continue to bargain willingly over alternative submission dates. Stand your ground and refuse to budge from your required date. This places the burden on the other manager to comply or face the alternatives whatever they might be. Compromise is always preferred to confrontation, but whether you're bargaining over a multimillion-dollar contract or due dates for reports there comes a time when you have to stand your ground.

CHAPTER 5

PREPARING FOR PROBLEMS GREAT AND SMALL

There are many things that may affect the outcome of any negotiation you participate in. Fortunately, however, most negotiations involve only a limited number of issues and are relatively straightforward. It's only on a rare occasion that you may run into a situation where it seems that anything and everything goes wrong at once. In any event, whether your next negotiation is simple or complex, most of the hassles can be controlled with a little bit of preparation. This chapter deals with a number of important points to consider that will lessen the likelihood of something going wrong.

USING FLEXIBILITY TO GET WHAT YOU WANT

Everyone enters into negotiations with a set objective in mind. It may be to buy or sell something, or for any other number of purposes. What's often ignored, however, is that flexibility is required if you want to achieve your objective. After all, the party you're negotiating with may have an entirely different idea as to what's reasonable in terms of reaching an agreement. Therefore, if you aren't willing to have some flexibility in your strategy to get what you want, it will be difficult if not impossible to reach a negotiated settlement.

Q: How should you go about establishing a flexible negotiating strategy?

A: The first thing you want to do is establish acceptable limits for reaching agreement which you won't ordinarily deviate from even if it means an agreement can't be reached. For example, if the negotiation involves price, decide the maximum price you will pay if you will be the buyer, or the lowest price you will accept if you're the seller. It's important to do this beforehand, since what frequently happens is that when negotiations take place, there's a temptation to pay more as a buyer or accept less as a seller during the closing moments of negotiations. This happens when the other party makes a final offer that is close enough to entice you to deviate from your objective in the interests of reaching agreement. Experienced negotiators routinely expect people to make this choice at the end, and unless you have established your limits beforehand, it's more likely you will bite at this bait. What people should do in this situation is to refuse the offer that will force the other party to concede in order to reach an agreement. Let's look at how this works:

Background

Melissa M., the facilities manager for a midsized corporation, is negotiating with a supplier for landscaping services. She has reviewed quotes from several sources before initiating negotiations with one firm. Before sitting down with the owner of the business, she has determined that $15,000 is the limit she will pay for the work she wants to be done. The supplier starts off by asking for $20,000, while Melissa's opening offer is $14,000. After some back-and-forth discussions about what the work will consist of, the seller offers to do the job for $17,500. Let's pick the discussions up at this point.

The negotiations

Melissa M.: "$17,500 is more than I'm willing to pay. Can you get that figure down to $15,000?"

Supplier: "The best I can do is $15,500."

Melissa M.: "$15,000 is all that's budgeted for this, so it's that or I'll have to explore other options."

Supplier: "This doesn't give me any profit at all on this job, but if you'll split the difference, we can settle at $15,250."

Melissa M.: "It's $15,000. Do we have an agreement or not?"

Supplier: "Look, give me $15,099 which will just about cover my costs."

Melissa M.: "Stop trying to squeeze another cent out of this. It's $15,000 or nothing."

Supplier: "Well all right. I guess I don't have any choice."

COMMENTS

By establishing her limit of $15,000 before negotiations began Melissa didn't even think about accepting anything beyond her limit. However, if she hadn't decided the maximum amount she would pay beforehand, it's very possible she would have agreed to the $15,500 offer or at least the subsequent offers, which were even lower.

The tactics of the supplier are typical negotiation ploys to extract a few more dollars out of a deal. First, the supplier tried to split the difference and when that failed a final pitch was made at $15,099. This last offer, which was only a few dollars higher than Melissa's position, is sometimes known in negotiation jargon as "picking up the loose change."

Q: You're talking about a flexible strategy, yet it seems pretty rigid to refuse to pay a few more dollars to reach an agreement. Can you explain this?

A: You remain firm only when you get to the point in negotiations where you have offered the best deal you can from your standpoint. This will generally be after some long and hard bargaining has taken place before you make what is your last offer. It's this very tendency to look at an offer which is slightly above what you planned to pay as a buyer as "only a few dollars" which causes people to cave in and accept it. In fact, this is the sort of argument you'll frequently hear from the other side when they say something such as, "Why are you being so stubborn about a few dollars?"

This same argument also applies to them, so when you receive such a complaint an obvious response is, "If you think it's just a few dollars, then there's no reason why you shouldn't accept my offer." Of course, every dollar counts to the other negotiator, and it should to you also, so don't cave in and deviate from your position at the last moment.

Q: If I start off with my best offer, then there's no room to negotiate, so I'll be making what's essentially a "take it or leave it" offer. Isn't this unrealistic?

A: It sure is. When you establish your negotiation position, you want to leave yourself flexibility to make adjustments in your position as negotiations move along. Essentially, your first offer should be what you consider to be the best deal you could possibly hope to get. For instance, in the preceding example, Melissa M.'s opening position was $14,000, although she recognized that she would go to $15,000 if need be. In fact, in determining your starting position as well as your outer limit, you need to decide what concessions you can make during negotiations. This gives you the flexibility to move toward agreement as negotiations proceed.

Q: Why not just give your best offer, have the other side do likewise, and be done with it?

A: That's fine if the other party is going to be as realistic as you are. It also works when you're buying standard items with a set price. But in situations where the price or other terms are flexible, if you throw your best offer on the table, the other party is likely to counter with an offer significantly different. This leaves you no room to negotiate and makes it more difficult than if you gave yourself some leeway.

Q: Many times, there are changes made during negotiations in terms of what is being bought or sold. Quantities, specifications, and other elements are all adjusted from what was originally contemplated. Therefore, why isn't it simpler to just go into negotiations without a preplanned position, since you'll probably have to adjust it anyway?

A: This is actually one more reason why you should plan your strategy beforehand. Naturally, you can't foresee every turn a negotiation may take, but by establishing your limits and looking at possibilities where you can make concessions, you're in a better position to make decisions if changes take place during the negotiation meeting. If you wing it from the start, the odds are that any decisions you make will be hasty, and there's a far greater likelihood that some of the adjustments in your negotiation position won't be in your best interests.

Q: Why not be straightforward right from the start and tell the other party what your position is and ask for their best offer? That way you can work out any differences together.

A: This is a very reasonable approach from a theoretical standpoint. However, it assumes the other person is going to be just as candid as you are. But where does that leave you if they decide to take advantage of your openness? The chances are they will come back and assert their best offer is something that is completely different from yours. The end result is an expectation you will make some concessions from your original position to reach agreement. As a result, you may end up paying more than if you gave yourself a cushion with your opening offer.

Of course, there are circumstances in which this type of straightforward approach will work, especially if you're negotiating with someone you have dealt with in the past and know that you both are willing to shortcut the back-and-forth bargaining. However, for the most part, it pays to be wary about putting all your cards on the table at the outset if you hope to get a reasonable deal.

Q: Where does a flexible negotiating strategy fit in when you're trying to bargain to attain personal goals such as a salary increase or a promotion? It seems that there's no bargaining involved at all, but simply a request on your part and a refusal by your boss.

A: It will be as you say if you approach it that way, but with a little bit of planning on your part, you can achieve personal objectives with a little bit of negotiating of your own. For example, if you're looking for a promotion, before you approach your boss, think about what his or her objections will be and have answers to counter them. In addition, when you hold the discussion, if the boss says a promotion isn't possible right now, try to get commitments as to what you have to do to enhance your prospects. If you do this, at a later date you will be able to go back and plead your case again. By being able to point out that you've upheld your end of the bargain, your boss is more likely to look favorably upon your request. There isn't much that you can't negotiate if you make the attempt. Furthermore, there's nothing to lose since the worst that can happen is that you'll get a "No" for an answer. Since that would have happened without your attempting to bargain, there's nothing to be lost by trying.

HOW TO HANDLE NONNEGOTIABLES—YOURS AND THEIRS

One of the biggest hurdles to overcome in any negotiation are those elements that either you or the other party to the negotiations consider to be nonnegotiable. These can become the subject of much controversy if either you or the other party desire changes made in these areas. For this reason, how you deal with any nonnegotiable item can impact upon the success or failure of the negotiation. Moreover, a dispute in this area can become long and drawn-out, so it's a subject that may sometimes require a bit of diplomacy to resolve.

Q: How should I handle nonnegotiable items in terms of discussing them with the other negotiator?

A: In the first place, never take the initiative to spell out what parts of your negotiation position are nonnegotiable. Doing this can only make it harder to reach an agreement. For one thing, the other party may accuse you of refusing to negotiate. Even more likely, however, is that the other negotiator will use your nonnegotiable items as a stepping stone to gain advantages elsewhere. For instance, the other negotiator may subsequently claim that one or more of his items are also nonnegotiable when you start to press for concessions. In fact, a savvy negotiator may falsely make this claim in an effort to later say something such as, "I'm willing to make a deal on my nonnegotiables if you will with yours." This tactic can put you in a tight spot by making you look unreasonable. Alternatively, the negotiator may seek concessions from you in other areas in exchange for recognizing the nonnegotiability of your items.

Q: What criteria should I use to identify what I consider to be nonnegotiable?

A: Broadly speaking, any term or condition that you consider to be an absolute necessity in the final agreement. In general terms, anything that's so important that if it's not in the agreement then you won't conclude the deal. However, great care should be taken in identifying items as nonnegotiable, since in the give-and-take of negotiations, reasons may arise which make the item negotiable after all. For example, let's suppose you are negotiating an agreement that has certain technical specifications that you determine can't be altered. As negotiations proceed, however, the other side offers a radically different technical approach that will give you a better product than your own specifications. What earlier was nonnegotiable now becomes very negotiable. The point is that things aren't always as nonnegotiable as they seem once negotiations get underway, so limit any such items to the absolute minimum.

Q: What do I say when the other party is looking for changes in something I consider to be nonnegotiable?

A: The best approach is to be as casual as possible about the matter. Try to phrase your response to indicate your position on the issue can't be altered unless there is some form of substantive concession that would coax you into considering it. Since the other party isn't going to concede anything of that sort of significance, this essentially puts the matter to rest without you actually stating it's nonnegotiable. This tactic avoids having to argue about why the item isn't negotiable.

On the other hand, there are occasions when it's practical just to spell right out that the item isn't negotiable. For instance, if you are buying a product that you need delivered by a set date, then just say the delivery date isn't negotiable if the issue is raised. This is especially true when negotiations are nearing the wrap-up stage, where there's little likelihood that not revealing something as nonnegotiable would have any impact on concessions or other trade-offs.

Q: I recently concluded negotiations on a project where I had a couple of items that were nonnegotiable. At the end I had to make concessions in other areas in exchange for the nonnegotiability of my items. Did I get shafted?

A: Maybe, maybe not. It depends upon the value of your concessions. This commonly happens when the other negotiator knows you have nonnegotiables. If the nonnegotiables were sufficiently important, and even with the concessions your agreement was favorable, then you came out all right.

Q: Are there other alternatives to making concessions in exchange for keeping certain items nonnegotiable?

A: There are a couple of other possibilities that are worth trying. One is to trade off your nonnegotiables against those of the other party. If none have been identified, then look for concessions you can make that are of little significance to you but of major importance to the other side. Some of these issues may have been revealed during the course of negotiations.

Another possibility is to tough it out by asserting that you have already made significant trade-offs equivalent in value to what the other side gave you in return. Therefore, your item isn't nonnegotiable, but if any changes are made in it, you want something significant in return. State what you want in terms of something you know the other side isn't about to agree to, such as a 30% price reduction. Incidentally, make sure what you're looking for will compensate you for surrendering the nonnegotiable status of your item in case the other party unexpectedly agrees to your terms. Otherwise, you will be placed in the unenviable position of having to backtrack on what you said.

THE DOs AND DON'TS OF WRITTEN PROPOSALS

Many business negotiation situations will require the preparation of a written proposal. This will be true not only for outside negotiations, but also for budget requests or other internal matters that are an important part of your managerial duties. Preparing a proposal can be a time-consuming endeavor, yet taking shortcuts can be costly. Therefore, whether you're preparing a proposal yourself, or are having it done under your supervision, it's worthwhile to take the time to do it right. Otherwise, your negotiations may be destined to fail before they even begin.

Q: I have an ongoing problem in the area of proposal preparation with people who work for me. No matter how much I counsel them otherwise, they continually work on a proposal until the last minute. This has always resulted in careless mistakes, but something happened last week which really has me in an uproar. We were late in meeting a deadline for proposal submissions and as a result are being excluded from competing on a project we were interested in. I know people work up until the last minute to try and have the best proposal possible. However, our track record indicates this isn't working out. What can I do to solve this problem?

A: Rushing to complete proposals probably results in more errors than anything else. Sometimes it's inevitable that a proposal will have to be prepared in a hurry, especially if you have been given a very limited time to respond. However, for the most part it's poor planning combined with a desire to cram every conceivable idea into the proposal. As a result, someone decides at the last minute that something else should be added and in doing so errors are made. At times the mistake is in failing to relate a change in one part of the proposal to other sections of the proposal that may be affected. For example, a technical requirement is added without making any adjustment in the costs proposed. This kind of an error can cause a real problem since the person evaluating the proposal doesn't know that carelessness caused the costs not to be reworked. Instead, the reviewer assumes the proposal is inaccurate because of a lack of knowledge. This sort of error can easily result in an unsuccessful proposal.

To overcome these bad habits, you should establish internal deadlines for proposal completion well ahead of the submission date. Furthermore, much of the proposal work can be done well ahead of time, with only a few crucial elements being worked on at the last minute. To ensure responsibility for proposal preparation, every proposal should have someone designated as the proposal manager. This person should also have decision-making power as to what goes in and what stays out. Otherwise, there will be internal bickering between departments and other hierarchies when a proposal involves the joint efforts of several groups.

Q: **My boss criticized me recently for a proposal I sent her requesting the purchase of some office equipment. She complained about it being confusing with all the numbers I had in it to prove the cost effectiveness of the equipment. Yet she's always telling people they have to justify the need for any expenditures. Is there any way to improve these presentations without leaving out essential information?**

A: Your problem is a common one with all kinds of proposals where numbers are interspersed with the text. On occasion it makes for difficulty in comprehending either the narrative or the numbers. One good way to avoid this is to put any extensive presentation of numbers in a separate section.

Q: We're preparing a proposal for submission, and there's a lively internal debate going on over whether or not to point out a couple of problem areas with using the approach we recommend. We know how to overcome these problems if they should arise, but some of our senior managers feel we're better off not even mentioning the matter, while others such as myself want to point them out. Who's right?

A: You are. Whenever there are potential problems with a proposed approach, it's better to point them out along with your recommended solutions. By doing this, you show not only that you recognize the problem, but also that you know how to solve it. By avoiding the issue, you run the risk that a reviewer may be aware of the problems, and assume you aren't aware of them or are trying to hide the difficulties. If that happens, it doesn't bode well for your proposal.

Q: Our company has been asked to prepare a proposal for a large-scale project. In reviewing the requirements, the technical people who work for me think there's a better way to do the job than what the requirements are asking for. Should we propose our approach, respond just to the requirements, or do it both ways?

A: This is an area that often causes unnecessary problems. At times the proposal requirements are ignored and the substitute approach is proposed. On other occasions, the two are intermingled in such a way as to cause confusion. The best approach to take in these situations is to respond directly to what was requested and attach a separate section containing an option to do the work differently. Be sure to specify that you will do the work as proposed, but are offering the other approach as an alternative.

It's important to handle these matters in this manner, since no matter how good your alternative is, the party requesting the proposal may want it done the way they asked. By handling the issues separately, you give them a clear-cut choice without running the risk of eliminating yourself from contention.

Q: Could you summarize the elements of a good proposal?

A: Briefly, a good proposal must

- *Be concise.* A good proposal contains everything needed in the shortest possible format.
- *Be accurate.* Even minor errors plant seeds of doubt in the reviewer's mind.
- *Be convincing.* If you want to win, you have to prove you're better than anyone else.
- *Be creative.* Ideas that people haven't thought about will stir their imagination.
- *Be readable.* Your ideas shouldn't be buried amid technical jargon and fanciful claims.
- *Be targeted.* The right proposal addressed to the wrong person is a waste of time.

TACTICS TO PREVENT CARELESS MISTAKES DURING NEGOTIATIONS

The pressure cooker atmosphere of a negotiating session can easily lead to mistakes being made as suggestions are bandied about, offers and counteroffers are made, and deadlines may be looming in the background. Fortunately, there are a number of measures you can take to avoid making careless errors no matter how stress filled a negotiation may be.

Q: Are there any surefire ways to prevent mistakes being made during negotiations?

A: Although there are no guaranteed ways to prevent errors, properly preparing before you begin to negotiate will give you a big head start in that direction. This means establishing your negotiation objective and carefully selecting and briefing anyone who will be participating in negotiations as a member of your team. In short, know what you want to accomplish before you begin to negotiate. This, along with establishing your negotiation limits, will prevent you from accepting an unsatisfactory deal.

Q: During negotiations I often find myself getting confused about who said what. This is especially true in technical discussions that I don't particularly understand, but instead rely on my technical people to figure out. I sometimes wonder if I'm losing control of the situation. Is this a common feeling, or is it just me?

A: In negotiations involving complex issues where a number of people may participate in negotiation meetings it's often difficult to keep track of the players without a scorecard. This isn't something that you should worry about. You don't have to remember everything that's said. What you are concerned with are issues that directly impact upon the negotiations.

On occasion, a negotiator will deliberately try to fog up the issues with long dialogues by technical members of his team about the virtues of this or that aspect of a proposal or the superior quality of a product. For the most part all you want to be aware of here are any inconsistencies in all this chatter that will pinpoint it for what it's worth—which is usually very little. In fact, there are advantages to be gained by these technical exchanges. They give you a chance to be thinking about what you will say next in terms of moving the negotiation along. So don't worry about not being knowledgeable about every technical issue discussed at a negotiation session. That's precisely why you have your technical team members along.

Q: I'm certainly cognizant of the need to avoid making careless mistakes, and I do my utmost to prevent that from happening. Yet, as you know, if anything can go wrong, it usually does, and sometimes mistakes are inevitable. What I'm concerned about is what I can do to minimize the impact of any mistakes that are made. Any suggestions on this?

A: As with any mistake, the best approach is to acknowledge the error, apologize for it, and take whatever measures are necessary to correct it. The most common mistakes made during negotiations are in making hasty calculations that result in mathematical errors. Unfortunately, the later they're discovered, the more difficult it is to correct them. Aside from that, you also have to convince the other party that a mistake was made and that you're not pulling a fast one. For this reason, be prepared to show the other negotiator the details of where the error was made.

It helps to prevent errors of this nature if you keep a written record of interim agreements made as negotiations proceed. Another approach is to make all interim agreements tentative on a final reconciliation when the negotiation is completed in full.

TIP: If a minor mathematical error is discovered, you may want to eat the costs rather than incur the headache of trying to get it corrected. This is especially true if the amount is insignificant in terms of the whole package, and you are well on your way to negotiating a favorable deal. There's little to be gained by muddying the waters over peanuts.

HOW TO ASSESS THE OTHER NEGOTIATOR'S GOALS

Establishing your negotiation objectives is, of course, crucial to your success, but it's almost as important to know the goals of the party you plan to negotiate with since this will influence your bargaining strategy. Naturally, the goals of both parties are pretty basic in most business dealings and consist of buying or selling something or other. In some instances, however, the other negotiator may have underlying goals that aren't apparent on the surface. Being able to recognize these is helpful in making decisions during the negotiation process.

Q: How do you go about figuring out what your negotiating opponent's objectives are before negotiations begin?

A: When you're planning your own negotiation objective, take the time to think about your opponent's expectations. On the surface this may be obvious, such as to buy or sell something to you. However, you want to take your analysis deeper than that. For example, what price is the person most likely to be willing to pay? What are the apparent negotiating strengths or weaknesses? For instance, are you negotiating with a large company that has the clout to impose their terms and conditions, or is it a small company seeking to establish a working relationship with your company. What, if anything, do you know about the individual who will be doing the negotiating? Does the person tend to be candid or can you expect to confront a number of negotiation ploys?

Thinking about all these factors will help you to determine your own strategy in countering objections during negotiations. Of course, your opponent's goals will surface more clearly when negotiations begin, but to the extent possible, it helps to learn what you can before the fact. It's even worthwhile to just think about the forthcoming negotiations from your opponent's viewpoint. If you were in their position, how would you approach the forthcoming negotiation? Looking at it from the perspective of the other party assists you in determining how you will present your arguments.

Q: Of what value is it to analyze the goals of the party I will be negotiating with?

A: This helps you match your goals against your opponent's objectives. Doing this lets you find the areas where you can readily agree as well as the issues that are most likely to cause disagreement. In many situations the price to be paid will be the major issue in dispute. Even here, thinking about your opponent's objectives may allow you to come up with possible concessions that will help resolve the pricing issue. For instance, if you know that just-in-time delivery is important to the other party, then you can offer this in exchange for a higher price. The possibilities, of course, will vary, but thinking these matters through will give you a sound basis for beginning the bargaining.

Q: I recently failed to reach agreement with someone, and in thinking it over afterward, it may have been because I wasn't very flexible about deviating from my negotiation position. I set my goals beforehand and just stuck with them. This resulted in negotiations breaking down without any agreement being reached. Should I have handled this differently?

A: The essence of a successful negotiation involves compromise. There's certainly nothing wrong with striving to achieve your goals, since that is your prime objective. In doing so, however, you have to be able to convince the other negotiator of the merits of your position. Being too rigid about your negotiating position ignores the give-and-take that's part and parcel of the negotiation process. Therefore, you have to have the flexibility to compromise when necessary to reach agreement. You may not always get a superdeal by doing this, but you're pretty well assured of a fair deal, which is far better than no deal at all.

PROCEDURES FOR DEALING WITH HIDDEN ISSUES

As in other aspects of life, things at the negotiating table aren't always what they appear to be. You may run into a situation where the other party to the negotiations has a hidden objective in mind. This may or may not impact you, but if you don't feel right about something taking place during negotiations, you better probe a little to find out what's going on. Otherwise, you may find yourself with what appears to be a good deal that subsequently turns out to be a can of worms.

Q: The company we're negotiating with has offered us rock bottom prices on the item we're buying. Being suspicious as to why their price is so low, we carefully checked their finances. The company is in good financial shape and has a good track record for quality and on-time delivery. The only problem I noticed was that their business is a little slow right now. I asked about this and was told it's something of a cyclical nature and their backlog is always low during the summer. Should I have cause for alarm over the unusually good deal we're getting?

A: Not particularly from the facts you have revealed. There are times when the negotiation position of the party you're dealing with may raise your suspicions. Nevertheless, although you should always seek answers about anything that appears out of the ordinary with the negotiating stance of the other party, it doesn't necessarily follow that there's a problem you should worry about. The other side may have reasons for their negotiating posture which are of little or no concern to you. For example, as in this situation, low prices being offered may result from a company's desire to maintain production levels during a traditionally slack period. A situation such as this is one of the rare times when you shouldn't look a gift horse in the mouth.

Q: How do I go about detecting a hidden agenda on the part of the other negotiator?

A: What you want to watch for are signs that something is amiss. This isn't always easy to detect, and you won't always be successful in detecting any covert motives on the part of the party you're negotiating with. In fact, as previously mentioned, it may not be something of any concern to you. That doesn't mean, however, you shouldn't remain alert to the possibilities, since someone else's secret agenda could be a potential problem for you. For example, if a company is experiencing financial difficulty, it may offer you a good deal because it needs all the business it can get. Yet the possibility exists that they may not be able to perform any agreement that's negotiated.

As for detecting signs of potential trouble, they can be unveiled by researching the company you're dealing with. Financial statements, credit reports, public documents, or information on prior dealings with others all offer potential clues. On the other hand, it may be something as subtle as a negotiator who is too willing to go along with everything you suggest. In fact, on occasion, it may be nothing more solid than your gut reaction that something just isn't right. When this is the case, try to probe deeper to see if you can uncover anything out of the ordinary.

Q: **What action should I take if I suspect something just isn't right with what the other party is proposing?**

A: It depends upon the circumstances. If you have some evidence of something being wrong, raise the issue if it's feasible to do so. For example, if you have discovered that a company has a history of late delivery, bring this fact up and see what kind of an explanation you get. In some instances, there may be valid reasons, while other times you may not be satisfied with the answers you get. If you're not, you have to decide whether the problem is something you're willing to risk by going forward with a negotiated agreement. One good way to protect yourself is to build in provisions in the written agreement to guard against the potential problem you're concerned about.

Q: **I'm a division manager within a large corporation, and I've had my purchasing people dump a serious problem in my lap. The vice-president in charge of corporatewide purchasing has adopted a hard-line attitude about dealing with suppliers. His edict boils down to cut costs and improve quality and on-time delivery. This sounds sensible enough on the surface, but it's being carried to the extreme to the extent that good suppliers are being squeezed to the point where several are threatening not to do business with us anymore. My purchasing people have complained to me about this. Our division has always striven to maintain good supplier relationships, and this has resulted in our having a network of top-notch suppliers. This is now threatened, and I'm not sure of how to handle this problem. The vice-president is one step above me on the management ladder, so I can't arbitrarily ignore him. Any suggestions on how to deal with this?**

A: If you do nothing, you're in a losing situation either way. If your supplier network deteriorates, vendor costs, quality, and delivery will all suffer, and the blame will rest on your shoulders. On the other hand, you have a political problem if you ignore the edict handed down. The vice-president's surface agenda is to improve vendor performance, but he may also have a hidden agenda, which is to look good at anyone's expense, which in this case consists of both your purchasing function and the company's suppliers.

That said, your problem may not be as bad as it seems. Sooner or later, the realization will set in topside that your vice-president is causing more problems than are being solved. In the short term there may be overall improvements in the purchasing picture, which make this executive look good. However, over the longer term, supplier dissatisfaction will inevitably reveal the foolishness of not maintaining good supplier relationships. What you want to do in your division is survive the short term until the policy situation is changed by the vice-president easing up, leaving the company, or being asked to resign.

The solution would appear to be minimal compliance with the directive. Have your people work with suppliers to cut costs and maintain quality and delivery as much as possible. But don't do it at the expense of giving suppliers the option of having to choose between losing money to keep your business or dropping your company as a customer. Improving supplier relationships won't come about by adopting unreasonable terms and attempting to impose them arbitrarily. In fact, in any negotiation, arbitrarily imposing unreasonable terms on the other party will inevitably lead to problems of one sort or another.

HOW TO MAKE YOUR POINT WITHOUT BEING ARGUMENTATIVE

Concluding satisfactory agreements goes far beyond having command of the factual situation and mastering negotiation skills. No matter what, negotiations boil down to two parties reaching joint agreement, and that isn't easy to do if one of them is argumentative. Nevertheless, it's necessary to make your point and to counter the arguments of the person you're negotiating with. The trick is to be able to do so without hostility, and in such a way that the other negotiator isn't inspired to respond in anger. A major key to negotiation success is the ability to control your emotions. When there's a lot at stake in a particular negotiation session, it's easy for people to become frustrated, which can easily escalate into anger.

Q: There's one person I do some negotiating with who is purposely antagonistic. I sometimes react with anger myself in an attempt to discourage him from this type of behavior. Is this the right thing to do?

A: As you may have discovered, anger begets anger, so rather than discouraging the behavior you don't like, you're encouraging it to escalate. It's not always easy to remain calm when someone badgers you, but doing so allows you to concentrate on the negotiations. Furthermore, since you recognize the person's attitude as a negotiation ploy there's even less reason to lose your composure.

Q: **Why are some negotiators deliberately argumentative when it only serves to anger people, rather than get them to make the compromises that are necessary for negotiations to succeed?**

A: There are a number of possible reasons. First, some people operate under the misguided belief that the key to negotiation success is to bully the opposing party into submission. They do this in the hope that people will become flustered and make careless mistakes. It's also done in an attempt to obscure the fact that the basis for their negotiation position is weak. Being unable to defend their cause on a factual basis, they become argumentative in an attempt to keep you from asking questions that would expose the weaknesses in their position.

Q: **I know it's in my interests to avoid provoking the opposing negotiator, but how can this be avoided when you want to object to what they said?**

A: First, most people are professional enough to know that you're objecting to their negotiation position and not attacking them personally. Beyond that, it's the manner in which you take objection to something that can arouse someone's ire. Therefore, how you phrase your objections is the key to making your point without being argumentative.

Q: **What are the techniques for rejecting what someone says without causing rancor?**

A: Consider the following ways when you must reject proposals made by the other negotiator:

- Couch your objection in the form of a conditional "No" rather than an outright rejection. That way, you are offering to accept the negotiator's suggestion if he in turn accepts what you propose. For example, "I'll pay the shipping costs only if I can choose the method of shipment." When you do set a condition be precise about it, and be sure the negotiator understands that your acceptance of what he wants is contingent upon acceptance of your condition. Incidentally, if you have no intention of agreeing with what was proposed, you can make your condition one that is too burdensome for the other party to accept. If you do this, be careful not to make it so outrageous that it will provoke the anger you're trying to avoid.
- Another method of rejection is to give it the appearance of near acceptance. With this approach you're agreeing with what was said except for certain qualifiers that render the suggestion unacceptable. These are phrased such as, "That's not a bad idea, but . . . ," and you go on to outline why you can't accept it.
- Be as positive as possible in turning people down, saying "That might work under certain circumstances, but what we're looking for is. . . ." Presenting your rejection in this manner doesn't convey a blunt attitude that can trigger resentment.
- When you turn something down, always try to present an alternative to what was presented. And if it's at all possible look for ways to incorporate some aspect of what the other negotiator suggested into your proposal.
- Naturally if you're continually refusing everything that's suggested, it's inevitable that tempers will get a little short. Furthermore, the other negotiator may accuse you of being arbitrary and refusing to negotiate. Therefore, try to be flexible in accepting some of the terms proposed. A good way to do this is to accept those things that are relatively insignificant while refusing those you can't live with. Whenever possible, combining the acceptance of something with the rejection of another item will work out well.
- If a particularly touchy subject appears ready to turn the discussion into an argument, try to shift the discussion to a less heated topic. This is also a good time to suggest a coffee or lunch break to diffuse matters before they get out of control.

- A good general approach is to let the other negotiator know that even though there are a number of points of disagreement, you're confident that by working together solutions can be found. Sincerity in itself can often serve to prevent the potential for heated arguments.

Q: I'm always hesitant to reject anything outright during negotiations for fear of alienating the person I'm bargaining with. As a result, I tend to leave everything controversial open until the end and then have a difficult time finalizing agreements. How can I avoid this?

A: When you're negotiating, you can't let your emotions get in the way of what you're doing. This is true when it comes to getting angry, but it's equally valid when it comes to the need to reject any proposition made by the other negotiator that you don't agree with. It's human nature to want to be liked, but when you're negotiating, you can't let this desire hinder your ability to bargain effectively. Furthermore, respect and consideration work both ways, so it's reasonable to expect the opposing negotiator to refrain from anger when you express your position. Incidentally, don't appear to be indecisive about rejecting something, since this will only encourage the negotiator to argue the issue even more.

WHY PERSONALITIES CAN MAKE OR BREAK A DEAL

The bottom line on reaching agreement hinges as much on the personalities of the people involved as on the subject matter of the negotiation. Two people who don't like each other very much aren't going to make the compromises necessary to reach a mutual understanding, unless one or both of them are able to curb their feelings to negotiate successfully. Beyond mutual dislike, there's also the need to avoid getting involved in an ego contest where each negotiator tries to outduel the other in getting the best deal. Even more basic perhaps, but of paramount importance, is the need to communicate effectively without hostility.

Q: I negotiate once in a while with a high-level manager who apparently thinks every negotiation is a contest in which someone wins and someone loses. It's extremely frustrating, and I'm not quite sure of how to handle this situation. What I've been doing in the past is refusing to budge an inch, since he refuses to do likewise. Obviously, our negotiations never seem to get anywhere. Is there another way to deal with someone like this?

A: The best way to avoid getting drawn into an ego contest is to ignore the personality involved and focus on the subject matter of the negotiation. In fact, someone with a big enough ego may be so wrapped up with his or her self-importance that you can achieve a better deal than if they concentrated on the task at hand. To be successful here, do a little bit of ego stroking with comments at the right moment about how tough a negotiator they are, how they know how to get things done, and so forth. These people tend to be suckers for flattery, and sometimes they're susceptible to accepting compliments instead of concessions. If so, you can negotiate yourself a good deal by avoiding getting involved in a verbal tug of war.

Q: Are there any tried and true ways to gain an advantage by having an upbeat personality? I'm a pretty friendly person, but I don't know whether I'm hard-nosed enough when it comes to bargaining with people.

A: Being hard-nosed has nothing to do with negotiation success, and it shouldn't be confused with the ability to not be bullied. Being friendly in and of itself also won't guarantee victory when you're negotiating with someone. Nevertheless, treating your counterpart with courtesy, and showing respect for his or her opinions, can pay dividends in a number of ways. For one thing people are far more willing to listen to someone they like, so it increases your opportunity to present your position to a receptive listener. In addition, it's more likely to gain the cooperation of the other negotiator in working together to solve any roadblocks to reaching agreement.

Q: One of the problems I run into when negotiating involves people who don't appear to listen to what I say. They seem to be so confident that their position is the right one that anything anyone else says is ignored. Is this common?

A: This is a fairly frequent occurrence with inexperienced negotiators, and it comes about when people become so preoccupied with their own negotiation objective that they have no interest in what the other party is saying. There are a couple of real dangers to doing this. For one thing, by not listening they lose the chance to pick up information that may cause them to either modify their position or aid them in attacking the other person's negotiation stance. Besides, this sort of attitude begs the other negotiator to reciprocate by ignoring them.

Q: What kind of tactics can I use when I think I'm not getting my point across? Sometimes people seem to tune me out unintentionally.

A: First, try to pinpoint why the other party is losing interest in what you're saying. It might be something as simple as fatigue, especially if negotiations have been going on for an extended period of time. If this is what is happening, it's a good time for suggesting a short recess in the meeting. Something else to watch for is that people aren't paying attention because the discussion is becoming too detailed. This can happen when there's an extended presentation of numbers that support some financial aspect of your position.

Probably the most prevalent reason you're not being listened to is that the other negotiator has no interest in what you're saying. This can be caused by the negotiator having a set position on the subject you're talking about or something as basic as the person being a poor listener. To regain people's attention, try shifting the focus from the subject you have been discussing. Changing the topic will generally grab someone's attention, but if this doesn't work, try asking a question that will force the other negotiator to respond.

Q: Although I don't know if it's a part of their personality, I have noticed that negotiators seem to have different styles of negotiating. Is this something I should be looking for, and what, if anything, should I do about it?

A: Concentrate on your own negotiation goals no matter how the other negotiator plays his or her hand. Nevertheless, it can be helpful if you notice the other negotiator has a particular style in terms of negotiating mechanics. For example, one negotiator may seem bent on wrapping things up quickly with little discussion of details, while another person may plod along endlessly discussing each and every item at length. Being able to detect a discernible pattern allows you to structure your negotiating approach to take advantage of it.

Q: How do I go about taking advantage of different negotiating styles?

A: If the other negotiator questions every minor detail, concentrate on having solid documentation to support your position. If you're readily able to back your assertions with documentation, you will develop a high degree of credibility with this type of negotiator. On the other hand, if your support documents are not adequate, it will make it that much more difficult to sustain your negotiation position. You'll also need an extra dose of patience when you're dealing with someone who uses this form of negotiating to make decisions.

When you encounter negotiators who are more interested in a quick settlement, extensive documentation supporting your position is less of a factor. Here, the emphasis will be on reaching a quick agreement, and this approach is often characterized by a series of rapid-fire back-and-forth offers and counteroffers until agreement is reached. What you have to guard against here is the possibility of making a careless mistake, so if necessary slow the process down to give yourself time to adequately evaluate the situation.

Although it's not always true, detail-type negotiators tend to be involved with buying situations and are looking for documentation supporting prices, while the fast-and-loose negotiating style is more likely to be found on the selling side of the negotiating table. As for taking advantage of a negotiator's style, it's not something that can be programmed, since many negotiators shift their tactics to meet the needs of the subject matter of the negotiation.

WHEN AND HOW TO ADJUST YOUR NEGOTIATION POSITION

Some negotiations flow rather smoothly and agreement is reached without too much difficulty. At other times, especially in complex negotiations with a number of issues in dispute, you may find yourself having to make adjustments in your negotiation position in order to reach agreement. How you go about doing this can have a significant impact on the type of deal you end up with.

Q: Adjusting my negotiation position seems like a buzzword for having to settle for less than I wanted when negotiations started. Is this true?

A: First, your prenegotiation planning should determine the minimum deal you will accept. Your initial offer, however, will be far more favorable to you than that, and it should represent the best deal you can hope to get. Nevertheless, this opening offer shouldn't be so unrealistic that it will be thought of as insincere.

To illustrate, if you are negotiating to buy something for which you're not willing to pay more than $200,000, but would like to pay a bargain basement price of $180,000, then the latter figure is the one you would use for your opening offer. The flip side of the coin is that the seller may determine that $200,000 is a bottom-line selling price, but would hope to get something more like $220,000. Conceivably, your negotiations will bring you both to an agreement somewhere around the $200,000 figure. It's between your opening offer of $180,000 and your maximum price of $200,000 that you will be making adjustments in your negotiation position. So to answer your question, adjusting your position means having to make compromises in terms of moving from your opening offer, but it doesn't contemplate paying more than your maximum price. It should also be pointed out that this can apply to any negotiation situation, including those where there aren't price considerations.

Q: **I know I'll probably have to make some serious adjustments in my position once negotiations begin since our company is proposing to do business with a much larger corporation and I know they'll take advantage of this. How can I minimize the concessions I make and still complete a deal with these people?**

A: Establish your negotiation limits before you start and stick with them. This is the key no matter what your negotiating situation is. Unsatisfactory deals result when people fail to establish limits before negotiating, or exceed them by rationalizing that what's offered to them is better than the risk of no deal at all. You can minimize the concessions you make by having confidence in your position and recognizing that the other party wants a deal too or they wouldn't be negotiating. Of course, if the only reason someone is bargaining with you is because they feel you can be taken advantage of, then you don't want to do business with them anyway. Always keep in mind that if someone is trying to force an unfair deal on you during negotiations, they will be just as unscrupulous in any future dealings you have with them.

Q: Our company is involved in on-and-off negotiations to sell a segment of the business. One company interested in purchasing this business unit has suggested swapping one of their divisions that would complement our business in another product area rather than doing a straight cash transaction. This is a radical departure from what we were thinking when we first started negotiating. It seems like an attractive proposition though, so we intend to explore it. One thing it does, however, is throw our entire negotiating game plan out of whack. Should we just rework out entire negotiating strategy?

A: Obviously, you have to substantially revise your negotiating strategy, since you not only have to determine if the proposed swap is viable, but also the value of the unit being offered. It may or may not be better than a cash deal, or it may call for cash in addition to the swap. Therefore, when your analysis is complete you may have several negotiation alternatives to propose.

Although not on this scale, many times during negotiations, issues are raised that require adjustments in a negotiating position. It may be due to something substantive recommended by whomever you're negotiating with, or your own realization that there are factors your original position didn't take into consideration. On other occasions, adjustments may be made by both parties in an attempt to devise solutions to what appears to be an unworkable problem. Whatever the reason, there are certain safeguards to take when you're contemplating any extensive changes in your negotiation plans.

For one thing, take the time to evaluate substantive changes to be certain you're getting a reasonable deal. In the back-and-forth trading that takes place during negotiations, a major change may be proposed that has greater implications than are realized at the moment. You have to keep in mind that the other party may have spent a considerable amount of time analyzing the change before they proposed it. Therefore, you should insist on taking whatever time is necessary to be sure you understand the ramifications of the offer.

HOW TO UNRAVEL APPARENT DEADLOCKS

There are times when negotiations reach a stalemate with neither party willing to budge from their position. When this point in the process arrives, there are only two alternatives left. One is to call the deal off; the other is to search for a way around the deadlock. More often than not, especially if the other negotiator is equally anxious to conclude a deal, the two parties working together can cobble a solution together.

Q: **In a recent negotiation we reached a stalemate, with neither party willing to accept the other's final offer. In the end, I conceded and accepted what the other side was offering. Should I have done this?**

A: There's no problem with accepting someone's final offer if it's within your negotiation limits. Sometimes negotiators will hold firm on a position hoping their counterpart will blink first and accept the offer. At this stage of a negotiation, it's usually a question of who has the greatest perseverance. If the positions are reasonably close, it may be worthwhile to be the one to compromise rather than invest the time and energy in waiting for the other party to cave in. That's a judgment call that has to be made based upon all the circumstances surrounding the impasse. As an alternative, these situations are candidates for offering to split the difference if the disagreement involves monetary matters.

Q: **I recently negotiated with someone who was easy to deal with until we tried to agree on a final price. Then I couldn't get her to agree to any change in the price even though I was just looking for a minor concession. I finally conceded, but I found it odd that the other negotiator was willing to risk not making a deal over an insignificant sum of money. Am I missing something?**

A: Only the extra amount of money you gave away at the end. Actually, the negotiator's obstinacy could have resulted from one of two alternatives. As previously mentioned, she could have been standing firm waiting for you to make a move. Or she may have been given an edict by a superior not to exceed a certain amount of money. In either case, she was successful in achieving her objective.

On occasion, negotiators have limits imposed upon their authority to negotiate. Sometimes they will reveal this when an impasse threatens because of their inability to move beyond a certain dollar figure. When you encounter this problem, proceed as if it didn't exist. It's not your responsibility to adhere to guidelines imposed upon your counterpart. Hold your ground, and let the negotiator go back with the message that you won't give in. That leaves the next move up to them.

Incidentally, a tactic sometimes used by negotiators is to say that their boss or some other authority has imposed restrictions upon them when this isn't true. The objective, of course, is to convince you that the terms are the best you will get. Don't fall for this gimmick, and if you want to be hard-nosed about it, insist that the person imposing the restriction negotiate with you. This usually will send the negotiator scurrying to hold a meeting and then to come back to you with some form of compromise offer.

As an alternative, you can try to obtain concessions in other areas to offset the concession the negotiator wants you to make in the deadlocked area. If the negotiator really is stuck with an edict, it may be possible to extract significant concessions in other areas, especially if the negotiator is reluctant to go back to his or her boss over the deadlocked issue.

Q: Are there any tried and true rules for dealing with deadlocks?

A: First, you want to identify what's causing the deadlock. At times this will be obvious, while on other occasions you may be forced to speculate, since the actual motive may be something entirely different from the reason given by the negotiator. You then want to explore alternatives to break the deadlock, with or without making any concessions on your part. Other than that, it's basically a question of exploring the possibilities to see if something can be worked out. Usually it can, but there will be occasions when an impasse can't be resolved and an agreement is never finalized.

HOW TO USE DEADLINES TO CLOSE A DEAL

When negotiations seem to be making little progress, you may think about imposing a deadline for reaching agreement. As it happens, you may not go beyond thinking about it since there's always a genuine concern about what to do if the other party ignores your ultimatum. Although this is certainly something to be concerned about, it shouldn't be the overriding consideration in whether or not to impose a deadline.

Q: **If I have pretty much exhausted every avenue for reaching agreement and the opposing negotiator continues to stall, should I give a deadline for accepting my final offer?**

A: It's probably a good approach, but the primary consideration is whether or not you have viable alternatives if your deadline is ignored. What it boils down to is that the better alternatives you have, the less you have to lose. The same holds true for your counterpart in terms of accepting your offer or letting the deadline come and go. If the opposing negotiator has other options available if the deal isn't made, there will be less urgency to comply with your ultimatum. In most situations, however, where a deal is stuck on dead-center and there is little to be gained by further discussions, imposing a deadline forces both parties to make hard decisions on what to do next.

Q: **If I impose a deadline don't I run the risk of negotiations breaking off without a deal being completed?**

A: That's a possibility that may happen sooner or later anyway. By imposing a deadline, you at least force a decision. Besides, even if your deadline passes, there's nothing to prevent you from reestablishing contact and reopening negotiations.

Q: **Is there any other downside to imposing a deadline date?**

A: If you are forced to contact the other party to reopen negotiations after your deadline has passed without acceptance of your final offer, your threat of no deal being made has passed. Consequently, your credibility in terms of issuing ultimatums is weakened. Furthermore, the other side may perceive your renewed contact as a sign you're anxious to make a deal. They may try to take advantage of this. Conversely, if they're anxious to reach agreement it could work in your favor, since they may try a little harder to compromise, especially if they were worried about losing the deal ever since they let your deadline pass.

Q: **What if I have an actual deadline to meet that requires a deal to be completed by a certain date?**

A: If possible, don't let your opposite number know about it when negotiations begin. If you do, this may be used as a tactic to extract last-minute concessions from you. In some circumstances, it may be impossible to keep your deadline a secret until the last moment. For instance, if you're negotiating to buy items that are needed by a certain date, the other side obviously knows when the contract has to be agreed to in order to produce the items to meet your schedule. Even in this or similar situations, however, you can protect yourself to some extent. For instance, let the other side think your deadline is sooner than it actually is. That way, even if they stall until the last minute, you will be able to casually continue to negotiate past the deadline date. Once your counterpart sees that you didn't panic and make last-minute concessions, you should be able to get a reasonable deal fairly soon thereafter.

WHAT TO DO WHEN YOU ARE GIVEN A DEADLINE

As a manager you're used to being confronted with deadlines. Of course, they can always create problems for you, and even more so when you have one in a negotiation situation. On the bright side, when the party you're bargaining with has a deadline to meet, you have a real opportunity in terms of getting a favorable deal.

Q: **In a recent negotiation, I knew my counterpart had a deadline date by which negotiations had to be completed. As a result, I thought I'd be able to get a little better deal by stringing things out until the last minute. As it turned out, when the deadline arrived, we couldn't reach agreement, so the negotiations broke off never to be resumed. I was surprised to say the least. Why would someone not make any sort of compromise at the last minute when they are faced with a deadline?**

A: Although it may help you to get favorable terms when you're negotiating with someone who has a deadline to meet, there's no iron-clad guarantee. For one thing, the other party may have alternatives to making a deal with you. In fact, although it may not be what you're told, your counterpart could be conducting simultaneous negotiations with others. Even when this isn't so, good negotiators won't let the time pressures of a deadline force them into accepting unreasonable terms and conditions. So even where you might be able to gain some advantage from a deadline, if you press your luck too far, it may backfire on you.

Q: Just last week the person I was negotiating with told me he had to have an agreement by last Friday, as the books were closing for the fiscal quarter and the contract was going to be included in that quarter since that was where it was budgeted. He maintained that if it wasn't finished, the funding for the project would be withdrawn. As it turned out the deadline came and went and the guy just kept on negotiating without even saying anything about the deadline. As of this time we haven't concluded a deal, but talks are continuing. In fact, it looks like it will take a while to agree to something, since I have a number of questions, and I'm having trouble getting answers from this guy who supposedly was in a big rush to get the deal done. What I want to know is how could someone be so cavalier about a deadline? If I missed one, I'd probably be looking for a job.

A: One possibility is that the negotiator's actual deadline hasn't arrived yet. It may well be that the date you were given was in advance of the actual deadline, which is why the negotiator is so casual about it. It does not happen very often, but on occasion a negotiator will either say or imply that he or she has a deadline to meet. In truth there may be no deadline at all, but the negotiator may be using this as a tactic to speed negotiations up. One reason this is done is to discourage people from asking too many questions about what the negotiator is proposing. Therefore, always exercise caution when someone lets you know about a deadline, since there may be very good reason for you to take the time to properly evaluate all aspects of the proposed agreement.

Q: Are there specific techniques to follow when you want to maximize your advantage because of the other party's deadline?

A: The specifics of any situation will to some extent determine what you do when the other party is under time pressures to complete the negotiation. The following guidelines will help in most instances:

- Do not attach any significance to the other party having a deadline to meet.
- Do not give the appearance of stalling when you're negotiating.
- When you're given a final offer, counter with something more favorable to you.

- Be nonchalant if the other side gives you an "accept now, or forget it" ultimatum.
- Do not be greedy and overreach in trying to get a good deal.

Q: Isn't it unreasonable to take advantage of someone's deadline pressures?

A: What you want to do is get a reasonably good deal. You don't, however, want to push too far for a couple of reasons. First, the other party may decide not to deal at all. Second, if you force someone into taking an unfair deal, it may cause problems for you later.

CHAPTER 6

KEEPING NEGOTIATIONS ON TRACK

As a negotiation moves along, there will be any number of matters that come up that can throw it off course. Sometimes, it's just a question of calling a recess to give you a chance to collect your thoughts. In other instances, the discussions may start to wander off course or, even worse, be focused upon an issue you would prefer to gloss over. Besides these factors, you have a serious task to perform in defending your negotiation position when it's challenged by the other side. And if that's not enough of a headache, you have to learn how to separate fact from fiction in what the other negotiator is saying about his or her position. All in all, it isn't always easy getting from beginning to end when you negotiate, but if you work at it, you'll get there a lot quicker. Let's look at how you can do just that.

WHEN TO CALL A RECESS TO REGROUP

You may experience moments during a tough negotiation when you wish you were a thousand miles away. Perhaps the other negotiator is probing an area you don't particularly want to discuss, or maybe you just need to gather your thoughts. Whatever the reason, there are times when you should call a recess to get things back on track.

Q: Once in a while I'll negotiate with someone who wants to establish a set time to adjourn for coffee breaks and lunch. Should I object to this, since it takes away my flexibility to suggest taking a recess when it's to my advantage?

A: This isn't any big deal, so I wouldn't make a major issue of it. Even if you do want to take a recess at some other time, there's nothing to prevent you from doing so. It's always nice, however, to have as much control as possible over every aspect of the meeting. Furthermore, if things are going particularly well for you when the scheduled times roll around, it would be preferable to keep the discussion going. Therefore, when set break times are suggested, you might want to say, "Why don't we play it by ear rather than having a set schedule?" It's unlikely you will get any argument about this.

Q: Can you outline the various reasons for taking the other negotiator to lunch? It may come in handy to me, since our accounting people are always scrutinizing T&E (travel and entertainment) expenses.

A: There are a couple of very good reasons such as establishing a good working relationship and the opportunity for private discussions, not to mention common courtesy. The last instance is especially true if the people you're negotiating with are from out of town.

Q: Although I have never done it, I've often wondered whether or not I should offer to take my negotiating counterpart to lunch. Are there advantages to doing this?

A: It's always a good policy to do this unless you have more compelling reasons for using the lunch break for working on your negotiation plans for the afternoon meeting. For one thing, taking the negotiator to lunch allows the two of you to establish some personal rapport. This can come in handy in diffusing difficult negotiation problems that may arise. At other times, lunch together allows the two of you the opportunity to discuss issues informally on a one-on-one basis. This is especially valuable if there are other people involved in the negotiations who are muddying the waters in terms of getting an agreement wrapped up. Sometimes a negotiator will level with you at lunch about behind-the-scenes influences on the proposed agreement.

Q: What do you mean by behind-the-scenes influences?

A: They can vary, but perhaps the other negotiator's technical people want to do something that isn't feasible from a negotiation standpoint. They may have been talking this viewpoint up during negotiations with your own technical people. Knowing this isn't something that can be negotiated, you can avoid revamping your negotiation plans to suggest ways to accommodate these technical changes. What you learn, if anything, will vary with the situation, but the important point is that lunch presents an opportunity for such exchanges to take place in confidence.

Q: What are the basic guidelines covering when you should call for a recess during a negotiation meeting?

A: The most common motives for calling for a recess are the following:

- A recess gives you a chance to regroup if things aren't going your way.
- You can reassess your negotiating position if you think changes are in order.
- A recess can be used to research something that came up during negotiations.
- In a large-scale meeting, you can talk privately with team members.
- When negotiations are lengthy, a recess will help battle fatigue.
- It's a good way to give both sides an opportunity to examine the respective offers.

HOW TO STEER DISCUSSIONS IN THE RIGHT DIRECTION

When a negotiation meeting is underway, it's to your advantage to be able to steer the discussions in a direction most favorable to you. Naturally, your counterpart also has this goal in mind, so you can't just haphazardly talk about what you want when you want to. With a little thought, however, there are several ways you can get the discussion back to where you want it to be if it starts to drift toward subjects you would rather not discuss.

Q: I just returned from out of town where I spent two days negotiating a deal that should have been completed in two hours. The other negotiator kept getting interrupted every time I was zeroing in on accomplishing something. What can I do to avoid these situations in the future?

A: You have to be direct about it when continued interruptions are interfering with a negotiation meeting. This apparently happened so often to you that it was simply a case of someone not scheduling his work so the meeting could be completed without interruption. If the interruptions had been less frequent, it might have represented good tactics by the other negotiator, since a handy interruption is one of the best ways to shift the focus of a discussion that isn't going your way.

Whenever discussions are focusing on some weakness in your negotiation position, you want to steer the talk in another direction. A well-timed interruption can do this, but it has to be done in such a way that another subject is raised as a result of the interruption. One way to do this is to briefly excuse yourself, then come back and say something urgent has come up that will require your attention for a few minutes. When the meeting resumes, start right in talking about another aspect of the negotiations instead of going back to the touchy subject. Be sure to do so in a convincing way so the other party doesn't become suspicious.

Q: What's the best way to go about shifting the focus of the discussion from a topic you don't want to discuss?

A: Try to ease off the subject without drawing any attention to your reluctance to discuss it. For example, say something such as "Before we get to that, Jim, let's go over . . . " and then start talking about something else. If you can quickly and unobtrusively shift the discussion, the topic might not be raised again, but even if it is, you will have had a chance to gather your thoughts on how to deal with it.

Q: Suppose negotiations get hung-up on some sticking point so that the discussions seem to drag on endlessly. Although everything eventually gets resolved, a lot of time is wasted on one particular issue. The funny thing is that it seems when the tough issues get left for last, they seem to get wrapped up without as much hassle. Is there a reason for this?

A: Once a negotiation has some momentum, the issues become easier to deal with. For one reason, the parties are likely to be more cooperative in working together to solve difficult issues once they have agreed on other topics. The mutual feeling becomes one that a lot of time has been invested in reaching agreement on a number of issues so it would be foolhardy to throw everything away over one troublesome topic.

In certain instances, reaching agreement on other terms and conditions makes it easier to reach common ground on the tougher topics. In fact, agreeing on other things first sometimes minimizes or eliminates what would have been a difficult issue if it had been discussed earlier. For this reason, it's worthwhile when a topic starts to bog things down to suggest that the discussion move on to something else.

SENSIBLE WAYS TO CIRCUMVENT A BOTTLENECK NEGOTIATOR

It can be extremely frustrating to discover that the biggest impediment to reaching agreement isn't the issues themselves, but rather a bottleneck negotiator who won't agree to anything. The reasons for this are varied, ranging from inexperience to indecisiveness. Whatever the cause, it's necessary to work around this individual to accomplish your objectives.

Q: One of the biggest bottlenecks for me is another manager within my company. She consistently throws up road blocks by citing "this" company policy or "that" company procedure, and so forth, as justification for holding things up. Is there any conceivable way to negotiate around this with her?

A: One tactic you can try is to give a little to get a little. In other words, when something is relatively minor, agree to her suggestions. This may build up enough goodwill so that when you have something of importance, you can do a little bargaining over compliance with the policy she's using as justification for holding things up. Point out where the policy doesn't apply in your situation. Furthermore, if she gives several reasons for her dissent, then argue them all individually, thereby winning some while losing others. You may still be slowed down, but at least not to the extent you were before.

Of course, if circumstances are such that there's anything concrete you can use as a bargaining tool, be sure to do so. If anyone under your management does any work for this manager, you can counter with your own slowdown to use as a trade-off. Finally, as with any external negotiations where a negotiator becomes a bottleneck, work around her if possible, or go over her head if necessary.

Q: I'm negotiating with someone who insists on clearing every minor decision with a boss. What's the best way to deal with this?

A: This can be a real problem, since the person you are dealing with is a conduit for someone else who is the behind-the-scenes negotiator. Many business negotiations require the agreement to go through various approval and sign-off channels. For the most part, however, these are mere formalities, and they don't seriously impact upon what was negotiated. But in a situation where someone else is the decision-making authority on every minor item, then you have to protest this procedure.

Tell the person you're dealing with that you're not going to continue until you can deal with someone who has the authority to reach agreement with you. If you're hardheaded enough about this, then either the negotiator will start making some decisions or someone else will join the negotiations. It's prudent to be cautious about taking this course unless it's absolutely necessary, since you don't want to alienate someone unnecessarily. Therefore, when you seek to get someone else involved, use as much diplomacy as possible to do so.

If it's feasible, suggest that both you and the other party bring someone in to assist. This takes the onus off of your suggestion, and it is not likely to arouse any animosity.

Q: I often confront negotiators who claim they have to clear something with their boss. Inevitably, they come back and say it isn't acceptable and then they make a counteroffer more favorable to them. How can I deal with this ploy?

A: A quick way to attack this gimmick is to insist that the person who finds your offer unacceptable tell you firsthand. Otherwise, you will be nickel and dimed to death with this tactic. Incidentally, if you want to retaliate against this technique, start claiming you have to clear any of their offers with your own boss. Then come back with a counteroffer which is even lower than what they originally refused. When they protest, you can really enjoy saying something such as, "It's too bad my initial offer wasn't accepted. I knew how hardheaded my boss is when it comes to negotiating anything."

Q: **One person I deal with is extremely indecisive. As a consequence, it's tough to make any headway in agreeing on anything. What's the best approach for dealing with an indecisive negotiator?**

A: Someone inherently indecisive is the last sort of person who should be negotiating anything, since even if they were offered the best deal in the world, they probably couldn't make up their mind whether or not to accept it. On the other hand, you can be successful with this type of individual if you make it easy for them to agree with you. To do this, avoid giving them a lot to think about. If possible, structure your offer so there's only one decision to make, which is to either accept it or offer an alternative. Even if they can't or won't make the decision themselves, it will be taken to another level where it can be acted upon.

THE PROS AND CONS OF TRADING CONCESSIONS

If there is one area that ultimately determines how well you come out of any deal, it's your ability to trade concessions. The less you have to give up, and the more you receive in return, will control how good a deal you come away with. For this reason, this is an area where you shouldn't bargain in haste, since a careless error can be costly.

Q: **How do I decide what concessions I can make during negotiations?**

A: Your basic planning in this regard should take place before you begin to negotiate. First, decide what you won't concede under any circumstances. This will essentially be the least acceptable terms under which you will still go through with an agreement. It will include not only financial terms, but any other necessary requirements such as technical specifications, delivery terms, and anything else you require to be part of the agreement. Once you have done that, anything else is more or less negotiable and therefore eligible to be considered as a possible concession.

You should go beyond this, however, and try to rank anything you might concede in terms of its importance to you, as well as its value to the person you will be negotiating with. The relative worth won't necessarily be the same. For instance, you may not have too much concern about payment terms, while the other party may place great significance on them. This is somewhat speculative before negotiations begin, and the negotiations themselves may reveal issues that are of primary value to your counterpart, although you would never think so beforehand. Therefore, the relative merit of concessions can't be fully assessed until negotiations take place.

Nevertheless, taking the time to think through the possibilities beforehand will prevent careless giveaways when negotiations commence. By preplanning the concessions you can make, you are far less likely to concede more than you have to in order to reach an agreement. On the other hand, during negotiations, don't be reluctant to make any concession—planned or not—as long as it yields a net gain in reaching your ultimate objective, which is, of course, a satisfactory agreement.

Q: I have a negotiation in process where we are pretty far apart in terms of price. The other side is looking for us to relax our product specifications in exchange for accepting our price position. Relaxing the specifications isn't a problem, but in crunching the numbers, the price should be even lower than where it is now if we do that. In effect, we appear to be giving something up that is out of proportion to what we would gain. How should this be handled?

A: Offer to relax your specifications based on your cost figures factoring in the new price. Even though the other side won't gain financially, that may not be their objective. Perhaps they are better prepared to produce the item with the revised product specifications. You can never equate what the value of a particular concession is to someone else. What's of little or no value to you may be of extreme importance to them. For this reason, this is an area where you can benefit by making some astute trade-offs.

Incidentally, whenever you negotiate, always treat every concession you make as a significant one. That way, you will be able to get maximum benefit from trading off items that are of minor significance to you for substantive concessions by the other party.

Q: When should I make a concession?

A: Only when you have to. Don't be hasty about making concessions, since before you know it, you will have traded off everything you can and still be left with a gap to close to reach agreement. Furthermore, when one party starts to make concessions, right from the start the other side assumes the opening offer wasn't close to what would constitute a reasonable deal. It boils down to the more concessions you make, the more that are expected to be forthcoming. Hold off on making any concessions until the other side offers to make a significant adjustment in their position in return for some form of trade-off from you. The specific trade-off they ask for will also clue you in as to where their priorities are in terms of getting concessions from you. If you're lucky, they will be something that's of secondary importance to you but of prime value to them.

Q: **I have a negotiation that's hung up on an issue. The fact is that I could readily concede the point since it's not of great value to me. It would, however, result in me giving up a concession without getting anything in return since the discussions aren't far enough along to trade this off for something else. Is there a way around this?**

A: One way to work around this is to make the concession contingent upon reaching agreement on something else later. For example, say something such as, "I'll concede on that to move things along, Joe, but it's contingent upon us being able to reach agreement on . . . " (whatever the issue is you want to tie to the concession). Not only does this get you over the hurdle of an early impasse, but it gives you an advantage when it comes time to discuss the issue you tied the concession to.

Q: **It seems to me that negotiating one concession for another concession is a long and involved process. Wouldn't it be more expedient to just make a package deal all at once to reach a quick agreement.**

A: Many business negotiations are relatively simple and don't involve a great many issues on which the parties differ. Here it's easy to close any gap between the two positions. In other negotiations there may be a wide variance in the respective positions, and there may be a large number of issues where the parties differ. In these cases, it's not always either practical or possible to tie everything up into a neat little package.

Q: **Soon after a recent negotiation of mine started, the other party offered to lower their price 10% in exchange for me including more favorable payment terms in the contract. The problem is that lowering their price 10% doesn't solve anything since the price was 30% too high to start with. How are situations like these handled?**

A: What you have here can be called a mirage or illusory concession since what you're seeing is a concession in appearance, which isn't a concession at all. This is quite common especially early on in negotiations. What happens is the party starts with an inflated position and then offers to lower it somewhat in exchange for a concession of real value on the part of the other party. When negotiations begin, never give up anything of value until you get to the point where the other side's negotiation position is within reach of what you consider to be acceptable terms. Since most negotiation positions have built in fat, little of value is being traded away until this fluff is eliminated. To guard against getting stung this way when you're offered a concession, ask yourself these questions:

- What is the value of the concession to you? Every negotiation is different, so even a concession that you might consider valuable in one instance may be of little value to you in a subsequent deal.
- What does the other side want in return for granting a concession? Your objective in granting any concession should be to maximize what you get in return for any concession you make.
- Is the promised concession real or illusory? This is of special concern when what is promised may require the cooperation of a third party. One example would be some form of bank financing or government assistance. These are beyond the control of the other party, so there's no guarantee the promise can be fulfilled.

Q: **I'm being asked to make a trade-off of concessions, but the concession I'm getting consists of additional work to be done during the**

performance of the agreement. How do I protect myself to ensure the promise is carried out.

A: This isn't a problem as long as you spell out what will be done in the written agreement. Many concessions involve aspects of performance that will take place after an agreement is signed.

Q: What happens if I concede everything I can and there's still a gap remaining between my position and the opposing position?

A: You have to stand firm on your final offer and try to persuade the other side to accept it. You should always try to keep something in reserve to concede in the latter stages of negotiations to close a deal. Otherwise, you will end up in this sort of bind.

HOW TO KEEP MINOR ISSUES FROM HOLDING THINGS UP

It's one thing to reach an impasse over a major issue, but it's pointless to let every minor detail impede progress toward reaching agreement. Yet this is what can happen if one or both parties expend their energies on winning every point, regardless of its importance to the agreement as a whole. Quibbling over minor issues develops for several reasons. One is an ego-driven attempt to out-negotiate the other person. Another is a failure to focus on how the issue in dispute relates to the total package that's being negotiated. A third reason, which arises early on in a negotiation, is caused by each negotiator trying to establish a pattern of being firm, and as a result neither negotiator is willing to be seen as the first one to make a concession. Regardless of the cause, it's crucial to move beyond getting bogged down in minor issues. Otherwise, a dispute over an otherwise trivial point can escalate into a contentious debate that threatens to derail the whole deal.

Q: Top management is doing its utmost to encourage team-based decision making within our company. As a result, several other managers and I are assigned to a task force on preparing a policy to implement a greater degree of teamwork throughout the corporation. Talk about irony. Here we are establishing a policy on teamwork, and the group can't agree on anything. Since we were told to iron out any differences ourselves, as a group we have little choice but to resolve matters. The major problem seems to be that a couple of managers refuse to yield from their positions on even minor issues. How can we (the majority) negotiate with these obstructionists? After all, we don't have anything to offer them in return for their concession on these issues.

A: This represents one of the fallacies of what constitutes a negotiation. People tend to think of such things as labor negotiations, diplomatic treaties, or the exchange of money for goods and services as the basis for negotiations. They often don't recognize the negotiating possibilities in less structured circumstances. Nevertheless, people are often negotiating both in the performance of their jobs, as well as their personal lives, sometimes without even recognizing it as such. For example, two friends trying to decide where to go to lunch can result in an informal negotiation where they agree to let one person choose the restaurant today, and the other individual to make the selection on the next occasion. The point is to not overlook the negotiation possibilities in any given situation.

As for the specifics in this instance, there is a very effective issue to use as a negotiation tool with the obstructionist managers. Since the vast majority of managers on your task force are in agreement, suggest to the two holdouts that they write a minority opinion to be included in the task force report to top management. This should quickly bring them into line, since as you inferred it looks pretty bad when a committee on teamwork policy can't reach agreement. Furthermore, since the majority are in agreement, a minority report will spotlight the two managers as not being team players. Once they see the apparent dangers in what is suggested, it's quite likely they will quickly jump aboard the majority bandwagon.

What you have done from a negotiation standpoint is furnished consideration in the form of not spotlighting them as not being team players in exchange for their concession in accepting the majority view. A concession can be an agreement to refrain from doing something that has a negative impact on the other party, and not just the granting of something favorable.

Q: I have a negotiation where we have been spending a lot of time discussing what to my mind at least is an insignificant issue. I suggested we put it on the back burner temporarily and come back to it later. Is this a proper approach to take?

A: It certainly is, and the nice thing is that it may not even come up again, unless it really is a major issue from the viewpoint of the other negotiator. If it is, then you're in good shape, since you stated it's not of any real value to you. If it's of value to the other side, then you can use this as leverage to swap for a major concession in return at a later point in the negotiations. This is why you have to use extreme care and not haphazardly agree to something because it isn't important to you. That's only half the equation, with the other half being its importance to the other party. If they value something that you don't, then it's a useful issue to use for a favorable trade-off.

Q: The person I'm negotiating with suggested that we shelve several minor issues until after we have reached agreement on the two major points on which we have differences. Should I go along with this?

A: Tackling the one or two major issues first is a viable alternative that is often ignored as a matter of human nature more than anything else. Whether it's the paperwork on your desk, or disputed issues during negotiations, the tendency is to do the easiest things first and postpone tackling the tough tasks. Whenever anything newsworthy is being negotiated that draws the attention of the media, you will frequently see periodic reports from both sides that progress is being made, although the major issue has not been resolved. What you're hearing in effect is that minor points are agreed on, but the heart of the matter remains unresolved.

Despite this tendency, forging ahead and negotiating the major issues first will make it that much easier to resolve any minor issues later. After all, once the major issue is agreed upon, neither side to a negotiation is about to negate an agreement over a secondary matter. So although they may be more difficult to resolve, leaving the major issues until the end serves no valid purpose, and in fact can lengthen negotiations by stretching out the amount of time spent on relatively insignificant matters.

SEVERAL WAYS TO SHIFT THE FOCUS AWAY FROM YOUR WEAKNESSES

You may start a negotiation knowing full well that certain aspects of what you propose are weaker than others. Whatever the weak points of your negotiation position may be, they present no particular problem unless they're picked up on by the other side. To keep it that way, you have to be prepared to shift the focus away from these weak spots if the other negotiator starts to ask questions that are targeting the deficient areas.

Q: We're negotiating a contract that will require our company to expedite delivery of certain items. Our recent record on meeting delivery dates has been spotty because of certain production problems that have now been cleared up. What I'm concerned about is how to keep this issue from being raised. Are there any techniques that will help in this regard?

A: The basic approach you want to take is the same as for any other negotiation, which is to maximize your control over the conduct of the meeting. Basically, what you want to do is be the one who is controlling which topics are discussed—which from your point of view are the issues of importance to you. Keep asking questions that require detailed responses so the other negotiator is spending the bulk of his or her time defending his or her negotiation position.

Of course, this can't go on indefinitely, but when the other negotiator starts asking questions that target your weak points, immediately shift the discussion toward the strengths of your proposal. Do this as effortlessly as possible so as not to arouse suspicion. It's also important not to send nonverbal signals that indicate you're uneasy over a particular issue. Therefore, if one of the weaknesses is raised as an issue, reply with confidence and try to move the discussion to another topic by saying something such as, "That's no problem at all, but before we get into that let's talk about. . . ."

Q: It seems I'm continually on the defensive whenever I negotiate, as I'm spending most of my time defending my position. How can I turn this around in future negotiations?

A: The best way is by doing what other negotiators are doing to you, only do it a little better. Hone in on the weaknesses of your opponent's position every chance you get. Even when the discussion may have switched to another topic, whenever there's a pause in the discussion, refer back to a questionable area and ask for further clarification. Just as you have experienced in the past yourself, if you're spending your time defending your own position, you don't have the time to probe too deeply into the other side's proposal.

Q: The party I'm negotiating with is extremely uneasy about a certain aspect of my proposal to the extent that I'm seriously concerned about whether or not a deal can be made. What can I do to put him at ease?

A: If you have a particularly worrisome area that causes concern, you may be able to resolve the difficulty by offering some form of concession. Try to tie it into the particular problem that is causing the difficulty. For instance, perhaps a penalty clause if delivery dates aren't met will satisfy someone who is concerned about an ability to meet certain dates. Whatever the issue may be, there's always a way around it if you give it some thought and come up with a creative solution. Be careful when you do this, though, since the other negotiator may not be as concerned as it appears, but is instead looking for some guarantees that provide a better deal without costing anything.

Q: Our company has a good chance of getting a contract to do a large amount of work for a major corporation. The basic reason we have been contacted is because the other company's engineers are impressed with our technical capability. I'm having a problem closing a deal, though, because the other negotiator is unhappy with our costs. She doesn't seem to understand that because it's largely high-priced technical talent, the costs are going to be higher than if we were doing the job with lower-priced people. All she keeps saying is that perhaps we should use less-expensive people to work on the project. The fact is that we're getting the work only because of the people we're using. As it turns out, the strength of our proposal has been turned into a weakness by the other negotiator. How can I convince her of that?

A: The best thing to do here is to let her own people convince her. This is a classic situation that arises where a lack of communication within a large company sometimes leaves the person doing the negotiating looking at the project from a different perspective than the people who want the work done. If this negotiator had technical people accompanying her for the negotiations, this problem wouldn't have come up. What you want to do is have your technical people get in touch with their counterparts and let them know what's happening. In the meantime, suggest to the negotiator that you would be glad to use lower-priced people to do the work, but before that adjustment is made, it might be better for her to check it out with her own technical people.

SAVVY WAYS TO SUPPORT YOUR POSITION

It's to be expected that people you negotiate with will work hard to attack your negotiation position to get the best possible terms they can. Conversely, the better the job you're able to do in defending against these assaults, the more likely you are to negotiate a favorable agreement. The more unassailable your position, the less chance there is that you will have to make significant concessions to reach agreement.

Q: I'm being badgered about some of the costs contained in my proposal. The other negotiator insists that our overhead rate is too high. What's the best way to defend this?

A: You can use a couple of tactics with this sort of a problem. Argue that your overhead rate is irrelevant, since your price is reasonable. Price is the issue here, assuming that the agreement will be at a fixed price. Some negotiators like to probe costs on an element-by-element basis, hoping to nibble away at the total price in this fashion.

Another approach is to state that no one else takes exception to the rate, and you aren't going to respond in detail unless the other negotiator can offer evidence to support the claim that it's too high. This approach puts the negotiator on the defensive. This is a justifiable position on your part since your overhead rate is based upon the elements that are contained in it. It will vary widely from company to company, so there's little evidence it's too high based on an assertion by the opposing negotiator.

Finally, if you think it's in your interests to do so, you can have your accountants go over the figures with accounting people representing the party you're negotiating with.

Q: Is there a good general way to support my negotiation position?

A: On an overall basis, throughout the negotiation strive to emphasize the strong points in your position and downplay any weaknesses that can be seized upon by the opposition. Although the specifics of what you're negotiating, as well as the issues being raised by your counterpart, will largely determine your response, there are several good techniques you can call into play when appropriate. These include comparisons with competitors, but be certain you can prove your company's superiority, or your claims won't have any credibility.

Any documentation that will support your position is another good way to justify your position. It can be in various forms and from internal or from outside sources. Incidentally, if you're proposing to furnish services of some sort, testimonials from satisfied customers are an excellent form of support. Other possibilities include product demonstrations, lengthy experience and overall corporate reputation, or one-of-a-kind expertise if that is in fact true.

Q: My counterpart has asked for documentation to support some of our claims. Should I furnish it, and if so, to what extent?

A: As long as the questions being raised are valid, and it isn't just a fishing expedition, you should furnish any necessary documentation to support your position. The exception would be if the data requested are proprietary information or are in some other way inappropriate to furnish to an outsider. Beyond furnishing the data, it's also beneficial to be sure it's complete and to provide it as quickly as possible. The sooner you can satisfactorily respond to requests of this nature, the quicker the questions will be put to rest.

Q: We frequently submit lengthy proposals to customers that then become the basis for negotiation. Inevitably, we spend a great deal of time defending the terms and conditions we have proposed. What are some of the basic tactics that can be used to support the information in a proposal.

A: First and foremost, in preparation of a proposal, one of the prime considerations should be how you will respond to any aspects of the proposal that are likely to be questioned. In a general way, any of the following strategies can be used to defend proposal terms:

- Assert what's being questioned is a standard practice which is accepted by others.
- Provide backup documentation that offers additional support for your proposal.
- When feasible, justify a provision as necessary to meet local, state, or federal regulations.

- Offer proof that the item in question is for the customer's benefit, not yours.
- Claim that a provision is standard company policy imposed on a corporatewide basis and applies to all customer agreements, not just this one.
- If you can't convince the other party, try trading off some other item as a concession in exchange for retaining the provision.
- Flat out refuse to change the offending item if your negotiating position is strong enough to sustain it.

Q: Whenever I advocate anything within my company, I experience a lot of difficulty in convincing other managers to accept my position or to adopt my ideas. Never mind not being able to negotiate, I can't even get a fair hearing. Any suggestions on how I can improve in this area?

A: A resistance to change along with the self-interest of other managers can make it difficult to persuade others to accept ideas that aren't of their own creation. As with more formal negotiations, one of the key elements is to do some planning before you even approach others. This can be overlooked, especially if what you want to implement is easy to understand and offers obvious benefits. As you have discovered in the past, however, you have to be able to counter objections.

As a starter, be your own critic. Then decide who has to be convinced and try to determine who will furnish the greatest opposition to your ideas. This should give you a pretty good idea of the size of the selling job you have to do. You can also try to neutralize the opposition by incorporating the suggestions of others into your position. This will increase the base of your support. Finally, whenever feasible, present your case in person rather than in a written proposal. That way you can counter objections right away, and it provides less time for opponents to organize their opposition.

PINNING DOWN YOUR OPPONENT'S FACTS

You may find that the information you're given to support someone else's negotiation position is one of two extremes. It's either negligible or nonexistent, or you're practically buried in paperwork. The complexity of the negotiation may account for this, but in some cases it's nothing more than the negotiation approach being taken by your counterpart. Whereas one negotiator may feel that the less information you have, the fewer questions will be asked, another negotiator may decide the way to win is by burying you in so much detail you won't be able to sort anything out. In any event, whether it's one extreme or the other, or somewhere in between, your task is to get all the facts you need to make an informed decision on what is being offered to you. That isn't always as easy as it might seem, so you may find persistence to be your best weapon in ferreting out the facts.

Q: I'm in the middle of negotiations with a hard-headed negotiator who refuses to provide any information to support his position. How should this be handled?

A: Try one more time and be specific about what you are looking for. If your request is refused and no valid reasons are given, call off the negotiations. Tell the other negotiator that there's no point in going any further unless and until you get the information you need since you can't negotiate properly without it. Let it be known that you will be happy to resume negotiations if you get the data within a reasonable period of time.

On occasion you may run into a negotiator who will stonewall giving you anything at all. Even your objections may not bring results, especially if the negotiator thinks you will stop asking for anything once you're convinced it won't be furnished. The only way to cope with this situation is to break off negotiations. When this is done, you may even see a change of heart before you get out the door, but if that doesn't happen, you will likely be contacted within short order. Fortunately, these situations are the exception rather than the rule.

Q: I need some information, but unfortunately I don't know what to ask for in terms of specific documentation. I'm afraid I'll be turned down if I make a general request, so how should I approach this?

A: If you are cooperative and establish good rapport with your counterpart, there usually won't be any problem in obtaining information. After all, it's in the interests of both parties to work together toward reaching agreement. That doesn't mean there won't be sharp disagreements on the merits of the respective positions, but a negotiator is always willing to furnish anything that further supports his or her position. The only time you have to worry is when you get refusals, since the reason may be that the documentation won't support the position that's being taken. Be open and candid with the negotiator about what you're looking for. He or she can then determine what will best meet your needs. Don't be hesitant about doing this since it simplifies matters for the other side to be able to give you what you want rather than have you continually asking for additional data.

Q: My opposite number gives me information when I ask for it, but it's always minimal and never completely answers my questions. Should I make an issue of this?

A: There's no point in getting involved in a heated debate over this, since it won't get you what you want and will only serve to anger the other party. What you want to do here is to continue to ask for additional information until you are satisfied.

Q: In going over some data given to me I discovered a computational error that will result in a $5,000 advantage to me if it isn't discovered. Should I tell the other negotiator about this or just ignore it?

A: Should you be honest or not is really the question. Good negotiating and good judgment go hand in hand. In all likelihood the error will be picked up anyway, but by being ethical and pointing it out, you will be a step ahead in reaching an agreement without sacrificing either your ethics or your reputation for integrity.

WHAT TO DO WHEN YOU CAN'T AGREE ON AN ISSUE

No matter how hard both parties work at negotiating an agreement, a point may be reached where there's no room left for further bargaining. Both sides may be at the limit of their respective negotiation positions with nothing left to concede. It's tempting at this time to want to toss in the towel and forget about reaching an agreement. Despite the obvious feelings of frustration, however, there are still ways to work things out if you can come up with the right approach.

Q: My negotiating opposite and myself have reached our negotiation limits, and we find ourselves $10,000 apart on price. I'm not about to budge and neither is she. What are our options?

A: The best thing to do is for the two of you to sit down and explore potential ways to solve the problem. Alternatively, if the other negotiator isn't interested in doing this, then work at it on your own. One possibility whenever price is the hang-up is to revise the requirements of what is being bought. For example, can the specifications be changed so the item is less costly, or is a less expensive version available. If the money problem concerns the total amount and the unit price is acceptable, perhaps fewer units can be purchased. It's generally not too hard to find solutions to an impasse over money if both sides are willing to be flexible about making any necessary adjustments.

Q: My negotiation is hung up on price, and the other party suggested we split the difference of $50,000. There's no way I can absorb $25,000 even if I thought it was reasonable, which I don't. I would be willing to move $10,000 just to get the deal done. How can I convince the buyer to move $40,000 from their existing position?

A: There's no iron-clad rule that says any difference in price remaining between the two parties near the end of a negotiation has to be split equally. What you have to do is offer to move $10,000 and let the buyer raise the price the rest of the way. Incidentally, you don't have to convince the buyer to move $40,000, but only $15,000. The buyer by offering to split the difference has already indicated a willingness to raise the price offered by $25,000. Assuming the other party agrees, you have conceded $10,000 of the original difference of $50,000, and they have absorbed $40,000. Here's how you want to make this suggestion:

You: "Since you've indicated you can go up $25,000 by splitting the difference, that leaves us only $25,000 apart. Unfortunately, I've lowered my price as much as I can, so I can't absorb the other $25,000. However, I appreciate your efforts to get this agreement signed, so I've talked to top management to get approval to drop another $10,000 if you will raise your offer another $15,000 to reach agreement."

Of course, the other party didn't initially offer to raise their price $25,000, but did so contingent upon you dropping your price an equal amount. So if they agree, they would be absorbing $40,000 of the $50,000 gap in the respective positions. Nevertheless, the possibility exists for such an offer to be accepted if they are convinced you won't budge any further and the price they would be paying is within their acceptable limits. Frequently, negotiators offer to split the difference in price positions in the hope of getting a favorable price, knowing full well their offer will be refused. So this is by no means an extraordinary way of settling a situation such as this.

Q: What do you do next in a situation like the preceding one if the other negotiator won't go beyond an equal splitting of the difference to close the gap?

A: Although hope springs eternal, you can't deposit it in the bank, so if your proposed settlement is refused, you have to look for another way to resolve the dispute. Assuming you have no more room to move in terms of a price concession, look for another way to add value to your offer so your counterpart will pay more, or alternatively search for a way to take something out of the package to lower your costs. The specifics will vary, but such things as better payment terms, stretching out delivery dates, relaxing specifications, and any other number of factors are potential considerations. On occasion, a significant revamping of the subject matter may be called for. The important point is to realize that there's generally a way to work around any stalemate if both parties to the negotiation are willing to work together to seek a solution.

Q: I've been trying to negotiate something with another manager for weeks and am getting nowhere. Should I just give it up or are there other options?

A: Whether you quit trying or not depends upon how badly you want to reach agreement. If it's important to you, there are a couple of possibilities you can try. One is to look for a way to make it worthwhile for the other manager to work something out with you. For instance, are you overlooking reasons why it would be in his or her interest to go along with what you want? If you can come up with something along this line, it could be a convincing argument for you to use. To do this effectively, you have to look at the situation from the viewpoint of the other manager. It's easy to assume that since you see the wisdom in a particular course of action, other people will view it in the same light. That isn't necessarily the case, since everyone looks at things from their own point of view and with their own self-interest in mind.

A second possibility is to bring pressure to bear on the individual to work out an agreement. Perhaps you could get a more senior manager to intervene. If you take this course of action, you want to try and work it in such a way that there's no indication you initiated the action that puts pressure on the manager to resolve the matter.

CHAPTER 7

MASTERING KEY NEGOTIATING SKILLS

Success in negotiations is closely tied to the ability to be an effective communicator. You have to know when to talk and when not to. And unless you ask the right questions, you're certainly not going to get the answers you need from the person you're negotiating with. Furthermore, no matter how good a communicator and negotiator you may be, there may come a time when mistakes are made. That's understandable in the heat of a complex negotiation, but you have to know how to recover from such mishaps.

One good way to do that is by practicing a little public relations. Although it's not generally given much thought, it's a lot easier to do business with people you like. And if you display an air of cooperation and negotiate without hostility, your counterpart will be more disposed toward working with you to get the deal done. This, of course, doesn't mean you have to agree with everything that's said, only that it's just as easy to bargain hard while being pleasant—and often more profitable. Let's look at some of these issues up close and personal.

UNCOMPLICATED WAYS TO BE PERSUASIVE

You may think you're offering the person you're negotiating with a great deal, and it may even be true. That, however, isn't what counts, since it's how the other person views your offer that will influence whether or not a deal can be struck. Besides, in most negotiations what you're offering is a much better deal for yourself or your employer than it is for anyone you're negotiating with. Therefore, for better or worse, you have a selling job to do if you want to gain acceptance of your offer on the most favorable terms. So the better the job you do in persuading people to see things your way, the more likely it is that the negotiations will work out to your advantage.

Q: **I'm not very good at glad-handing, back-slapping, or even casual conversation, so for me, being persuasive isn't one of my strengths. Given these personality traits, how can I succeed in persuading people of the value of what I'm proposing to do?**

A: You can be quiet and laid back and still be effective at persuasion. In the first place, you're seeking acceptance of what you're proposing, not a social friendship. Therefore, you want the emphasis to be on your proposal—not on yourself. For this reason alone, an unruffled demeanor helps you put the spotlight on what you're offering. This avoids the possibility of someone being overwhelmed by an outgoing personality to the extent that they pay only secondary importance to what is being proposed. Furthermore, what you want to emphasize are a belief in what you're proposing and a knowledge of the facts surrounding it, so although you should be courteous, you don't have to be outgoing.

Q: **One of my assignments in my management position is to set up a temporary interdepartmental task force on quality issues. Naturally, I want to obtain the best people possible to serve on this working group. What I'm encountering from managers when I seek candidates from each department is a reluctance to assign anyone worthwhile to me. When I mentioned this to the VP who gave me this assignment, he said, "You can work it out. One of the reasons you were given this project was your negotiating skills." The problem is, I don't have anything to negotiate with. What can I offer a manager to make it worthwhile to lose a good worker for two weeks?**

A: Before you can persuade anyone to do anything, you have to figure out how you are going to do it. There are a number of intangibles you can use in this situation as persuasion tools. One would be to convince managers of the importance placed on this project by top management. You can also point out that the person assigned will be the key resource in the manager's group in terms of knowledge about quality issues and any relevant polices and procedures that will be implemented.

Tell managers that unless they assign someone in whom they have confidence, it could be a real headache for them when it comes time to implement quality-related recommendations. And casually point out that, since they're selecting the individual who participates, the burden for failure will fall on them. You can reinforce your personal pitch by preparing a memo for these managers emphasizing the importance of the project and essentially reiterating what you tell them personally. For added weight, prepare it for the signature of the vice-president. This backs them nicely into a corner without ever realizing you're the source of this inspiration. With this strategy, you can complain to any manager who tries to dump a dud on you and your task force. That's not likely to happen, however, since this approach won't leave any manager wanting to take the risks.

This particular situation shows how intangibles can be used in negotiations. Without anything being mentioned about negotiations or bargaining, that is what is taking place here. In exchange for not getting in hot water with top management, each of the managers will assign a top-notch worker to the task force. You might argue that the managers weren't negotiating since they didn't have anything to bargain about. They did, though, since they would have assigned a dud to the project, as opposed to being persuaded to assign a higher-caliber employee.

Q: It seems to me that the basic elements of a negotiation, such as offer, counteroffer, consideration, and acceptance, that would make this a legitimate negotiation are lacking here. Isn't that so?

A: All the elements of a bona fide negotiation are present—or would be depending upon the initial reaction of each manager. Let's look at them separately.

- The offer: to train a competent worker in quality issues.
- The consideration: the manager having someone in his department conversant with corporate quality issues.
- The counteroffer: a second-rate worker selected by the manager.
- The negotiations: The task force leader letting the manager know only a competent worker would be acceptable and an unspoken threat to make the manager look bad by telling the vice-president he was being uncooperative.

◆ The acceptance: providing a top-quality employee.

Q: Based on this, then, it would appear that negotiations often take place without either of the participants recognizing it as such. Is this true?

A: Quite true. The tendency is to think of business negotiations as the exchange of money for goods and services. In short, bargaining over the price to be paid. This is only one aspect of negotiations. In reality, managers are frequently negotiating at one level or another, often without even recognizing that negotiating skills are being used.

Q: When you talk about the need to be persuasive in negotiations it raises a question in my mind as to just who you are supposed to persuade. I raise this question since the person negotiating with me may not be the ultimate decision maker. How can I possibly persuade someone I'm not even dealing directly with?

A: First, the negotiator you are dealing with is the surrogate representing the ultimate decision maker, assuming that the negotiator doesn't have the final say. Therefore, in persuading the negotiator to reach agreement on terms, you are dealing with someone who has the confidence of the decision maker. For this reason, negotiators aren't often overridden at higher levels, although it does happen. Furthermore, a good negotiator is skilled at selling what's been agreed to within his or her own hierarchy.

Given the importance of the negotiator in selling the agreement within his or her organization, it's prudent to try and establish good rapport with this individual. This is especially true where you're in a position to dictate terms in a negotiation to the extent that the other negotiator may be displeased. The negotiator won't try to kill such a deal outright when seeking higher approval, since it would be difficult to criticize a deal he or she negotiated. Nevertheless, if the party doesn't think they got a reasonable agreement, it's unlikely they will work to prevent anyone else from scuttling the deal. Therefore, if you're negotiating from a position of strength, this is one reason why you don't want to overplay your hand.

Q: Are there tactics you can use to persuade any behind-the-scenes decision makers? This is a fairly common problem for me, since our technical services organization has a lot of competitors that do business with the same companies we deal with. As a result, they have their own supporters within each of these companies, which means there's always the likelihood of someone trying to kill one of our proposals behind the scenes.

A: The best tactic here is to cultivate your own sponsors within these companies. Your technical people who deal with their counterparts on a daily basis are in the best position to do this.

Q: One problem I've run into in the persuasion area is deciding who the target audience is when a proposal is being prepared. If the proposal is targeted at technical types, the language used may be confusing to those not familiar with the field. However, if it's generic enough to be understood by everyone, then the technical people may find it to be unsophisticated. Who should be the prime target when writing a proposal?

A: If it's just a question of technical versus nontechnical people in terms of readership for a proposal, there shouldn't be a problem. The technical section should be separate from the cost and administrative aspects of the proposal. Therefore, there won't be any overlap in the audience you're addressing. This does raise a general problem, though, which is the avoidance of jargon and profession-specific terminology in proposals where it's neither necessary nor called for. At times, people talk and write in the language of their profession, which isn't practical or useful when submitting a proposal to someone not familiar with the terminology.

Q: Could you summarize some useful pointers on being persuasive?

A: Several practical ways to convince people of the benefits of your negotiation position are

- Know the details of your negotiation objective.
- Project confidence in what you're doing.
- Strive to maintain good working relations with your counterpart.

- Determine the decision maker and target your pitch toward that person or persons.
- Support your arguments with any objective evidence you can muster.
- Show respect for the other person's position even though you disagree with it.

WHAT TO DO IF MISTAKES ARE MADE

The undertaking of negotiations—the need to closely monitor everything that's said and the task of steering the discussions toward a successful conclusion—is difficult. It also includes an awareness that careless mistakes may be made during the many back-and-forth exchanges that take place. These mistakes can be embarrassing, and if they're not discovered soon enough, they can even be costly. For the most part, however, most errors are miscues resulting from hasty computational errors or a misinterpretation of something that was said. Success in coping with errors during negotiations involves a double-barreled policy of prevention, along with a bit of diplomacy if you say or do the wrong thing.

Q: When going over the figures after completing a negotiation, the cost analyst assisting me discovered a major discrepancy in the data furnished to us by the party we were doing business with. Although I can't prove it, the error was buried in the backup detail in such a way that I suspect it was deliberate. It represents a large amount of money, so I have to do something about it. Fortunately, an agreement hasn't been signed yet. How should this be handled?

A: First, your suspicions about the error being deliberate shouldn't be brought up with the other party since you can't prove anything. Therefore, all you could hope for by mentioning it are an angry denial and a hostile climate, which will make it even more difficult to correct the situation. It may well be that the error was accidental since many proposals are prepared in haste at the last minute, which makes it easy for errors to be made.

As far as correcting the situation, call your counterpart and explain the error. Give him or her the revised figures your people have computed and have them verified. Assuming that the other party agrees with the figures you can then proceed to include them in the agreement.

If for some reason the other party doesn't agree with the figures, arrange to get together for another negotiation session. What you have to watch for in a situation such as this is someone coming back and saying something such as, "Even though the amounts were in the wrong category the total amounts are correct. They should have been included under. . . ." In effect, the negotiator doesn't want to make the adjustment in the total amount as a result of correcting the error. Instead, he or she tries to justify the error as a misplaced number rather than an erroneous number. This isn't likely to happen but it can. Aside from outright dishonesty, the negotiator's motive may be self-interest. This is particularly true if the amounts are significant and the previously agreed amount has been publicized within the individual's organization. The negotiator may try to cover up rather than have to admit this error to his or her boss.

Unless there is substantial justification to back up such a claim, either insist that the final document contain the revised figures or don't go through with the agreement. If your decision is the latter, be certain someone at a higher level than the negotiator is made aware of the situation before you call the deal off. This will guard against an unscrupulous negotiator taking advantage of the situation by telling his own people you canceled the deal for some other reason. That way, the culprit won't be able to cover up the fact that an error was made, and you may be able to salvage the agreement by dealing with someone else.

Q: **I made a minor computational error that will cost us a few dollars if it's not corrected. I'm reluctant to bring it up now since we're in the final stages of negotiations, and it would involve a great deal of recompilation. It would also require changes in the formal agreement, which has already been drawn up in draft form. What should I do about this?**

A: With insignificant errors, you're frequently better off just forgetting about them. In this instance, if you want to earn a bit of goodwill, tell your counterpart about it, and say that you're just going to eat the loss. On the other hand, if your embarrassment would be greater than the goodwill to be generated, don't even mention it.

Q: **I've discovered a major error I made that will substantially increase the costs of a proposed agreement for the party I'm negotiating with. Fortunately, negotiations haven't been completed yet, but I'm afraid**

of the reaction I will get. Is there such a thing as a good way to deal with something such as this?

A: About all you can do is admit your mistake. Apologize, and if the error isn't obvious, provide sufficient evidence to prove that it was an honest mistake. If there's any way to simplify correcting the problem, offer it as a suggestion. Even if the other negotiator initially reacts with anger, don't lose your composure.

Q: Sometimes there's a lot of confusion in deciding who agreed to what after a negotiation is completed. At times it has resulted in redoing the completed agreement before having it signed. Is there any way to safeguard against this?

A: It's always prudent to take notes of tentative agreements reached as the negotiations move along. Then, at the end go over everything agreed to item by item to be sure there are no disagreements. This is far preferable to trying to make changes after an agreement is prepared and is being circulated for approval prior to being signed off.

WHEN TO TALK AND WHEN TO LISTEN

To get what you want when you are negotiating, you have to be able to communicate effectively. As you know, convincing people isn't always easy under any circumstances, but it's even more difficult in negotiations. After all, you're trying to sway someone whose objective is to convince you, not to be convinced by you. So while you're knocking yourself out making your pitch, the person across the table is looking for ways to poke holes in your arguments. Of course, your goal is to return the favor when the other person is commenting on the virtues of his or her negotiation position.

Moreover, although you want to be convincing, you also have to be careful about what you say to avoid misunderstandings. Therefore, you have to walk a fine line between promoting your negotiation position and being straightforward enough to be understood. Beyond that, you have to develop a keen sense for separating fact from fiction in what the other party is telling you. So although all your communication skills will come in handy, the basic key is knowing when to talk and when to listen.

Q: I must negotiate with a person who never lets me get a word in edgewise. As a result, I have a difficult time getting my points across. Is there an effective way to deal with this?

A: As you know, some people just like to talk. That isn't necessarily a disadvantage when you're negotiating with someone who is talkative, since you're able to learn a lot by listening carefully to what the other person has to say. For example, you may be able to detect inconsistencies in what is being said, or facts may be revealed that you can use to good advantage.

On the other hand, you want to keep control of the negotiation so you can focus the discussion on what you want to talk about, which for the most part will be the virtues of your position and the inadequacies of your opponent's negotiating stance. Therefore, the key is to try and maintain control of the discussions. Therefore, whenever you feel the other party is dominating the conversation to your detriment, interject with questions that put them on the defensive. By forcing them to defend what they're saying, they will soon be more than happy to let you have your say.

Although as a rule you don't want to interrupt someone, if you have a particularly verbose person to deal with, try politely interjecting with a question by saying something such as, "Excuse me, could you clarify something for me?" Then go on to ask a question that targets what you consider to be a weak point in the other person's arguments. Although you want to avoid being rude, you may find yourself having to be forceful if someone is trying to dominate the discussion. So even if you have to put etiquette on the back burner for a while, make sure you're getting the chance to be heard.

Q: Whenever I want to discuss a certain issue when I'm negotiating, I frequently find people deftly shifting the discussion to a different topic. It's often done in such a subtle way that I can't bluntly say something such as, "Wait a minute. We haven't finished discussing what I'm talking about." Is this common?

A: It sure is, since everyone wants to avoid talking about any issue that's not to their benefit. Therefore, when you find this happening, the odds are that you want to discuss a topic that your counterpart would prefer to bypass. The simple way to deal with this is to raise the issue whenever you can. If people shift to another topic rather than discuss what you're bringing up, counter this by raising the issue at any point without concern for whether the discussion is on something else at the moment. If someone interjects and says, "That's not what we were talking about," reply by saying, "There's no point in discussing that until we finish talking about. . . ." This sends the message loud and clear that until you have resolved the issue you want to talk about, nothing much else will be accomplished.

Q: There's a certain manager I deal with who is always trying to make me look bad by asking loaded questions. What's the most effective technique for responding?

A: Loaded questions are designed to put you on the spot. They can take various forms and the specifics will depend upon the subject matter under discussion. A couple of examples are "Are you still having financial problems?" and "Have you solved your difficulties with late deliveries?" What you want to avoid here is a "Yes" or "No" answer, which confirms the assumption the person was making. Instead, give a direct reply in the form of a denial of the assertion such as, "I've never had financial problems" or "Our deliveries are always on time." Another approach is to hit the ball right back in the other person's court by saying something such as, "What are you talking about?" This then forces the individual to either state facts, which you can deal with, or back off by saying something such as, "Forget it, I guess I was mistaken."

Another form of tricky question you may have to contend with is of the "what if" variety, such as, "What if you can't finish the job on time?" Here again, make a positive reply rather than responding to the speculative question. A good way to support your arguments when you respond to speculation is by proving you have a positive record that negates any need to speculate otherwise. For instance, in response to the prior question, you might want to show you have a long history of completing every project on time.

Q: Is there anything special I should look for when the other person presents his or her negotiation position?

A: Try to sort out the areas where you are in agreement from those with which you disagree. In addition, pinpoint the issues on which you anticipate having the hardest time in reaching agreement. This approach will allow you to concentrate your negotiation efforts on the issues that really matter. Ask questions about anything that is unclear.

HOW TO ASK KEY QUESTIONS TO GET THE RIGHT ANSWERS

To get the information you need to make negotiation decisions, you have to count on your counterpart to give it to you. It won't always be done routinely, however, as your adversary will give you only what he or she wants you to have. Therefore, you will have to do some probing to get the answers you need. Let's look at how you can do this.

Q: What should you do when you get an unsatisfactory answer to a question?

A: You might want to rephrase your question, since it's likely that the person didn't fully understand what you were looking for. It's equally possible the person knew exactly what you were talking about and chose to ignore it, so keep asking additional questions until you get what you want. If you receive a general reply when you're asking for specific details, narrow the focus of your follow-up questions until you get the detailed answers you're looking for. Always avoid framing your questions in such a way that they can be answered with a simple "Yes" or "No"—unless, of course, that's what you expect as a reply. Whatever you do, don't become antagonistic if you're not happy with the answers. A little bit of patience and a lot of persistence may be necessary to get the information you seek.

Q: Are there specific tactics you should use that can help get the answers you need?

A: There are a number of techniques that you can use for guidance in framing questions. The following are tactics and examples of the right and wrong way to phrase questions:

- If you're looking for factual information, don't ask questions that provide leeway for someone to give you either a general reply or an opinion.

Bad: "Are a lot of labor hours required to produce that item?"

Comment: The response will likely be a "Yes" or "No" either alone or accompanied by the opinions of the respondent.

Good: "What is the exact number of hours required to produce each 236X gizmo? I would like to see your production time standards that document this."

Comment: Here, the question asks for not only the specific number of hours required to produce the item, but also the documentation that backs it up.

- Never ask questions in a demanding or threatening manner. It can encourage resistance to a request that otherwise might have been readily responded to.

Bad: "Give me the information by tomorrow, or the whole deal is off."

Comment: First, this is an open invitation to furnish less than a complete package of information and then claim there wasn't enough time to gather all the data. It also offers an opportunity for the other party to say right away that the data can't be gathered that quickly. This forces a decision to either call the deal off or ask how much time will be needed. If it's the latter, you know the respondent will reply with the longest time period that can conceivably be justified. As a result, instead of speeding things up, this tactic slows the negotiation down. It's a sound general rule in negotiations never to bluff unless you fully intend to carry out the threat.

Good: "If you can get the data to me by tomorrow, we'll review it over the weekend and be able to reply to you on Monday, since I know you're in a hurry to get this thing negotiated."

Comment: Rather than being demanding, this form of phrasing the request provides an incentive to respond promptly.

- Don't ask vague or misleading questions.

Bad: "Can you complete this job any sooner?"

Comment: This is an open invitation for the person to come back and say something such as, "Sure, but for every week we cut off the schedule, it will cost an added $30,000 for overtime costs." Alternatively, it will just bring a reply in the form of a question such as, "How soon do you want it done?"

Good: "We would like to have this job completed by July 10, without incurring any additional costs. Is that possible? If not, why not?"

Comment: Not only does this state the exact date on which the job is required, but it emphasizes no more money will be paid for expedited delivery. It also asks for justification if the supplier can't comply.

- When you ask for information, get a commitment as to when it will be furnished.

Bad: "Can you give us those figures as soon as possible?"

Comment: The answer here is likely to be one word: "Sure." There will be no compelling reason to furnish the information sooner rather than later. In fact, if it's the type of information the person would prefer not to provide, you may not get it at all unless you remember to follow up. And when you do, the reply will likely be that it's being worked on. It's at that later date that you will then probably impose some form of deadline. Meanwhile, a lot of time has been lost.

Good: "When will that information be available to us?"

Comment: A specific response will give you a time at which to look for the information. You will then have a legitimate complaint if it hasn't been furnished.

HOW TO COPE WITH VAGUE RESPONSES

Even though you strive to be specific when you ask questions, it doesn't necessarily follow that the responses will be equally forthright. After all, if what you're looking for will be harmful to the negotiation position of the person you're bargaining with, there may be a deliberate attempt to be vague in replying to your queries. As a consequence, you will have to be persistent enough to follow up until a satisfactory answer is received. Nevertheless, even though your patience may be tested, keep your composure, since getting angry isn't going to make the other person more cooperative.

Q: The other day I was getting imprecise answers almost every time I asked a question. Then, when I became insistent about getting some straight answers, the person I was dealing with went ballistic on me. As a result, I called the negotiations off. Was this the right thing to do?

A: The decision was a good one. Although you need to be persistent in pursuing answers and refuse to be intimidated, if you meet with a consistent unwillingness to be open and honest, you have to seriously consider whether or not to continue negotiating. Although a negotiator may drag his or her feet about giving you information, there will usually be at least a minimal effort to comply if you persist. When someone is unyielding and refuses to divulge anything, you have to recognize that there's probably good cause for doing so. It most likely is the knowledge that the information would make it unlikely you would continue to negotiate or at least would be looking for a markedly better deal. Therefore, rather than run undo risks, you are better off scrubbing the deal. You also have to keep in mind that if the agreement being contemplated would require ongoing work over a period of time, you would likely encounter problems all the way along.

Q: Another manager and I were bargaining recently over who would get what for their department in terms of some office equipment being made available by the phase-out of another group within the company. I couldn't get a straight answer out of this person to the simple question of how many people were in her department. My intention was plain, since I figured the computers could be shared based on the number of people who used them. All I can figure is that she wanted to get as many computers as she could, since they were newer models than what we are using. How do you deal with something like this?

A: This problem is easy to solve, since the answer to how many people work in that department is readily available from any number of sources within the company. This does point out, however, that in any negotiation where you're unable to obtain answers directly from the person you're negotiating with, there is the possibility of getting the information elsewhere. Even where it may be impractical or impossible for you to get the information you need, other people you work with may have contacts that can answer the question. For instance, technical members of a negotiation team may be able to learn things from their counterparts in a company you're negotiating with, even though the negotiator was reluctant to give it to you. Fortunately, not all negotiators take the precaution to brief negotiation team members about what they should and shouldn't reveal.

Q: There's a question that I want to raise during negotiations, but I don't think I'll get an answer since it would tend to strengthen my negotiation position. Should I just forget about raising it to prevent controversy?

A: Asking tough questions is part of the negotiation process so the question shouldn't be dropped. But since you anticipate an evasive answer, you might want to ask the question at a point in the negotiations where it would be least expected. Sometimes, when people are caught off guard by unanticipated questions, they will answer them before they realize it wasn't the smart thing to do.

TRIED AND TRUE WAYS TO PROMOTE COOPERATION

Despite a common assumption that negotiation success requires you to use craft and cunning to prevail over the opposition, the truth is that promoting cooperation is a far more effective way for negotiators to achieve their goals. It's a lot easier for both parties to accomplish their objectives if they are working together to solve problems rather than staunchly defending unattainable positions. This is, of course, even more meaningful when your bargaining is being done with other managers within your own company.

Naturally, encouraging cooperation may not always succeed and a more uncompromising stance may be required. Nevertheless, it's worthwhile to try promoting attempts to find a middle ground in resolving differences, at least until you know the other side isn't willing to be reasonable.

Q: **Some of the people I negotiate with are impossible to cooperate with. All they care about is achieving their own goals. Under these circumstances, of what value is it to try and work together to solve disagreements?**

A: It's to be expected that the negotiation objectives of both parties will differ in some respects. For example, in any negotiation involving price, the buyer wants the lowest price possible, while the seller wants the highest. Conceivably, they can bargain back and forth until they eventually reach a figure they can both accept. But what happens if they both reach their limit and there's still a gap in their price positions which neither party is willing to budge on. Quite simply, the choice boils down to no deal at all or searching for an alternative they can both live with.

What this might be will vary with the subject matter of the negotiation. It could mean buying a lesser quantity, more favorable payment terms, a change in the specifications, or any other number of possibilities. Conceivably, either party on their own might come up with an idea and suggest it as a means to resolve the price difference. However, a solution might be expedited if both parties worked jointly at exploring alternatives. A cooperative attitude toward negotiations doesn't mean forsaking your negotiation goals. Instead, it conveys a willingness to compromise when necessary and a recognition that working together may sometimes be necessary to overcome otherwise impossible obstacles to agreement.

Q: **Some people I negotiate with view me as the enemy during negotiations. How can I be expected to cooperate with them if a negotiation bottleneck develops?**

A: Your ultimate objective is to achieve your negotiation goals. To do this successfully, you can't let your emotions overrule logic. Whether or not you're happy with the negotiation tactics of others shouldn't get in the way of cooperating to resolve differences if that becomes necessary. Some people—especially inexperienced negotiators—use Attila the Hun as their negotiation role model. Then, as negotiations proceed and they discover you're not succumbing to their hardball tactics, some of these negotiators may adopt a more reasoned approach; others, of course, will continue their tactics right up until it becomes clear that serious hurdles threaten to derail a potential agreement. At that point, they too will attempt a more conciliatory posture.

It's important to recognize that you will confront different negotiating styles and personalities, since you generally can't choose who you will negotiate with. Therefore, you have to overlook the attitudes and personalities involved and concentrate on achieving your negotiation objectives. So no matter how unpleasant it may be to deal with someone, never let your feelings get in the way of working out a compromise to get what you want.

Q: In the past where some negotiations have been unsuccessful and even when stalemates occurred, the other negotiator showed no interest in exploring any possible way we could reach a compromise. Does this imply they placed more emphasis on their method of negotiating rather than on the desire to reach an agreement?

A: A few negotiators may never realize the need to compromise no matter what happens, and for them negotiating style will take precedence over substance. These folks aren't really negotiating, but essentially are adopting a "take it or leave it" stance. In other situations an unwillingness to compromise may be based on more practical reasons. For instance, reaching agreement may be of little or no consequence to the other party, since their reasons for negotiating may be substantially different from yours. One such instance would be a seller whose motivation is to reach agreement only if he or she can obtain an unconscionably high price. This could be for any reason, with one possibility being a heavy backlog of business that justifies maximizing profits on any additional business. You could even run into situations where the person is negotiating to test the market and has no intention of ever reaching agreement. Therefore, you may encounter a negotiator or two who chooses never to compromise, but these should be the vast exception rather than the rule.

Q: The bulk of any bargaining I do is of the informal type with other people in my company. In many instances, there isn't a lot of motivation for them to agree with me on anything. In fact, when it's someone who views me as a rival for promotion to higher-level management positions, there's actually incentive for them to arbitrarily disagree with me. How can I achieve cooperation under these conditions?

A: Although teamwork should be the rule within an organization, it's naive to assume this is always the case. As a result, there may be times when you have to do everything from pleading to playing hardball to get even minimal cooperation from others. In internal dealings where people don't have any compelling reason to cooperate with you it can be a problem to gain their cooperation. On the other hand, you have the advantage of dealing with these people regularly, which isn't as common in external negotiations. As a result, there are additional techniques you can use. Some of them, of course, apply to any negotiation situation, but they're most effective when you deal with the same people consistently. Consider the following:

- Learn the personality traits of individuals. They will offer clues as to the most effective way to deal with them.
- Show respect for the viewpoint of others and they may reciprocate.
- Don't make unreasonable requests.
- Look for ways to avoid placing stringent deadlines on anything you want done.
- Try to be flexible in deciding what has to be done to meet your requirements.
- Always remain calm even if you're provoked.
- Show understanding for the work pressures and deadlines faced by others.
- Look for ways to compromise on what you need.

Q: It's not so much any deliberate attempt to undermine what I'm doing that gives me trouble. What I constantly have to confront are routine objections such as, "I'm too busy to do that right now." How can I overcome these hassles?

A: Try to develop as many strategies as you can to counter this reluctance. For example, giving people plenty of advance notice doesn't put you in the position of being the person making unwelcome demands. Furthermore, don't treat everything you want done as the most important project in the world. There are only so many times you can go to the well when you're pleading how urgent something is. Once you have exceeded your limit, anything you want done will be treated routinely. This can cause real problems when you do have a priority project. Another approach is to look for ways to cut back on what you need done so it doesn't require as much time to do it. All in all, being reasonable about reaching compromises will give you a better shot at achieving the cooperation you need when you're dealing with others.

HOW TO GET DISCUSSIONS BACK ON TRACK

It can be a long and twisted path from the start of negotiations to the finish. The very complexity of a negotiation can account for this, which is understandable. At other times, unexpected delays and interruptions can take place. For instance, complying with a request for supporting documentation may take longer than expected. The inability to reach a compromise on individual issues can result in extended discussions that slow things down. Even when the negotiation itself is going well, a negotiator disposed to digress from the topic under discussion can impede progress. Often, the pace of the negotiations isn't of any great consequence; however, there are occasions when it can be a cause for concern. The need to meet a deadline is one such possibility, but even where no specific reason exists, keeping things moving along can avoid unforeseen problems that wouldn't have arisen if everything had stayed on track.

Q: I meet regularly with another manager to negotiate interlocking work schedules. Even when we have disagreements, we're able to iron them out amicably, so I have no problem in that regard. What is irritating is the tendency of this individual to want to discuss everything under the sun rather than just doing the schedules. As a result, I usually spend two hours a week doing something that could be completed in fifteen minutes. I hesitate to say anything, since if I get a negative reaction I could end up spending more time trying to get agreement on the schedules than I presently waste. Is there anything I can do about this?

A: There are several schemes you can try that will resolve your time-eating discussions. Nevertheless, before you do anything, you may have to decide whether or not it's worthwhile to do anything. If, as you say, working out the schedules could be very difficult if the other manager was hard to deal with, the extra time spent chatting may be a worthwhile investment on your part. You can't overlook the human angle here, and your trouble-free negotiating may be linked with the fact that you are a willing listener for the other manager. People are less likely to give a hard time to those they like, and since this person is a confirmed talker you may be one of only a few people who don't cut the person short. Unfortunately for you, there's a sound business reason for not doing that. That being the case, you may just want to count your blessings and enjoy the conversation.

Assuming you do want to go forward with cutting back on this downtime, you can do anything from gradually cutting the length of time down to revamping the procedure so you're only minimally involved. One possibility is to work out the schedule and send it to the other manager for concurrence. If only minor adjustments are needed, perhaps they could be worked out by phone. Another alternative is to send a trusted deputy in your place. Finally, you may want to look for a solution that eliminates the meetings altogether, such as possible computerization of the whole process. The details of what you do will depend upon the specifics of your situation, but the important point is not to overlook the personal relationship aspect of the situation. In every negotiation, the rapport developed between the negotiators will be a significant contributor to the ease or difficulty of the negotiation.

Q: Are there any common methods for getting negotiation discussions back on track when they start to wander off course?

A: One of the typical reasons negotiations bog down is a tendency to spend an inordinate amount of time on resolving differences in minor issues. You can do something as simple as look at your watch and say, "Let's see if we can reach agreement on some of these issues, or we'll be here forever." Then, make a suggestion for settling one of the issues in dispute. Just focusing the discussions on reaching agreement will tend to pick up the pace. If that's not practical, the best approach is to suggest that the item be put aside to be resolved at a later time.

If the discussions have just generally drifted off course, you can usually bring them back in focus by asking a question that keys on an issue in the negotiations that is of major importance to the other negotiator. Incidentally, don't overlook practical reasons that may be causing the discussions to drag. Perhaps the meeting is being unnecessarily interrupted by third parties. This is apt to happen when the meeting is held in the office of one of the negotiators. If it's your office, you may want to consider moving the meeting to more private surroundings. Alternatively, if it's in someone else's office a suggestion to move elsewhere might be in order. Finally, if the discussions have been going on for a considerable period of time, fatigue may be setting in. This, in itself, can slow things down. When this happens, it might be appropriate to call it quits for the day. At least that way, people will be well rested when the discussions resume the following day.

HOW TO NEGOTIATE WITH YOUR BOSS—AND WIN

No matter how good a manager you are, the ultimate key to your success is being able to manage your boss. The most difficult aspect of doing that is being able to negotiate with your boss. Many managers don't even attempt to do so, instead pretty much accepting what the boss wants and leaving it at that. But you won't get very far in getting the resources you need to do your job by relying on the goodwill of a cost-conscious boss who looks at everything from a dollars and cents standpoint. With that sort of a perspective, any request is going to be met with a quick rejection. Therefore, although you may not realize it, until you learn how to negotiate with your boss, your ability to operate successfully will be limited.

Q: **I don't negotiate with my boss, and I don't see how anyone else can. I make a request and the boss either accepts it or rejects it. It's as simple at that. There is no bargaining involved. What do I have to negotiate with in the first place? The boss holds all the cards.**

A: Your boss is as dependent on your performance as you are on those who report to you. Even though your boss has to respond to other considerations when you want something from him or her, there is also a need to oblige your legitimate requests. Otherwise, your performance and/or that of the functions you manage may deteriorate, and this reflects on your boss. In short, a boss generally wants maximum performance at minimum costs on a consistent basis with the fewest possible hassles. In the broadest sense, this applies to any manager, right up to and including the top executives.

For your boss to be successful, he or she must provide the necessary resources for you to do your job. The problem arises because of other constraints, most notably, cost constraints of one form or another, imposed on your boss by those higher up in the management ranks. There's nothing astounding about this, since you too have the same pressures. The key to your success in negotiating with your boss is in your ability to justify why granting your request is more advantageous to your boss than turning it down. In other words, if you go to your boss seeking approval to purchase a piece of office equipment, if you can show that the advantages of buying it outweigh the advantages of not making the expenditure you will get what you want.

There are, of course, other factors that can't be ignored, such as no money being left in the fiscal year's budget or a blanket policy directive suspending the purchase of office equipment. However, the first factor is a matter of timing, which you should have taken into consideration, and the latter is something beyond your control. The other major factor not yet mentioned is that other managers will also be making requests for the same limited resources. Who wins? The one who can justify the request in terms that will show how it meets objectives that are beneficial to your boss.

Q: I still don't see where this is negotiating.

A: Let's look at it from a different angle. Let's imagine that your boss is the supplier of an item—a piece of office equipment. He intends to award this item to the person who can provide the greatest return on investment. This is defined as an increase in performance that will reflect favorably on your boss. There are several competitive bidders, all offering the maximum return on investment. These, of course, are you and competing managers who are also looking for additional resources, which in this example is a piece of office equipment. Who will receive the quasi-contract? The bidder (manager) who offers the maximum benefit to the boss. Therefore, what you are negotiating with the boss is to a large extent your ability to best utilize the resources you are looking for. And your success will largely hinge on your ability to be more convincing than other managers.

Q: Aren't there other factors involved besides simply justifying the benefits of giving you the resources you're requesting? I know people who can get almost anything from their boss whether they need it or not and others who have to beg for everything.

A: Purely factual considerations can't be isolated from the human element in any negotiation situation. As has been mentioned previously, it's a lot easier to get things done when you have good rapport with the person you're negotiating with. This is especially true when you're dealing with a boss, due to the closeness of the working relationship. Personalities come into play in determining who gets what no matter how objective a boss may try to be. Therefore, how well you get along with your boss will partially determine your success in getting what you ask for.

Q: **Since getting what you want from your boss is so dependent on justification, how do you know what sort of justification to use?**

A: You have to determine what's most important in the eyes of your boss. From your daily interaction with your boss, you will know what the boss is looking for in terms of overall performance. It may be increased productivity, improved quality, cost containment, or better customer relations. Whatever the combination, these are the factors you have to focus on when you want something from your boss. Try and look at any request you plan to make from the perspective of the boss. How will he or she perceive it? If it ties in with the goals the boss is emphasizing, then your chances of success are better than average. If not, you will get one of those "Sorry, but . . . " promises that are the stock in trade of any manager—as you well know from dealing with people who report to you.

Although it's of secondary importance, another component for success is knowing your boss's tendencies. There are good times and bad times to approach anyone with a request, and sometimes timing alone can make the difference. Therefore, it behooves you to know the best times for approaching your boss with a meaningful request. This applies not only to the boss's personal likes and dislikes, but also as to the specifics of the request. For instance, if your boss has recently been ranting about all the expensive computers floating around that are underutilized, it wouldn't be prudent to stroll into the office looking for approval to buy ten new computers. On the other hand, it might be an opportune moment to suggest buying some productivity-enhancing software. As they say, it's all in the timing.

Another tendency of a boss to consider is whether he or she prefers written requests or one-on-one briefings. Some bosses don't want anything to exceed a page, while others want every last detail in writing. Knowing your boss's preference and complying with it may not guarantee approval, but it will at least avoid an automatic rejection.

Q: What form of justification do I need to win my case when I make a pitch to my boss?

A: Whatever it takes to get the approval. The more substantiation you have for your position, the easier it will be to convince your boss. Plenty of facts and figures showing how your request will meet one of your boss's main goals is what will work the best. Don't forget that your boss may be looking at it not only from the viewpoint of satisfying him, but also the need to satisfy higher levels of management. So if what you're seeking will require your boss to secure higher approval, the quality of the support documentation will have to be sufficient to give your boss confidence that his request will be sustained. Otherwise, even though your boss may agree that your need is legitimate, he or she isn't about to forge ahead with what is considered to be insufficient support to make the case for your request.

Q: My department is in dire need of new machinery, but in view of the costs involved, I doubt I can gain approval. Am I better off asking for a couple of pieces of equipment or trying to replace everything at once?

A: Your best bet is probably to make a pitch for the entire package, but have a fallback position in the event your request is denied. The reason is that everything needs to be replaced, so you're better off alerting the powers that be to this fact. If you just ask for a couple of machines, later when you seek additional machines you will likely hear something such as, "You just bought two machines. What do you need more for?" When you give your explanation, it will sound a little lame and your boss may say, "You should have told me before and we could have gotten them all approved at once." That, of course, may not be true, but it's easy to say after the fact. Of course, as an alternative, you could talk it over with your boss and explain your dilemma. Since the expenditures will be substantial, a great deal of support will have to be prepared, so you may save some time and effort by this approach.

KNOWING WHEN TO HOLD AND WHEN TO FOLD

There's a point reached in certain negotiations where you have to decide whether to continue negotiating or call it quits. You have probably reached your negotiation limit with significant issues still unresolved. Any concession you're willing to make has been made, and offers and counteroffers have still left a gap in the negotiation positions which show little likelihood of being closed. This brings you to the brink of making some hard choices, which are essentially to walk away without a deal or to move beyond your negotiation limits to reach an agreement. There are many factors to consider in deciding which way to go.

Q: What are the considerations involved in going beyond your negotiation limit to reach agreement?

A: The most important negative consideration is that you will be settling for more than what you originally decided were the minimally acceptable terms you would agree to. In essence, you are agreeing to terms you initially concluded were unsatisfactory. A secondary consideration that can't be ignored is that your offer may be rejected, leaving you right where you were before you made the offer. In effect, you may have encouraged the other negotiator to try and coerce additional offers from you by simply standing pat. If that happens, even if it isn't a significant deviation from your original position, it's a giveaway that didn't gain anything for you. Alternatively, of course, making a final offer that goes beyond your established negotiation position may result in the other party accepting your offer and completing the deal.

In making a decision to deviate from your established negotiation position you have to weigh the merits of making a less favorable deal against the available alternatives if a deal isn't concluded. If the potential benefits from the agreement heavily outweigh the negatives, then you may want to go ahead and make another offer. It all boils down to an assessment of the risks and rewards in making your final decision.

Q: How do I refuse to negotiate beyond my established negotiation position?

A: You must firmly state that unless the other party is willing to accept your last offer, there's no point in negotiating any further. Assuming that the other party refuses, then at least temporarily the deal is off. Even here, though, the possibility still exists—however remote it may be—that the other side will contact you within a few days and accept your offer.

Q: What are the determining factors in deciding whether to make an offer that exceeds your negotiation position or walking away without a deal?

A: It all boils down to deciding whether a not-so-hot deal is better than no deal at all. If you have other satisfactory alternatives, then there's greater motivation for you to scrub the deal. On the other hand, if the deal has a great deal of potential, or your alternatives are negligible, then taking the deal may be the way to go.

Q: If someone is negotiating wisely, how can they get stuck in a position where they reach their negotiation limit without closing the gap in the negotiation positions? Shouldn't at least one concession be saved for a final offer?

A: It's always prudent that a final offer be made including some form of concession in an attempt to reach agreement. There is, of course, no guarantee this offer will be accepted. If it isn't, this is when you have to decide whether or not you will exceed your negotiation limits in an attempt to reach agreement.

Q: How do I break off negotiations if I decide I won't reach agreement on the terms that are being offered?

A: Do so in a matter-of-fact way without any display of bitterness or anger. What you want to do is leave an opening for the party to contact you if they later decide to accept your offer. This isn't as unlikely as it may seem, especially if they underestimated your determination to stand your ground on your last offer. If that's the case, they will likely contact you in a day or two.

It's admittedly not easy to walk away from a deal, and the emotional pull is toward offering just a little bit more in the hope that an agreement will be reached. It's this very tendency that shrewd negotiators use to wring better terms from those they deal with. So despite any misgivings you may have, when it's time to call it quits, don't hesitate to do so.

CHAPTER 8

TRADING BACK AND FORTH TO MAKE THE DEAL

The back-and-forth trade-offs that take place during negotiations are part and parcel of the process that will, it is hoped, lead to a negotiated agreement. How you handle these exchanges will to a large extent determine what sort of deal you end up with. Offers and counteroffers will be made and sometimes even be withdrawn. To be successful in this give-and-take requires a willingness to compromise when necessary and on other occasions to stand firm. In addition, you have to know how to recognize and call a bluff, or perhaps find something wrong with what otherwise appears to be a bargain. Beyond anything else, you may have to devise solutions to difficult problems to salvage an agreement. All these topics and others are covered in the discussions that follow.

HOW TO MAKE AND REJECT OFFERS WITHOUT CREATING RESENTMENT

From a negotiating standpoint, the eventual price will depend to a large extent on how offers are handled. Who makes the first offer, how offers are rejected and counteroffers made, all are part and parcel of the give-and-take that ultimately leads to a negotiated agreement. How well you manage this aspect of negotiations will influence how good a deal you get.

Q: Is it better to make or receive the first offer when negotiations begin?

A: In the first place, quite often the initial offer in the form of an asking price has been established by a seller before the actual negotiations begin. In these instances, negotiations commence with that as a starting point. Where it's feasible for either party to make an opening offer, there are a couple of advantages to having the other party go first. For one thing, you get the opportunity to see how close their offer is to what you consider to be an acceptable figure before you even begin to show your hand. This has a significant advantage, since if there's a wide disparity you know there is a lot of ground to cover to reach agreement. Knowing this, you can temper your counteroffer to leave plenty of leeway for some hard bargaining. Let's look at how this might work:

Background

Charlie Cheap and Freda Frugal are negotiating the price of a piece of custom-designed industrial equipment to be built for Frugal's company. Unknown to the other, they have each independently concluded that $150,000 would be a fair price.

Offers

Charlie makes an initial offer to build the equipment for $200,000, figuring he can get top dollar since it's a one-of-a-kind job, so it will be impossible for Freda to make price comparisons with anything comparable. Seeing Charlie's offer as being way out of line, Freda makes a low counteroffer of $100,000. To make a long story short, after extensive discussions and a series of offers and counteroffers, they finally settle at a figure around $150,000.

Comments

If Freda had made the initial offer, it's conceivable she might have offered something closer to her target price of $150,000, say, $130,000. When Charlie responded with his figure of $200,000, it would have made it more difficult for her to reach a final agreement at $150,000, since she would have had to get Charlie to move down $50,000, while she had only $20,000 to play with on the upside. Of course, these scenarios can all play out differently, but for the most part, you're better off getting an offer from the other side first, so you can structure your offer accordingly. A second potential advantage of having the other party make the first move is that they may make a very favorable initial offer that gives you a better deal than you would have received by going first.

Q: What are the advantages and disadvantages of splitting the difference after each side has made their initial offer?

A: The advantage is that if splitting the difference between the two offers will result in a figure both parties can live with, then it's a quick way to settle on price. It avoids the hassle of a lot of discussion of the relative merits of each side's proposed price. Splitting a price difference isn't feasible when one of the parties is a lot closer to their price target than the other party to the negotiations. For instance, if $50,000 is a reasonable price, and A offers to buy at $45,000 and B offers to sell at $65,000, then splitting the $20,000 difference results in a price of $55,000. A would then be paying $5,000 more than planned.

Q: If I am the one making the initial offer, how close to my target price should it be?

A: Your initial offer should be close enough to what you expect the final figure to be to have credibility. Yet you should leave yourself enough leeway to do some bargaining. A fairly reasonable first offer is easier to defend, and it tends to encourage the other side to make a credible offer. If you make an offer that's obviously out of line, then the other side will likely do the same thing. This makes for a lengthy negotiation session to get to an agreement.

Q: I recently had an experience where the negotiator looked me right in the eyes and said, "This is my best and final offer. Unless we can agree on it, we can forget about making a deal." As it was within the range I considered to be acceptable, a deal was agreed to. My question is: What should I do when I get a best and final offer that isn't acceptable? I'm not about to accept anything that's unreasonable just because it's a final offer. On the other hand, how can I turn it down without ending negotiations then and there?

A: A best and final offer isn't necessarily final just because someone says it is. It also isn't necessarily their best offer. More often than not, this is a negotiation tactic made for the express purpose of convincing the other party to accept an offer. It works only if you bite at the bait. If you handle the situation correctly, it won't be their final offer. The threat of breaking off negotiations is essentially a bluff, and you can find that out fast by calling it and rejecting the offer. Say something such as, "I can't accept that offer, but if you will accept . . . , then we can make a deal." This way, you are making a counteroffer that immediately puts the other party in the position of having to choose among three alternatives: accept your counteroffer, continue to negotiate and try to reach agreement somewhere between the "final offer" and your counteroffer, or state that negotiations are ending since the final offer wasn't accepted.

As an alternative to openly refusing a so-called "best and final offer," you can just try talking right around it. If the other party doesn't cut you short right away, this is a sign that they aren't going to call it quits. As a result, they may be willing to make an even better offer themselves or entertain a counteroffer from you. Incidentally, if you're the one making a final offer, make sure it is just that, and be prepared to call off negotiations if it isn't accepted. Otherwise, you will lose your negotiating credibility.

Q: **What happens if the other side does end the negotiations when their final offer is turned down? Is that the end of it?**

A: Any complex negotiation is subject to talks breaking off and then resuming. A threat to end negotiations is an intimidation tactic designed to force someone into accepting the offered terms and conditions. Sometimes the party making the threat doesn't even follow through with it. Even when they do, there are still two avenues open for negotiations to resume. One, they may contact you when they realize you're not going to give in to their demands. Alternatively, you can contact them to try and reopen negotiations.

Q: **Assuming the person I'm negotiating with does end the discussions when I turn a final offer down, how should I go about reestablishing contact?**

A: Contact them and attempt to get things started up again. Suggest that you get together and see what can be worked out to salvage the deal. If the other party doesn't appear to be willing to do that, you have to be prepared to offer some concession to get things rolling again. However, try to hold off on revealing what it is until you actually sit down for another meeting. If the other party goes to the trouble of meeting with you, it's a good sign they want to reach an agreement, but if you make your concession over the phone, you have nothing left to use as a motivator to get them back to the negotiating table.

Of course, there's always the chance that you will be turned down when you attempt to get things going again. Even here, however, you're no worse off than you were when negotiations ended, since you can always say you have thought it over and are willing to accept their final offer. If that isn't acceptable to you, and they still refuse to negotiate, then all you have really lost is a deal you don't want in the first place.

Q: When you receive an unacceptable counteroffer to your offer, what's the best way to respond to it?

A: If it's reasonably close to what you are willing to accept, you might want to stand pat and try and convince the other party to sweeten the offer a little more. Alternatively, you might suggest splitting the difference between the two positions if this will work out to your satisfaction.

If the counteroffer still leaves the positions quite a distance apart, there are several approaches you can take. First, you can make your own counteroffer to narrow the gap a little further and encourage yet another offer from the other side. If you do this, don't make too large a move from your previous dollar figure, since a small price adjustment will signal you are probably pretty close to your limit. Conversely, if you make a large dollar adjustment with your counteroffer, it may be interpreted to mean you have a lot of slack in your position to play with.

If the counteroffer consists of many different terms and conditions, analyze the offer in detail and see which, if any, parts of it are acceptable. Then, you can accept those aspects of the offer you find to be reasonable and continue to negotiate those that aren't. This has the advantage of allowing you to respond positively to your counterpart. You can say something such as, "Several aspects of your offer such as . . . are acceptable to me. If you can do something about . . . then we can wrap this up." Even though you have turned the offer as a whole down, the acceptance of parts of it puts a positive spin on what is essentially a negative response.

Whatever you do, avoid arbitrarily turning a counteroffer down, since it signifies your unwillingness to be reasonable. Give the reasons you find it to be unacceptable, and if feasible, counter with an offer of your own. If you just bluntly reject a good faith offer to reach agreement, it will make it very difficult to work toward a satisfactory conclusion to the negotiations.

Q: I'm looking to relocate from my management position in Memphis to a similar position in New York. I've received and accepted a job offer, and the compensation package is satisfactory, but there's no way I can afford comparable housing, since real estate prices in New York are substantially higher. I frankly didn't realize the difference until the job offer was received and I got serious about making the move. I'd like some form of adjustment to compensate me for the higher housing costs. Even though I have already accepted the offer, is it reasonable for me to reopen discussions?

A: This points out a problem that can happen in any form of negotiation where an offer is made and accepted without reviewing it thoroughly beforehand. Whether it's a personal negotiation such as here or one conducted in a business capacity, the euphoria of wrapping up what seems to be a good deal can lead to a hasty decision. In fact, the better the deal appears to be, the more likely this is going to happen.

In answer to the question, you should raise the issue, since it's not insignificant. It's entirely possible something can be worked out to your satisfaction. Then again, was the compensation package you were offered high enough to take the difference in living costs into consideration? If it was, then you probably aren't entitled to any special consideration. It all boils down to how badly the company wants your services and your ability to be convincing. In any event, when you raise the issue, they certainly won't be impressed with your ability to think things through before you make decisions.

Q: I'm about to start negotiations on an agreement that has to be wrapped up quickly, although the people I'll be negotiating with don't know that. Is there any way I can structure my offer to get a quick acceptance?

A: There are a couple of strategies you can use to encourage the quick acceptance of an offer without any extended discussions. One is to have a substantive reason why the deal has to be completed quickly. You have to be careful here, though, since you don't want to make it advantageous for the other party to stall, hoping your urgency to settle will get them a better deal. For this reason, it's better to use some form of justification that's beyond your control. For example, perhaps some circumstance or event that will negate the need for the contract if it's not signed by a certain date. Whatever it might be, make sure it's believable or you will virtually guarantee the other party will drag their feet until the deadline date, waiting for you to blink and offer them a good deal at the last moment.

A second possibility is to offer some form of incentive to encourage quick acceptance of your offer. For instance, perhaps you can promise more favorable payment terms or other form of financing on the condition your offer is accepted by a certain time. If you do this, be sure to emphasize that the incentive is available only if the acceptance takes place before the deadline.

Another way to wrap things up quickly is to state at the beginning of negotiations that you are going to make a blanket offer encompassing all the terms and conditions that can be accepted or rejected as a whole, but not as to individual terms. State that your offer will be very favorable to encourage acceptance. Then make a fair offer that could conceivably be accepted. This approach avoids having to spend a lot if time bargaining over the individual terms and conditions. Whether or not it's accepted will, of course, be dictated by how favorable the offer is viewed by the other party as well as the inclination of the other party toward avoiding a lengthy negotiation.

WHAT TO DO WHEN AN OFFER IS WITHDRAWN

The withdrawal of an offer, either by yourself or the other party, can cause all kinds of problems when you're negotiating. The reason why offers are made and then withdrawn are varied. In some instances, it's nothing more than a negotiation tactic, while on other occasions there may be valid reasons for an offer to be pulled off the table. Frequently, it's a function of the negotiation process itself where the negotiator isn't the final approving authority for an agreement and changes are mandated by behind-the-scenes decision makers. Whatever the basis for an offer withdrawal, how you handle it is crucial to salvaging an agreement.

Q: The person I'm negotiating with has just told me his offer will be withdrawn if I don't accept it by tomorrow afternoon. What are my options?

A: The obvious one is to accept the offer, which should be done only as a last resort, and assuming it is an offer you can live with. If this is indeed true, then the best way to handle it is to wait until shortly before the deadline and then make a counteroffer fairly close to what the other person has proposed. Say something such as, "Your offer is pretty close to what I can live with. If we can make it . . . then we have a deal." This approach puts the onus on the other party. If there is a legitimate reason for them to have imposed a deadline on their offer, they are under pressure to make a deal. For this reason, they may accept your counteroffer, which gives you a more acceptable basis for agreement.

On the other hand, if they are just stringing you on, they may well say, "It's either my last offer or nothing." Depending upon the circumstances, you can then accept their offer or refuse and leave them with the choice of continuing to negotiate or following through with their threat.

An alternative approach to take if the deadline offer was unacceptable to you is to state that whether or not they withdraw the offer is up to them, because it's unacceptable to you in any event. Tell them that if they wish to continue to negotiate a fair deal, they should give you a call. If they were just bluffing, they will either continue to negotiate at that point or call you shortly after their withdrawal deadline has passed.

Q: My situation is somewhat similar to the previous one, except that the other side made me an offer that was contingent upon my acceptance within seventy-two hours. They told me this was necessary, since their main supplier of components was raising prices in a few days, and unless they could place an order before then, higher prices would have to be paid. These components do constitute a major cost of the agreement being negotiated. Am I locked in to accepting their offer or else having them come in with a higher offer if the deadline passes?

A: Obviously, they should have documentation they can show you confirming that supplier prices will go up. Assuming this is true, then you have to look at their offer as it stands versus what it would be with the higher prices. You should then offset that against where you stand in terms of the rest of the costs contained in the proposal. If you have major differences elsewhere, then you shouldn't lock yourself into accepting an offer because of the supplier price increase.

One way to approach this is to make them a counteroffer that is fair in terms of the other costs that are in question. If they won't accept it, then state that you can't accept their offer. Further state that if they withdraw it, you will not negotiate any other offer that contains higher supplier prices than you have already been given. State that their supplier increases are their problem, not yours. Frankly, your counterpart has probably already locked in the existing prices with the supplier, and the price increase is just a gambit to get you to agree with their terms. This should force them to negotiate a reasonable agreement with you before the supplier deadline.

Incidentally, there are all sorts of gambits used as negotiation ploys in an attempt to panic someone into accepting an offer. This includes alleged price increases as in this case. Of course, sometimes there may be valid reasons why an agreement has to be withdrawn if it's not accepted by a certain date. But when someone gives you this sort of ultimatum, the important point is to verify its truthfulness. This shouldn't be hard to do, since if the other party is telling the truth, they will be more than willing to prove it. On the other hand, if they're trying to string you along, you will encounter resistance in obtaining proof to back up their assertion.

Q: I recently finished negotiating an agreement and the other negotiator has just told me that she would have to give me a new offer since she had been unable to get approval for the agreement from top management. It burns me up to find that I have a deal one minute and don't the next. How should I react to this?

A: It can be frustrating when business deals are scuttled or changed as they go through the approval process. Nevertheless, approvals beyond the level of the negotiator are standard practice and are to be anticipated. In most instances, the approvals result in ratification of what was negotiated or at worst some minor changes in terms and conditions. However, there are times when substantive changes requiring renegotiation are recommended by those in the approval cycle. The first and foremost requirement when you're confronted with such a situation is to refrain from expressing anger.

In brief, the proper approach is to renegotiate what has to be worked out so you have a proposed agreement that satisfies you. You should then insist that it be fully approved before you take it to your people for approval. This will guarantee that you will be going through your own approval cycle with an agreement you know is valid.

Q: What do I do when the other negotiator comes back and tells me what was negotiated is unacceptable to his superiors and then offers me something unsatisfactory?

A: The bottom line is to turn it down. The other negotiator then will have to go back to his people and either get approval for the original deal or get them involved in the negotiations. This is an area where you have to be careful, since it's a standard trick to use the "my boss won't agree with this" argument to try and extract a better deal from you. You have to call this bluff by refusing it.

WAYS TO LOOK FOR LOOPHOLES WHEN BARGAINS ARE OFFERED

In either your personal or professional life you have undoubtedly experienced any number of instances where someone has told you about the great deal they got. Sometimes to your displeasure this conversation takes place in relation to something you have either purchased for your personal use or negotiated in your business capacity. It's almost a certainty that in 99.9% of these cases, the so-called better deal you're hearing about is pure exaggeration or else the comparing of apples and oranges. Needless to say, the very people who tell you these stories never have a tale to tell of having been burned by a bad deal. The fact is, especially when it comes to business negotiations, bargains are few and far between. Therefore, when one appears to be in your grasp for the taking, you better proceed with caution.

Q: The supplier I'm negotiating with swears up and down that I'm getting a bargain basement price. He's even given me figures showing what competitors charge for the same item. What bothers me is that I don't see how one supplier could have prices so much lower than anyone else. Am I being too skeptical about this?

A: You may or may not be getting a lower price, but you have to do a little digging to make that determination. First, it's pretty standard for claims about lower prices to be made when that isn't necessarily true. It isn't always a case of out-and-out lying as much as it is a little bit of stretching of the facts. The price may indeed be lower, but the competitive item it's being compared with may not be comparable. The competitive item may have added features or other value-added functions that justify the price differential.

Market conditions also change, so it's conceivable that competitors' prices were higher last month than the price you're currently being quoted. What the supplier may not be telling you is that his prices were also higher in recent history. A price may indeed be lower than a competitor's even for almost identical items, but what is it based upon? Are you being given competitive prices for the same quantity? Ancillary charges can also influence price variations. Perhaps the competitive prices include shipping charges, while the supplier you're negotiating with has broken his out separately.

On the other hand, it could be that this supplier's prices are indeed lower for specific reasons. Perhaps this supplier is the low-cost producer in this field. Maybe the supplier is quoting you lower prices to fill slack time on production lines. Whatever the reasons, asking some questions, along with a little research, will determine how good a price you're actually getting.

Q: I'm being told that prices are increasing next month, so if I don't accept the offer being made right now, I'll lose out when I have to make a purchase at a later date. My problem is that the offer before me is about 10% higher than it should be. On the other hand, if prices increase 20% next month, then I'll be in worse shape than accepting the overpriced offer right now. Am I in a lose-lose situation where my options are to get stiffed now or get stiffed later?

A: One of the most common pitches made is to buy now to beat a price increase. Take this factor right out of the negotiating equation by telling your counterpart you're not interested in what's going to happen next month. What you're concerned about are unreasonable prices being proposed right now. Stick to your guns and negotiate this agreement without regard for what might happen later. The odds are the negotiator is using this argument since he has no other alternative to defend the price he is presently quoting. If you agree to an inflated price, assuming you make future purchases with this supplier, you'll be paying any price increase on top of the inflated base price you agree to now. Of course, there are valid reasons for buying in anticipation of a price increase, but this is separate and distinct from paying an unfair price now to beat a future price increase. And that's the problem you have in this negotiation.

HOW PROBLEM-SOLVING CAN SAVE A DEAL

Negotiations sometimes get hung up over a particular issue that threatens to derail a deal before it's even agreed upon. Sometimes these obstacles are the result of a basic disagreement between the two parties on a particular point. At other times, the actual problem may be something other than what appears to be holding the negotiations up. Frequently both parties working together can arrive at a mutually agreeable solution that resolves the difficulty, but now and then you will have to go it alone in seeking an answer to the dilemma.

Q: I'm in middle management in a large financial services corporation, and I'm trying to resolve a problem with another middle manager. I'm trying to negotiate with him on a reasonable basis, but he refuses to be accommodating. In talking with other middle managers, I've learned they have experienced similar difficulties. To make matters even worse, what this guy has done in the past gives me cause for concern. I've been told of a couple of instances where he refused to agree to any form of compromise. Then, when higher management got involved because nothing was being resolved, he quickly pinned the blame on the other managers for refusing to cooperate. Needless to say, I don't want this to happen here. We both report to the division manager, but I don't want to go to him, since it will look like I can't solve my own problems. Since I can't negotiate any sort of agreement with this person, how can I get this problem resolved or at least protect myself from being the scapegoat?

A: You actually have two problems, the one you are trying to resolve as well as the person you have to deal with to resolve it. To start with, look for ways to cut your problems from two to one. Specifically, think about how this problem can be handled without dealing with the other manager. Can you go to a subordinate or work around this individual in some other way?

If that's not feasible, come up with your own solution to the problem and then go see your mutual boss. Mention the problem, give him your suggested solution, ask what he thinks of your idea. If he approves, then it becomes his solution as well as yours. Then you can go to the problem manager and say something such as, "Joe Schmidt (the division manager) thought it would be a good idea to do such and such." Presenting it as the boss's idea prevents him from objecting to it. He may, of course, be unhappy that you cut him out of the loop, but that's his problem, not yours.

Q: The person I'm negotiating with has confided in me that her boss is second-guessing what we have already agreed to. Specifically, he wants an unrealistically high profit, and I'm not about to agree with that. Obviously, the negotiator can't override her boss, so how do I handle this?

A: First, try to establish that it is the boss objecting and not just a ploy to extract a few extra dollars from you. Tell the other negotiator the boss should enter the negotiations since he isn't delegating negotiation authority to her. Assuming he shows up, let him know quickly you have no intention of altering your negotiation position. If he doesn't accept your offer, break off negotiations. Then, if it's practical for you to do so, get a senior manager to contact top management at the other company about the problem. Chances are this will work to good effect, especially if you do business regularly with this company or they are anxious to get your business on this particular project.

There's often second-guessing behind the scenes of many negotiations. Most of the time, it's of the harmless Monday morning quarterbacking variety, but occasionally there's outright meddling. This puts both negotiators in a bad position. In any event, you have to turn down any unrealistic change in what has been negotiated.

Q: Are there any specific problem-solving techniques that are useful in negotiation situations?

A: The first step is to identify the problem. Unfortunately, in negotiations the problem isn't always obvious. For instance, you may have made a very attractive offer during negotiations only to have someone appear to be stalling about accepting it. They may actually be giving you an excuse for their reluctance that is masking the true cause. The reason will vary with the circumstances. Perhaps there are people behind the scenes who oppose the agreement, or maybe the negotiator is just stalling while simultaneous negotiations are taking place with someone else.

You have to analyze the situation carefully to see if you can detect what the problem is. Naturally, if you suspect something is amiss, you can always ask, and sometimes your counterpart will level with you. In any event, once you have identified the problem, you have to explore possible alternatives to solve the problem. Sometimes you and the other negotiator can work together on a solution. At other times, you may have to put your own creativity to the test to come up with the answer. For the most part, however, negotiation problems can be worked out if both parties are firmly committed to reaching an agreement.

THE RIGHT WAY TO CALL ANY BLUFF

One of the most common techniques used by negotiators is bluffing. It can be used in a variety of ways, ranging from issuing deadlines, to breaking off negotiations, to pronouncements that this is the final offer. Bluffing can be successful or an abject failure depending upon how it's used and what the response is. One thing for sure is that it shouldn't be treated casually, no matter which end of the bluff you're on.

Q: I've got a supervisor who works for me who has threatened to quit if she doesn't get a 10% pay raise. I tried to explain that wasn't within the pay guidelines so she was asking me to do the impossible. I hate to lose this person, since my department is already short one supervisor. However, I think she was bluffing in an attempt to negotiate herself a pay raise. Do you agree?

A: Whether she was or wasn't will be determined by whether she quits or not. This does point out one important aspect of bluffing. A bluff isn't going to be effective unless it convinces the other party that you will carry the bluff out if necessary. For example, in negotiations one party may threaten to break off negotiations if an offer isn't accepted. If the other party doesn't balk and accepts the offer, the bluffer has to follow through and end negotiations. Otherwise, he or she has lost credibility and won't be taken seriously. Put simply, a bluff is only as good as the ability to carry it out. For this reason, you should never bluff in negotiations unless you're willing to carry out your threat.

Q: How can you determine if a party is making a genuine threat to end negotiations or is just bluffing with no intention of following through on their warning?

A: If it's easy to figure out, then it isn't a very good bluff, since the success of a bluff lies in its ability to be convincing. There are several things you should look for in negotiation situations to help decide whether someone is sincere or just bluffing. First, how important is this negotiation to the person? If it will be of much greater significance to the other party than to you if the negotiations fail, then it's probably a bluff. They may even carry it out to the extent of breaking off negotiations, but if they really want an agreement, they will likely contact you. You must also consider the alternatives available to the other party. If other arrangements can be made to meet their needs, then they might mean what they say.

Beyond the facts of the situation, you also have to consider the human factor. If you're negotiating with someone who is particularly volatile, they may well follow through on a threat even if the facts of the situation would indicate otherwise. This is especially true if they are a relatively inexperienced negotiator and would be more inclined to let their emotions rule over reason.

Q: The party I'm dealing with has given me a "it's this or nothing" offer. I really want to reach an agreement, but the offer is so unreasonable it would be foolish for me to accept it. Any suggestions?

A: Keep right on talking and ignore the ultimatum. Sometimes this works, especially if the other party is just bluffing. But even if you're unsuccessful and the negotiations end, all you have lost is a deal you couldn't afford to make. That in itself can be considered a victory on your part.

WHEN TO STAND FIRM AND WHEN TO COMPROMISE

The back-and-forth exchanges of offers and counteroffers can sometimes become almost overwhelming. It's not always easy to know where you stand at any given moment during a negotiation, especially if a number of issues are being discussed simultaneously. Your success, however, depends on knowing where you are in relation to your initial negotiation position and how far you are from reaching the point where you are no longer in a position to concede anything further. If you aren't careful, you may find yourself in a bind, having reached your ceiling while not being anywhere close to reaching an agreement. To prevent this from happening, you have to know when to stand pat on an offer and when to offer to compromise and make some form of concession.

Q: One thing that bothers me about negotiating when I'm buying something is what I should do in terms of my initial offer. I'm afraid if it's too low it won't be taken seriously. On the other hand, if it's too high I may end up paying more than I need to. What are the criteria for establishing what your first offer should be?

A: This will vary with the situation. If you're buying something where the price is relatively stable, such as off-the-shelf items, your price should be relatively close to what has been quoted, since you know what the going price is for the same or similar items. In these instances, there generally isn't much to negotiate, and in fact, items are pretty much bought and sold at the asking price. Here, the marketplace itself establishes the price.

Nevertheless, even with these items there are on occasion negotiable points, and in some cases very spirited negotiations take place. This happens when the specifications differ from the standard item, unusual quantities are being purchased, special packaging or shipping requirements are imposed, or some other deviation from the norm is present. Therefore, if there are special requirements, the seller's asking price has obviously factored these considerations into the asking price. It's also reasonable to assume that the seller has padded the asking price to cover every possible contingency that might arise in meeting these requirements.

For this reason, your opening offer should be high enough to be realistic, but low enough to leave some negotiating room, since your goal should be a price that covers the minimum cost of complying with any additional requirements. The final negotiated price should end up somewhere between these two figures.

On the other hand, if you're buying something where the price is pretty much determined by the value the two parties place on the item, then you should allow much more leeway in your offer to leave room to negotiate. Here, your prenegotiation price position will serve as your jumping off point. This is the highest price you decide you will be willing to pay to reach an agreement. In using this to determine your initial offer, you have to consider whether or not you have already received an offer or price quote from the seller. If you have, your first offer should take into consideration how far from your target price that offer is. If it's relatively close, then make your offer enough below your target price to allow you to bridge the gap during negotiations without too much difficulty. However, if the asking price you have been given is substantially higher than your target price, your first offer should be significantly lower to give you leeway to close the gap.

Finally, if for some reason the seller hasn't given you any indication of what price would be acceptable, then you have to be guided by your judgment and whatever facts are available in setting your first offer. The offer should be low enough to give you negotiating room to gain agreement at your target price. Nevertheless, it should be high enough to give it credibility as a serious offer. For one thing, if it's reasonable, the seller may surprise you by accepting it. Of even greater importance, though, is that a credible offer will set the tone for the negotiations. If you make a ridiculously low offer, several things can happen. One, it may create a hostile environment right from the start, which will make the negotiation process very difficult. Second, the buyer may respond in kind by making an absurdly high offer. Third, even under the best of conditions, the large variance in price positions will leave a lot of ground to cover to reach an agreement.

Q: How do I go about standing firm on an offer rather than making a concession to close a gap in the respective negotiating positions?

A: There are a number of responses you can make when you have made an offer and it isn't strategically practical to make any concession. First, you should always be prepared to defend the validity of any offer you make. How you do this will be based on what it is that you're negotiating. In general, however, there are a wide variety of resources you can use to support your position, contingent upon which of them fit your particular circumstances. These include

- *Historical cost data.* Use financial data to show that the price you're offering is the same as that offered to others.
- *Price comparisons.* If appropriate, use comparisons with competitor's prices to show you are the low-priced supplier.
- *Documentation.* Provide any documentation that supports your negotiation position.

- *Proof of performance.* Provide records of on-time deliveries, quality standards, and other productivity-related evidence to buttress your position.
- *Customer tributes.* Include letters and other complimentary material received from satisfied customers that offer proof that your performance will equal your claims.
- *Third-party testimony.* Use experts to bolster your negotiation position.
- *Experience.* Prove you have a solid track record for performance over an extended time period.
- *Unequaled talent.* Demonstrate that your people have skills and experience which can't be matched elsewhere.
- *Novelty.* Show that your product or service is one of a kind and therefore justifies a premium price.

The long and the short of standing firm on your offer is to be able to support it against attack. A second part of your strategy is to constantly test the credibility of your counterpart's offer. By continually asking probing questions, you will be able to focus on the weaknesses in your opponent's position. This, combined with having solid support for your position, should gradually carry the day in achieving your objectives.

Q: I sometimes chuckle to myself when I'm negotiating since I run into people who are constantly defending their price position as being cut to the bone if they're the seller or as high as they can go without going bankrupt if they're the buyer. Yet in these same negotiations the offers and counteroffers are adjusted thousands of dollars at a time without blinking an eye. It would seem to me that if someone wants to plead how tight their price position is, they ought to take a cue from consumer marketing where you see almost every price end in ninety-nine cents.

A: This is a good point and one that is often ignored. If you want to add credibility to a price offer, have your computation end in an odd figure; not rounded off in thousands or even hundreds of dollars. For example, $48,443.42 looks a lot more convincing than $48,000 when you're pleading you figured your offer down to the last cent you can afford to pay. Even apart from that argument, it has a look of computational plausibility, where rounded figures suggest they were pulled out of thin air—which they often are.

HOW TO SHIFT YOUR APPROACH TO SALVAGE AN AGREEMENT

Even though you start bargaining with a clear-cut objective in mind, as the negotiations proceed you may find it necessary to make either minor or major adjustments in your negotiation position to reach agreement. This may be due to information you learn from the other negotiator or a change in your own assessment of the situation. At other times, it may be done to overcome obstacles that are standing in the way of an agreement.

Q: Several colleagues and I have been in meetings for a week with a group of managers from another division of the company. I'm the team leader for our group, which is trying to work out an agreement for a couple of projects that are being shifted to our division from the other group. I'm getting irritated since there are a couple of people on the other team who are constantly raising objections to every suggestion that's made. At this rate, these meetings will go on forever. What can I do about this?

A: Your best bet in a situation such as this is to get together privately with the other team leader and reach agreement on what has to be done. A good way to approach this is to suggest the two of you go out to lunch. Your counterpart is probably as anxious as you are to resolve matters, but is probably reluctant about being forceful, having to work with the people on a daily basis. It's reasonable to assume that these people don't want to lose the projects and are obviously out to put as many obstacles as they can in the way of an agreement.

Incidentally, this is the sort of situation that can develop in any negotiation meeting where there are a number of participants. One or more people may be slowing progress down to the point where you're better off having a private discussion with the negotiation team leader. This is also a good procedure to follow when there are sensitive topics to discuss or issues that may evoke widely differing opinions.

Q: I can't put my finger on it, but the other negotiator appears to be stalling. We just can't seem to reach an agreement on one particular issue. What's the solution?

A: Shift the focus to other issues in an attempt to keep the discussion moving toward an agreement. Sometimes negotiations get bogged down on an issue where one party is reluctant to commit to an agreement. Just getting off the topic to another subject can sometimes keep things rolling along. Later on, when you revisit the touchy topic, it frequently can be worked out without too much difficulty.

Q: My counterpart has made an unexpected offer that appears to be fairly attractive. It does deviate somewhat from what we were originally planning to buy. The item performs the same basic functions we were looking for, but it has more bells and whistles than we would be getting for the same price as the basic item. I'm being pressured for a quick acceptance. What are my options here?

A: Essentially tell the other negotiator the offer sounds attractive, but you have to discuss it with your technical people and others prior to accepting it. Tell him or her you'll need a day or two to do this. Unless your counterpart is pulling a fast one, there should be no objection to your suggestion. Any offer that differs markedly from what you were expecting to buy should be carefully reviewed before making a commitment, no matter how attractive it may seem. In fact, the better the deal, the greater the need to think about it. Bargains aren't waiting around every corner as you know, so when one appears on the scene, it pays to make sure it's as good as it seems to be.

PRACTICAL METHODS FOR USING OPTIONS TO YOUR ADVANTAGE

Although it's not an everyday occurrence you may have occasion to use options in an agreement. It may be at your initiative, or a suggestion of the other party. Whichever it is, options can at times serve a useful purpose.

Q: What's the difference between a priced and an unpriced option and what are the considerations in using either one?

A: Basically, with a priced option, the price to be paid is negotiated up front, while with an unpriced option, the price to be paid is negotiated at a later time. The most prevalent reason for using an unpriced option is when it's difficult to determine in advance what the price of the option item will be sometime in the future. It's most common where an item is subject to volatile price swings. Options are used for a wide variety of purposes, including to guarantee a ready supply of an item in the future, as well as lock in a price; assuming you use a priced option.

Q: A counterpart and I have been having a lot of difficulty trying to agree on prices for repair parts to be delivered to us over the next several years. Would it be feasible to include an unpriced option for these items in our agreement for the machines we're buying?

A: It's a good way to get around a sticky point such as this. Just be sure that the option provision is included in the resultant contract, as well as what happens if a price agreement can't be reached at a later date. Incidentally, it's sound business practice to have an attorney review any option provision. This is sometimes neglected, and it can be a costly oversight.

Q: I'm having all sorts of headaches trying to get an agreement negotiated. What happened is that the other party submitted a proposal to perform the services we were asking for, as well as an option for some additional services. Now, during negotiations, it seems they have lumped the costs for both what we requested and their option together. As a result, every time I question something pertaining to the basic proposal, it seems as if they're telling me that the questionable item belongs in the option. In other words, I can't seem to be able to segregate the option from our basic requirement, so it's virtually impossible to establish a separate price for each. Furthermore, we don't even know if we want to buy the optional services that were proposed. What can I do about this mess?

A: Right off the top, have them break out everything pertaining to their option from your requirement. They might well have done this deliberately in an attempt to coerce you to buy the additional services. Even if that's not the case, it's a sloppy way for them to propose optional services you didn't ask for. They should have included any option as a separate section in the proposal. The bottom line is that you want to negotiate the package you're looking to buy. If you then decide to add the option, that should be considered separately. Don't let them sell you on the proposition that lumping the two together will make it less expensive. If that's the case, it will still apply whether you negotiate them together or individually.

FOOLPROOF WAYS TO PIN DOWN AMBIGUOUS OFFERS

You may not have planned to play detective when you start to negotiate something, but you may find yourself feeling like one before you're through. Frustration can set in if someone makes offers you can't pin down in terms of specifics or in other ways is less than cooperative in helping you separate fact from fiction. But doggedness and persistence will get you what you need to know, even though it may not come your way easily.

Q: In negotiating an agreement for technical support services, I'm running into a situation where just when I think I have an offer to work with, the supplier keeps revising the costs upward with one excuse or the other. The reasons given are sound enough, but it was my assumption that all the work requirements were included in the basic offer so no adjustments should be necessary. The supplier says that his proposal responded to what we asked for and he would be glad to furnish just those services. The problem is that without including the add-ons at an additional price, we won't be getting the services we need. Frankly, our request for a proposal wasn't very specific, since we haven't used these services previously. Nevertheless, I feel the supplier should have anticipated what we were looking for and responded accordingly. What's the best way to resolve this mess?

A: The problem is that you never definitively determined what you were buying before you started negotiations. As a result, in attempting to negotiate, you're trying to hit a moving target in terms of the supplier's offers. This is bound to happen when someone starts to negotiate without being specific about what they're buying. As a result, there's a golden opportunity available to be sold far more than you need.

In your present situation, determine precisely what you need in terms of the technical services you plan to procure. Since you seem to be unsure of your needs, you can do this in conjunction with the supplier. Needless to say, if you're not careful, you may end up buying services that aren't necessary. Therefore, don't be shy about asking plenty of hard-hitting questions as to what is being proposed. Then have the supplier give you cost figures for doing this which you should review carefully. Then, and only then, are you in a position to begin negotiating.

This example is just one of many ways that another negotiator may try to alter your requirements to obtain some form of advantage. Therefore, it's important to be alert to the possibilities and to respond promptly when it happens.

Q: A group under my management has a top-priority assignment to complete under a very tight deadline. Since it was impossible to do with the number of people available, the manager in charge who reports to me came looking for help. Through our division manager I worked out arrangements for another division to loan us ten people for two weeks. Since only people with certain skills would be able to do the work, my people worked up a list of ten names in conjunction with supervisors from the other division. I now find out that it will be ten other people who will be reporting on Monday. My project manager is in an uproar since it appears that these are all either junior people or others without the requisite skills. I'm about to go into a meeting with the general manager who controls both divisions and my counterpart from the other division. I know my opposite number in the other division will say that ten people are ten people. Obviously he doesn't want to relinquish ten of the best workers over there for two weeks. I don't know what the reaction of the general manager will be, but if he goes along with the "bodies are bodies" argument, how can I argue the issue. It doesn't seem as if I have any ammunition to bargain with. Any suggestions as to how this can be approached?

A: You're sure to win if you can convince the general manager that the project won't be completed on time. You also have a way to make it worthwhile for the manager from the other division to be more cooperative. The fact is you are in a pretty strong negotiating position even though you don't realize it. Here's how to make your case. First, point out that using the inexperienced people will take longer to finish the project, as well as possibly jeopardize the quality. Furthermore, state that if the people being offered to assist are used, you will need them for four weeks instead of two, because of their inexperience and lack of skills. As the project is top priority the general manager isn't about to risk the deadline or the quality of the job. The other manager may put up a battle and be overruled. On the other hand, his arguments may not be too vigorous, since he will be facing the prospect of losing ten people for four weeks instead of two. Chances are, the general manager will point this out if there are strenuous objections.

This is just one of those situations where no matter what's being negotiated, there's the likelihood of someone trying to make changes to your requirements to your detriment. However, if as here, you're prepared to counter these ploys, you'll win out in the end.

Q: I have been offered a job that will require relocation from California to Texas. It's a logical career move for me and looks like a great opportunity. My prospective employer has said they will try to find a position within the company for my husband. My problem is that this is a pretty vague offer, which is really no more than a promise to see what they can do. Both of us have good positions now, mine in the financial area and his as an electrical engineer, so other than as a career move for me, there's no compelling reason for us to relocate. If my husband did land a job with the same employer, it would add another distinct advantage to our move, since we would be working at the same location. As it is now, he commutes thirty miles in one direction, while I go twenty miles the opposite way. Needless to say, that, along with long working hours, limits our time together. Is there a good way to pin down the promise to find a job for my husband before I commit to accepting this position?

A: Your best bet is to level with your prospective employer. Although they have probably made a good faith offer to try and find your husband a job, there's no compelling reason or sense of urgency for them to do so as long as they assume you are going to accept the position even if he doesn't get a job. The only negotiating chip you have to play is that whether or not he has a job will be a determining factor in your decision on accepting the position.

When you point this out, this may motivate them to work a little harder at coming up with something. In fact, if they want you badly enough, they may create a spot for him. Obviously, if the potential for hiring your husband is real, and not just shop talk, there may be present or planned openings available. If so, this may push them to hire your husband sooner rather than later or not at all. It may also motivate them to use their contacts with agencies, headhunters, and other prospective employers to land him a position with someone else in the area. In employment offers such as this one, and indeed negotiating situations in general, it's important to distinguish between vague promises and firm commitments. Otherwise, you will assume you're getting one thing while the actual performance will be something quite different.

Q: I'm trying to pin a person down on some terms we're negotiating, but she keeps saying, "We'll do the best we can, but we can't guarantee it." Her reasoning makes sense, but would I be wise in agreeing to something where there's only a general promise being made?

A: There are instances where ambiguous conditions are acceptable in agreements. Sometimes particular aspects of performance can't be pinned down with a lot of certainty. At other times a great deal of flexibility in what and how something is done is both justified and necessary. One common example would be various types of research, but you can have open-ended provisions applying to almost anything. It's not so much that some aspect of performance is spelled out in general terms that is the problem, but rather that both parties aren't aware that's the case. As long as both sides in a negotiation agree with what is being done, it presents no particular difficulty. It's when one side expects a definitive result and the other side believes best efforts are called for that trouble is brewing.

Q: Are there certain signs to look for which indicate the party you're negotiating with isn't leveling with you?

A: During negotiations a lot of so-called "huff, puff, and fluff" flow back and forth. Usually this is just the typical promotion of one's negotiating position. What you have to watch for are telltale signs that the negotiator is deliberately trying to deceive you, or at least is avoiding giving you the information you need to make an informed decision. Such things as false claims, failing to answer questions, not furnishing requested documentation, or misrepresenting facts are the type of actions that should sound a red alert. When you see this happening, push to get any information you need, and if it's not forthcoming, seriously consider the wisdom of doing business with this person. Where you do have suspicions, but decide they're not of sufficient magnitude to call it quits, take adequate safeguards to protect your interests in any agreement that is reached.

WHY BEING PATIENT CAN YIELD BIG DIVIDENDS

There are any number of reasons why negotiating with someone can make you tense and anxious to get the bargaining over and done with so you can get on with your other management duties. It may be the pressures of your job that don't allow you the luxury of indulging in lengthy negotiation meetings. Perhaps it's the need to reach agreement because of a deadline you have to meet. And then, perhaps you are just weary of listening to another party try to convince you their position is correct, even though you have logically presented facts proving otherwise. Whatever the reason for your fervent desire to wrap things up, it's to your distinct advantage to restrain these feelings, since patience and persistence are primary qualities for negotiation success.

Q: The person I'm negotiating with has from the start emphasized a desire to wrap things up quickly. I generally agree with that, but there's no imperative such as an urgent deadline forcing us to complete our bargaining in a hurry. Could this person have some hidden agenda I'm unaware of? I don't want to be forced into making a crucial mistake by rushing.

A: There are several possibilities as to why the other negotiator is in a rush. First, it might be nothing more than the individual's personality, his other business commitments, or a combination of the two. Then again, it may be a negotiation tactic being employed for a specific reason. The most common and benign reason may just be a ploy to try and force you into making careless mistakes and perhaps conceding more than you would if you had the time to think things through.

On the other hand, the negotiator may have very sound reasons for wanting to get a deal signed off. For example, maybe there are some serious flaws in what is being proposed that would give you cause for concern if you discovered them. Another reason may be that there are facts known to the other party that make the potential deal much more lucrative than you're currently envisioning. By getting an agreement under contract, this windfall won't be known to you and cause you either to reconsider making any deal or at least to significantly alter your negotiation position. For these reasons, it will serve you well to proceed deliberately, for no matter what the reason, the other negotiator's impatience may prompt him to offer you more than you would otherwise expect to get.

Q: My negotiation position is sound, but I really don't have much of anything to concede. In other words, I don't have any room to make trade-offs or offer concessions. Although I don't want to tell the other party this, it's pretty much a question of "what you see is what you get" in terms of where I stand. Since I don't have any wiggle room, how should I proceed?

A: You have to have a lot of patience, since you may have to repetitively justify your existing offer as the best deal anyone should expect to get. This means you may have to do some stonewalling if the other party makes any concessions and wants you to do likewise. To be successful, you want to alternate between stressing the reasonableness of your position along with poking holes in your counterpart's position. The more you can keep your opposite number on the defensive, the less time you will have to spend mounting a defense of your own position. Assuming that your position is objectively valid, you may ultimately succeed. In these situations, however, the possibility always exists that the other party will conclude you're just being unreasonable and refuse to bargain any longer. Therefore, this approach works only if what you're offering is a good deal on its face. Most people are reluctant to believe that accepting an initial offer is in their best interests. Then, again, there are consumer goods that are heavily discounted for which some people still pay list price. Perhaps the person across the table is one of those people.

Q: I was recounting the facts of a recent negotiation I had with another manager, and she kidded me about my tendency to be helpful as being a costly negotiating trait. What prompted this was my telling her how I had interrupted to help the other negotiator out when he was trying to explain a technical point to me. I did it as a matter of courtesy, since I'm experienced in the technical field and he isn't. My friend said if I had let the negotiator struggle on with the explanation I may have learned something that would have helped me during negotiations. Who's right about this?

A: It's impossible to tell without knowing all the facts, but as a general rule your friend is giving you good advice. When people from the other side of the negotiating aisle are talking, it's prudent to be patient and let them have their say. The more they talk, the more you learn. That's not to infer that you acted improperly, since nothing of significance to the negotiation might have been revealed. Nevertheless, it does pay to sit back and listen, since you never know when someone may inadvertently reveal something of value to you.

CHAPTER 9

DEVELOPING MUTUAL TRUST FOR SMOOTHER NEGOTIATIONS

Negotiating with others doesn't have to be the hassle that it's often made out to be. One of the keys to sensible negotiations is trust. This alone will help defuse sensitive issues. So where there is mutual trust to begin with, the negotiation process will be a lot smoother. However, even if there is no initial basis for trust, it can be developed as negotiations proceed. No-hassle negotiating also requires the ability to work around difficult issues and to keep minor disagreements from becoming major problems. These and other strategies for keeping negotiations civilized are discussed in this chapter.

HOW TO BUILD TRUST TO GET RESULTS

As any manager knows, building trust with employees is a complex and time-consuming endeavor. And as you might imagine, it's doubly difficult to do so with people you negotiate with. In the first place, unless you deal with someone on a regular basis, the opportunity to secure their trust over time isn't present. Perhaps of even greater significance is the fact that the negotiation process itself is conducive to inspiring suspicion in lieu of trust. Yet the very fact that trusting the person you're negotiating with is so uncharacteristic makes it a more valuable objective. Therefore, if you can earn the confidence of the person you're negotiating with, it will be much easier to reach agreement on even the most difficult of issues.

Q: Another manager and I are assigned to negotiate a number of interdivisional working procedures. He offered to prepare the memorandum setting forth what we have agreed upon. I'm uncomfortable with that, since three years ago he pulled a shady deal on me. Am I being unreasonable?

A: This is an example of how violating someone's trust will be long remembered. That's why it's so important to establish trust even when you're negotiating with someone on a one-time basis. Even though you never expect to deal with them again, there's always the possibility, however remote, of future meetings. Furthermore, taking unfair advantage of people during negotiations can have future repercussions beyond those who are immediately involved. When people feel they have been treated shoddily, they have no hesitation about reminding anyone who will listen that so-and-so can't be trusted to negotiate fairly.

As for the question being raised, you're not being unreasonable about proceeding with caution when dealing with anyone who has already stung you once. It's better to prepare the memorandum jointly to be sure you're both in agreement as to the contents. It should also be signed by both parties. Incidentally, there's also a hint of office politics being played here, since the other manager may want to prepare the memo individually, so as to take credit for working out the agreement.

Q: I represented our company at a business association meeting in which an agreement was reached to establish certain technical standards. Although I signed the agreement for our company, the responsibility for preparing technical documentation required by the agreement belonged to another department that isn't under my management. I relayed the information on what was required to the appropriate manager, but I'm now on the spot. Another meeting is coming up next week, and the documents were never prepared. I don't see how anyone at that meeting will be willing to reach any future agreements with me when I didn't come through the first time. What can I do about this?

A: They may not have much faith in you following through on your promises, which is a hazard every negotiator faces. If there is sufficient time remaining to have the documentation prepared before the next meeting, take whatever measures are necessary to have the other department do its job. If you have to enlist higher-level support to get action, then by all means do so. If the documentation isn't provided, it reflects on the entire company, even though you will be the person taking the heat.

In some negotiation situations such as this one, the negotiator is responsible for initiating action to comply with what was agreed to. The failure to follow through to complete the agreement destroys trust in both the negotiator and the organization he or she represents.

Another trust-related hazard is in the area of securing necessary approvals for what has been negotiated. Negotiators have varying levels of authority to negotiate on behalf of their employer. With any sizable business transaction, various approval levels are required. When someone at the approval level objects to a provision that has been negotiated, it often results in further negotiations.

Although the fact that approvals are necessary is routinely recognized in the business world, it's always troublesome to have to revisit previously negotiated terms and conditions. Therefore, whenever anything is negotiated that requires approval, the negotiator has a selling job to do in convincing people in the approval cycle of the merits of what has been negotiated. To some extent, you're going through a secondary negotiation arguing the merits of what you negotiated versus the lesser benefit or weakness of any recommended changes to the agreement.

Aside from avoiding the considerable hassle of trying to renegotiate changes made in the approval process, there's another advantage to being able to support what you negotiate. If you negotiate with someone on a regular basis, it's a real trust-builder if they know you are generally successful in sustaining what you negotiate. People are naturally reluctant to negotiate with someone who is habitually unsuccessful in obtaining approval of negotiated agreements.

Q: **Are there practices that can be followed to help build trust with people you're negotiating with?**

A: As a matter of fact, there are a few routine practices you can use that will encourage the level of trust that should assist in your working with your counterpart to reach a mutually satisfactory agreement. First, be willing to recognize that the other negotiator has objectives and goals even though you may not agree with them. You should, of course, be quick to point out weaknesses and errors in the opposing position. Nevertheless, if you do so in a respectful way without demeaning either the individual or what is being proposed, it will go a long way toward establishing the sort of rapport you may need to resolve significant differences in the respective positions. It also helps build trust if you are prompt about furnishing requested documentation in support of your position, assuming, of course, that the request is justified.

Q: A friend who does a lot of negotiating and I were discussing ways to establish instantaneous trust when you're negotiating with someone. After all, if the person doesn't even know you, it's probably assumed that your objective is to shaft them anyway you can in order to get a good deal. Where this attitude does exist, it makes it much more difficult to work together in resolving difficult issues. One of the things my friend does to overcome negative feelings is to question a point in his own negotiation position. He then proceeds to explain why even though it might appear to be questionable, it does in fact make sense. He does this when there is an obvious point that he knows the other side will eventually raise. He maintains that by raising the issue himself, it gives him an opportunity to explain it away, which is far more convincing than if the other negotiator brought it up. My friend swears that doing this really helps him establish instant credibility. What do you think of this idea?

A: This is, indeed, a creative way to foster trust. After all, when someone sees that you have the integrity to raise questions about what you're proposing, it gives you a lot of credibility. It also makes sense from the perspective of answering objections to the issue before they're even raised by the other negotiator. This way, you can dispose of a potential problem on your terms, rather than being placed on the defensive when your counterpart raises the issue. Nevertheless, this tactic has to be used with care. You first should be fairly certain it's an issue the other side would raise, and in addition, you have to defend it in such a way that it doesn't backfire and provide ammunition for your opponent.

Q: I'm going to be negotiating next week with someone who I'm told not only tries to intimidate people, but also can't be trusted to keep his word. How should I go about preparing for this?

A: Above all, worry about substance and not form, which means prepare your negotiation position just as you would in dealing with anyone else. It may well be that this individual will pretty much confirm what you have heard. Nevertheless, it's not good policy to prepare to fight fire with fire, since it may well be that your negotiation experience turns out quite the opposite from what you had been led to believe. There can be any number of reasons why things may be different. One is that what you're hearing may be sour grapes on the part of someone who didn't do a very good job negotiating. Perhaps this person was the one who turned a negotiation with the other person into a dogfight. Then, again, maybe the negotiator is more concerned about reaching agreement with you and will adopt a different approach. In any event, if you have any hope for establishing mutual trust, you should treat this like any other negotiation until your counterpart proves you wrong.

TECHNIQUES TO PARLAY SILENCE INTO SUCCESS

When the opposing party in a negotiation is talking, many negotiators are busy thinking about what they are going to say next. That is understandable, since there seems to be a general perception that the more talking you do, the more successful you are as a negotiator. While there are times when it's beneficial to plan your next move while your opponent is expounding on the virtues of his or her negotiation position, for the most part it's more beneficial to listen to what is being said. It's not how much you say that brings negotiation success, but how well you do at making your key points. In short, as with so many other things, it's quality—not quantity—that counts. In fact, there's something to be said for the benefits to be gained by remaining silent.

Q: How can you use silence effectively and at the same time still try and control the discussions so they focus on what you want to talk about rather than letting the other negotiator set the agenda?

A: The point is that there are certain situations and specific purposes for which silence can be a useful tool in achieving your negotiation goals. At these times, you may be better served by remaining silent rather than speaking out. One good example is when another negotiator is explaining his position. The longer he or she talks, the greater the possibility of you learning something that may be of value. For this reason, it's generally a good idea to refrain from interrupting with questions or to object to something that was said. This can always be done later. When you have someone rambling on, the likelihood increases of someone telling you something that otherwise might have gone unsaid.

Q: Beyond remaining quiet in an attempt to listen for inconsistencies or untruths about the negotiation position of someone you're bargaining with, are there specific instances when silence can be used effectively?

A: One such instance is when you have asked a question about some aspect of the other negotiator's position and the person is bumbling around trying to justify what you have challenged. When the person stops talking, the natural inclination is to take over the discussion. Instead, when the person finishes, don't say anything. If you just sit there with an expectant look on your face, the chances are the person will start talking again to fill the void. Without saying a word you have forced the person to continue to discuss a topic which they would rather forget about. By their inability to adequately defend their position, it makes it easier for you to win your arguments on this topic.

Q: There's a manager I work with who is an expert at communicating what he thinks without ever saying a word. For example, if you ask him his opinion on something, sometimes he'll just look at you and silently shake his head. Usually, he'll then smile and tell you what his objections are. But what I think about is that when he nods his head without saying a word, he's already told you what you need to know. Can nonverbal signals of this nature be used to effect in negotiating?

A: They can, but they should be used both carefully and sparingly, since they are easily subject to misinterpretation. For instance, if you want to register disagreement with something the other negotiator says, you might frown or grimace. This might be preferable at times to openly registering displeasure. One such occasion might be if you're unhappy with a price being offered, but don't want to offer objections to it at that particular moment. A frown can register your unhappiness without you having to say a word. Incidentally, you can also look for nonverbal clues from your counterpart. You have to be careful here though, since a savvy negotiator may use nonverbal clues to send a misleading signal.

Q: How about pausing when you say something to give it added effect?

A: There's nothing wrong with doing that since a brief pause in midsentence will tend to focus the attention of the listener on what you're going to say. In fact, it can be very effective when you want to make a point, especially if discussions have been dragging on for so long that attention spans are starting to slip.

HOW TO SHORT CIRCUIT DIFFICULT ISSUES

In many negotiations each party has several issues on which they are unwilling to concede. These are the touchy parts of any negotiation, since a total unwillingness to compromise on the part of one or both negotiators can be a deal-breaker. Conversely, if both parties are willing to be reasonable about their respective positions, the likelihood of resolving even the most difficult issues increases dramatically. Yet there may be a time or two when the respective positions on an issue are so disparate that even two negotiators who are otherwise willing to compromise find themselves boxed into a deadlock. It's at this point that the only solution to keeping the negotiation from ending in failure is to search for alternatives that will sidestep the bottleneck.

Q: Another manager and I are struggling to write an agreement that will cover the procedures for our two departments to work together. This document is necessary because there's a great deal of interaction between the two groups. This has caused a lot of problems in the past, where both supervisors and employees in both groups have had disagreements as to who is responsible for performing certain duties. The other manager and I have been able to reconcile our differences on most of the issues, but there are two on which we disagree. They don't concern anything that should cause a problem very often, but we want to cover every possibility for conflict that might arise. Any suggestions on how this can be worked out?

A: It's always prudent to be as specific as possible in nailing things down to prevent future disagreements. Having said that, it's also necessary to recognize that no agreement can cover every possible contingency. No matter what the subject matter of a negotiation is, future events or circumstances may raise issues that couldn't have been predicted beforehand.

Admittedly, your disagreement centers on issues that you can identify. Nevertheless, as mentioned, these aren't likely to cause disagreements very often—if at all. Even if they do, there's no reason why they can't be resolved by the parties involved if and when they come up. For this reason, this is a situation where the best solution to your problem is to just forget about putting anything about the disputed issues in your agreement. They can be dealt with as exceptions to the general working rules you're trying to establish. This assumes, of course, that the two of you can't agree on the simplest solution of all, which is to include provisions on one issue the way you want it to be written, with the second issue being handled as suggested by the other manager.

If you both feel something must be said about the issues in the agreement, you could list these two issues as exceptions in the agreement with a proviso that any disagreement on either of them should be referred to you and the other manager for resolution. Give this some thought, though, since such a provision may discourage employees from working out the differences themselves. After all, there's no incentive for them to tackle the problem if they can pass it on to you.

Whether you're negotiating something one-on-one with another manager as in this case, or with outside suppliers, customers, or anyone else, there are times when you have to be pragmatic and just completely ignore some sticking point. When you face this sort of scenario, decide whether it's preferable to have an agreement that ignores one or more troublesome issues or not to have an agreement at all. In most instances, some of the hardest issues to resolve are those that aren't that crucial to reaching a final agreement. More often than not, the issue has escalated into a topic of epic proportions because of the ego-driven need of a negotiator to have his way in winning the argument on the point.

Q: In preparing to negotiate a sales agreement with a customer, I envision several potential sticking points that could cause difficulty. As a way to circumvent this problem, I'm contemplating making a very favorable initial offer to wrap everything up with a blanket offer covering price, delivery, and all other terms and conditions. My offer would contain a very favorable price, but it would be predicated on acceptance of the total package as a whole. By doing this I can avoid getting involved in discussions of

the individual issues that could prove to be troublesome. Is this a practical approach and is it likely to be accepted?

A: There are instances where it's much better to negotiate on an all-or-nothing basis to avoid getting bogged down in haggling over all sorts of minor details. Since it simplifies reaching agreement and is a real time-saver, the recipient of such an offer may readily accept it. This is especially true if there aren't any issues of great significance to the party that would have to be resolved individually. After all, many people would prefer avoiding the hassle of back-and-forth bargaining if they are offered an easier alternative for reaching an amicable agreement.

Even when there are suggested terms and conditions a party might object to, if a significant concession is made by the party making the total package offer, this might adequately compensate for accepting less than preferred terms on other issues. In the situation cited, it's highly likely that the favorable price being offered will convince the customer to accept the deal as proposed.

This all-or-nothing approach can also be used during negotiations to circumvent issues that the parties can't seem to agree on. It may help to make such an offer as a way around the problem. Assuming the offer is reasonable, there's a strong likelihood it will be accepted.

Q: **I'm unable to reach agreement on one issue, which is the difference between reaching an agreement or forgetting about it completely. Every approach to resolving the difficulty has been explored. I'm now considering whether or not to concede the point in the interests of sealing the deal. Conceding the issue will give me less of a deal than I really want. On the other hand, there are long-term advantages to be derived from doing business with the company I'm dealing with. It provides a chance for future business, but beyond that it gives us credibility in the marketplace, which should open up other business opportunities. Am I wrong to accept a deal that isn't that good for these reasons?**

A: Whenever you look beyond the scope of the immediate agreement to justify its acceptance, you basically have to look at the risk-reward ratio. In short, will you gain more by accepting the agreement than you lose by rejecting it. There are certainly plenty of instances where agreements are reached based on the possibility of them serving as door openers. As long as you enter into a situation such as this with your eyes open, the risks may be justified. However, what you want to avoid is accepting such a deal based on nothing more than pie-in-the-sky speculation.

Q: The company we're negotiating with wants to include a provision in the contract providing for financial penalties if we don't meet certain performance objectives in doing the work. We refuse to sign any agreement that contains such terms. Are there any other ways to resolve this issue that may satisfy the customer?

A: One way to work around a difficult issue is to look for alternatives or trade-offs that will cancel out or negate the need to consider the issue. The specifics will vary with each individual situation. In this particular case, rather than a penalty clause that will cost you money, you might suggest putting a performance incentive clause in the contract. This would give you more money if you meet or exceed the measure of performance and cost you money if you don't. This should satisfy the demands of the customer, while at the same time give you an incentive to work harder to meet the performance measure.

Depending upon the circumstances, various guarantees, warranties, incentives, and penalty provisions are all possibilities for use as substitutes for issues that can't be resolved. Another approach that is useful in limited situations is a provision calling for arbitration or mediation to resolve a dispute. The main thing is that when you get hung up on an issue, there are ways to work around it rather than resignedly recognize it as a deal-breaker.

AN EASY METHOD TO KEEP CONFUSION FROM KILLING A DEAL

It's not always an easy task to keep everything straight during negotiations. This is especially true when more than two people are participating and/or a number of complex issues are involved. Trade-offs and concessions are made, the discussions jump from topic to topic, and interim agreements are reached on individual issues. Adding to the difficulty, one side or the other may suddenly make an unexpected offer that makes it even harder to keep everything in focus. Then, before you know it, a point is reached where neither party knows who agreed to what.

Usually, after a lot of piecing together and summarizing of the respective positions, everything gets back on track. It's not unknown, however, for negotiations to end without agreement because one party thought a commitment had been made which was being reneged on. Therefore, since negotiations are difficult enough as it is, it pays to avoid creating any unnecessary confusion, which is easily avoidable if the proper precautions are taken.

Q: **Just as it seemed like some progress was being made in a negotiation I'm conducting for some consulting services, quite unexpectedly the other negotiator proposed a substantial change in the way the work would be performed. This forced me to temporarily postpone any further discussions until we had a chance to reexamine the impact of what was being proposed. Is it unusual for changes to be proposed in this manner?**

A: It's not the norm, but it certainly isn't out of the ordinary. For one reason or another substantive changes in what is being negotiated occur during the bargaining process. These changes generally result from information revealed during discussions. These may cause one of the parties to recommend a different approach to doing the work, purchasing additional or lesser quantities of what's being bought, or any other variation, depending upon the subject matter of the negotiation. The reasons for doing this may vary from practical reasons that are revealed during negotiation discussions or something as common as seeing an opportunity for proposing additional business.

Whatever the purported reason for the change, if it's unexpectedly suggested by the party you're negotiating with, it behooves you to proceed with caution. After all, at a minimum this will alter your negotiation position, and it may even cause you to rethink whether or not you want to proceed with the negotiations. Therefore, as a minimum, whenever substantive changes are recommended by your counterpart, take whatever time is necessary to evaluate your position before proceeding any further. Otherwise, trying to change course in the middle of negotiations will at best cause confusion, and at worst it may prove to be costly.

Q: **Our company is expanding, and as a result I'm in the process of negotiating a lease for additional office space. I've received several proposals for space, have looked at possible sites, and am about to initiate negotiations with the one I find has the most potential for meeting our needs. I don't have a lot of time to spend on this, and there are numerous provisions to consid-**

er. How can I be sure of covering everything I need to consider, while avoiding discussions on anything that isn't significant to me?

A: No matter what you may be negotiating, one of the best ways to minimize the confusion associated with trying to resolve a large number of issues is to separate out beforehand what you can readily agree on, what can be resolved with a minimum of discussion, and what the major issues are. If you do this before negotiations begin, you will usually find that there are only one or two issues of substance that will require extended discussion. For example, in negotiating an office lease some of the potential items for discussion would include the following:

- What will the term of the lease be?
- When will it begin and end?
- What is the price per square foot and how is it calculated?
- How much usable space will you be paying for?
- What about subletting or early termination?
- Are there escalation clauses that may mean rental increases or additional payments for taxes, heat, or maintenance?
- What services will be provided in the areas of maintenance, heating, ventilating, and air conditioning?
- Who will pay for any improvements that are needed?
- What other businesses are tenants in the building?
- What about parking and/or access to public transportation?

If you look at these items you will see there are some that just require a quick answer, such as what other businesses are in the building and the availability of public transportation. These are just fact-finding questions with no negotiations involved. Others may require a minimum of discussion, such as the lease term and starting and ending dates. Then, there are a few items that you may want to do some serious negotiating on, such as the price, what improvements will be made and who will pay for them, and so forth. Whatever the subject matter of a negotiation may be, listing the potential issues and establishing their relative importance will help you keep from getting bogged down in extended discussions on minor issues.

Q: I ran into some trouble when concluding a negotiation last week. It was a pretty complicated deal and tentative agreements were being reached on individual issues as the discussions moved along. At one point—or so I thought—I had agreed to something contingent upon satisfactorily agreeing upon a related issue that we hadn't discussed at that time. As it subsequently turned out, the related issue became a nonissue when the customer (the other negotiator) requested certain changes in the items being bought. To make a long story short, I made a substantive concession and got nothing in return. I also think the other negotiator knew the changes would negate the issue at the time he traded concessions with me. Should I have objected to this?

A: What is there to object to? The issue you were worried enough about to make a concession on has dropped out of the picture completely, so it can't cause you any difficulty. The fact that it was taken out because the requirements changed is unfortunate, but it's always risky making a concession in exchange for something else to be agreed upon later. For one thing, something that is an issue early on in a negotiation for one reason or another may become a nonissue later. Second, there's no guarantee the other issue will ever be resolved, at least in the manner you anticipate. Finally, this practice of settling one thing now while leaving an issue it's tied to until later can cause a great deal of confusion and can result in disputes over who agreed to what and why.

For these reasons, the only time it's really practical to make a present concession for a future contingency is when you trade something meaningless to you to break an impasse early on in the negotiations, as was mentioned in response to a question in Chapter 6. That way, even if you don't get the issue to be discussed later resolved in your favor, you haven't lost anything. However, if you're making a concession of real value to you, it's preferable to trade off one item for another at the same time. If it isn't practical to discuss one of the issues at the present time, then set the other one aside and discuss them both later.

HOW TO GIVE GROUND WITHOUT GOING BROKE

In the average negotiation you have to give something to get something in return, so compromises and concessions will help move both parties toward a position they can both agree on. You may recall the discussion on the pros and cons of concessions back in Chapter 6. Here the focus is on how you can obtain the maximum value in concessions from your counterpart while conceding as little as possible yourself. How skillful you are in this back-and-forth horse trading will largely determine how much you have to give up to get an agreement. Fortunately, there are a few strategies you can employ to hold your own in the trading that takes place.

Q: It sounds great to be able to concede very little in exchange for major concessions on the part of the person you're negotiating with, but how realistic is it? Unless someone is really naive, they're not going to give something valuable away for little or nothing in return.

A: Your assumption is true assuming a given issue is of equal importance to both parties to the negotiation. This is seldom the case, and it's far more likely that a particular issue may have extreme significance for one party, but mean little to the other. For example, it might be very important for one side to get the proposed delivery dates changed, because meeting the delivery schedule would require adding a second shift, which would be expensive. The other side might not be overly concerned about stretching out the delivery schedule because they have sufficient inventory on hand to meet their requirements. For this reason, it presents the second party with an opportunity to obtain a concession on some point of real value in exchange for consenting to a change in the delivery schedule. If this happens, the second party will be extremely happy about receiving a valuable concession in return for a meaningless concession.

Does this mean the first negotiator got a bad deal? No, since a delivery schedule adjustment was extremely significant to him, and that, in itself, would justify making a meaningful concession to get it. It may be, however, that the negotiator didn't concede anything of importance to his position. As with the other negotiator, he may also have swapped something of little value. Therefore, it frequently happens that when concessions are traded, both parties may be giving up something relatively meaningless for something significant. This is essentially a win-win situation for both parties, which they may be individually viewing as a win for them and a loss for the other side.

A factor that is sometimes overlooked in negotiations is to assess the value the other negotiator places on particular issues. Any issue of importance to the other party is a candidate for substantial concessions. The failure to look at issues in dispute from the viewpoint of their potential value to the other side can result in giving up a lot more than you have to concede to reach agreement.

Q: How can you tell when issues are important to the person you're negotiating with?

A: Aside from obvious issues that the party may have indicated are important, the easiest way to tell is by how hard they press you to make concessions on a given issue. If a negotiator is adamant about making changes in a certain provision, it's obvious this is an important issue to him or her.

Q: I was dealing with a really obnoxious person last week, but I did get some satisfaction out of it. What happened was the guy was pressing me to concede on a particular point. It didn't really mean anything to me, and if I had been dealing with someone decent, I would have conceded the issue. Instead, I kept arguing the importance of handling the issue the way I wanted. To my surprise, the other negotiator kept upping the ante that he would trade off in exchange for this concession. I finally ended up getting a reduced price in exchange for something that was meaningless to me. Did I luck out or what?

A: It could have been luck, but it was more likely the ego of the negotiator. It's not an everyday occasion, but once in a while you may run into people who in their eyes have bested everyone they ever negotiated with. This ego-driven desire to win can cause them to make meaningless concessions if they think they are getting the other party to give in on an issue of great importance. For this reason, the higher the value you place on something, the more this person will give away to get you to make a concession on it. This is just one reason why you shouldn't generally concede things without getting something in return. The more you emphasize how important it is for you to have a disputed term or condition of an agreement settled to your satisfaction, the greater the chance of getting a meaningful concession in return—even if you're not dealing with an egotist.

Q: It's easy enough to know the importance to me of any concession I make, but how do I know the value of a concession I'm getting in return?

A: First, when you trade concessions, you want to swap your concession for a concession you know you want. You already know the importance to you of what you're getting. It's irrelevant whether or not the item is of any great importance to the other negotiator. In fact, early on in negotiations, trade-offs go fairly smoothly, since in reality each side is conceding points that don't mean that much to them for things that do. It's only when these concessions are disposed of that the going gets tough. This is why stalemates are most likely to occur near the end of a negotiation, since neither side has any fat left in their negotiation position. As a result, any further movement in either side's position involves conceding something they are reluctant to give in on.

You must watch for when the other side offers a concession you weren't looking for. Even though on the surface it may be appealing, be very careful about making any trade-off for it, since upon investigation it may not be as good as first indications would have you believe. For example, some concessions involve performance under the agreement when it's finally negotiated. If this is the case, be sure the written agreement contains adequate safeguards to ensure that you eventually get the concession you bargained for.

HOW TO BE CLEAR ABOUT STATING WHERE YOU STAND

There are enough hazards to overcome when you're negotiating without having the additional burden of misunderstandings. Due to the complexity of many negotiations, even though you think everything is being carefully covered, there is still the very real possibility of misunderstandings developing. Aside from the fact that they increase the amount of time needed to reach agreement, disputes of this nature can become controversial and in extreme cases even threaten to terminate the negotiations. For these reasons, it's crucial to be constantly aware of the need for clear communication.

Q: I had a serious disagreement with another manager over an issue I thought had been agreed upon, but as it developed later, he thought otherwise. What happened is that we were bargaining back and forth over several issues involving work being parceled out between the two departments. During the discussions, I agreed to assume responsibility for one project if he would accept the next similar assignment that came up. Two weeks later a similar project was given to me, and I forwarded it to him with a memo referring to our previous understanding. The next thing I know, he came barging into my office beet-red with anger and accused me of trying to pawn my work off on him. To make a long story short, I finally said I would handle the project in my group. How could I have avoided this fiasco?

A: The agreements reached should have been committed to writing and signed by both of you. If at the time the other manager saw no need for it, you should have prepared a confirmation memo yourself and sent him a copy. It would also have been helpful to send a copy to your boss. If that had been done, you would have had the evidence to support your position.

No matter whether you're bargaining with another manager or negotiating an agreement with customers, suppliers, or others, future promises should be committed to writing, since even if someone isn't being deliberately deceitful, memories fade with time, and people can misconstrue what was said earlier.

A problem similar to this is fairly common in negotiations. What happens is that one party agrees to something on the condition that the other party agree to something else when that topic is discussed at a later time. When the topic is finally covered, the first party brings up the fact that they have already agreed on how it will be handled. The other negotiator having forgotten about it—perhaps as a matter of convenience—angrily denies any prior agreement.

Consider two people discussing their respective viewpoints on the necessary quality control provisions for equipment that will be built under a contract they're negotiating. One negotiator finally says, "I'll accept your recommendations on quality assuming you agree with my standard payment terms when we get around to discussing them." The second negotiator agrees assuming without asking that payment is on delivery. Much later when they start to discuss payment, the first negotiator says payment is thirty days after testing and acceptance. The immediate reaction of the first negotiator is a vehement, "I didn't agree to that." Needless to say a heated disagreement ensues.

Misunderstandings of this nature are easily avoidable. Whenever agreement is reached on specific points, it's useful to restate the agreement to be certain both parties see it the same way. It also helps to make a written note of interim agreements made along the way so memories can be refreshed at a later time if that becomes necessary. Actually, if an agreement is fairly complex, it can be worthwhile to have the written understanding initialed by both negotiators. It may seem bothersome to submit to this sort of detail, yet the time involved is minimal compared with the headaches involved in unraveling a later disagreement.

Q: **I negotiate with someone who has a bad habit of trying to put words in my mouth. On more than one occasion she has accused me of agreeing to something I didn't say. The last time she did this I called her on it and she said, "I was talking about that five minutes ago and I mentioned we were doing it the way you wanted and you didn't say anything." To be honest she may have misquoted me and I failed to either agree or disagree when she did it, as she was engaged in a long discourse about a particular issue. How should you deal with something like this?**

A: This is a case of what you didn't say being as critical as what you do say. Whenever someone misrepresents your position, it's important to immediately deny it. Otherwise, it will be assumed that the misrepresentation is in fact your true position. This can cause a real problem if it involves an issue of importance. This is especially true if you don't discover the misrepresentation until late in the negotiation. This can happen accidentally in a lengthy negotiation where a large number of issues are discussed. It can also be caused by fatigue setting in and one party not paying close attention to what the other person is saying. Then, again, a dishonest negotiator might try to do this deliberately in an attempt to catch you off guard. In any event, whether it's an honest mistake or a deliberate attempt to deceive, it's easily preventable by always listening to what the other negotiator is saying and immediately correcting anyone who tries to misrepresent your position on the issues.

It's also important to be specific when you're negotiating. If you talk in generalities, even though what you say isn't misrepresented, it may be assumed to be negotiation shop talk. This is especially true when you want to indicate your intention not to waver from your stand on a particular issue. For instance, saying "I will not agree with that" sends a different message than saying, "I don't think I can go along with that."

METHODS FOR BEING FIRM WHILE STILL BEING FAIR

Despite the value of establishing good rapport with the other negotiator, whether or not you succeed, there will still come a time when you have to stand your ground and refuse to go along with what the other negotiator wants. The fact is there are two opposing viewpoints that have to be reconciled for an agreement to be reached. In many business negotiations, this is relatively easy, whereas in others it may appear to be next to impossible. Nevertheless, even under the most difficult conditions you can be firm without being hostile. In addition, if you have the good fortune to be in a situation where you have a decided advantage in setting the terms and conditions of an agreement, always strive to be positive rather than punitive. Taking unfair advantage of someone in a negotiation situation may bring short-term gains that may be offset many times over by the long-term damage it can cause.

Q: Occasionally I run into someone in a negotiation situation who loses control and becomes angry and argumentative. Are there any good ways to defuse these situations?

A: You must keep in mind that disagreements are the norm in negotiation situations. You may also be negotiating with people who aren't experienced negotiators. Aside from that, some people get frustrated more easily than others, and when there are problems in trying to reach agreement, these frustrations may boil over into anger. The crucial element is for you to remain calm no matter what. As long as you control your emotions, you can keep things from getting out of hand. After all, when someone blows his top, it shouldn't take long for him to realize how foolish he must appear to be. This is especially true if the person he's yelling at is sitting in silence waiting for him to run out of steam.

More often than not, the person's anger results from being unable to resolve a particular issue. In these instances, if you're able to suggest alternatives for resolving the matter, it may succeed in getting the individual to simmer down. You can also switch the discussion to a less emotion-laden topic and return to it in the future when things have quieted down a bit.

On the other hand, if the person persists in being hostile, you certainly can't be expected to subject yourself to an incessant torrent of nonsense. Therefore, under these conditions you may want to admonish the person by saying something such as, "If we can both maintain our composure, I'm sure we can work our way around the problems." Aside from letting the person know you won't tolerate the behavior, a statement such as this assures the person that the problem can be solved. If the bad attitude continues, you may have to threaten to break off the talks. If even that doesn't work, you may have to walk out of the meeting to send the message that you're not going to be subjected to any form of intimidation.

NOTE: You may want to refer to the section on how to make your point without being argumentative in Chapter 5 for additional ideas.

Q: **I go to great lengths to present my negotiation position in detail, with plenty of facts and figures. As a result, I'm always well prepared to justify and defend any aspect of it. For this reason, I get aggravated when people refuse to accept my position on issues, even though they are solidly supported by fact. Is there anything I can do about this?**

A: What you say may be true, but there are two sides to every story, especially when it comes to negotiations. It's quite conceivable that those people you negotiate with are equally convinced of the wisdom of their position. As a result, they aren't about to jump through hoops to accept your terms and conditions, no matter how logical they may be to you. All the documentation in the world won't carry the day in negotiations unless you're able to convince others of the virtues of your approach. To negotiate successfully you have to be flexible enough to honestly evaluate the position of the other negotiator and be willing to make reasonable compromises to reach agreement.

Q: **I recently had a negotiation where I went to my limit to reach agreement, but the other negotiator refused to budge. Only after negotiations broke off did I get a call agreeing with my position. Is this unusual?**

A: No, it isn't. Some negotiators will go to the wall in an attempt to extract one more concession out of you. As a result, you have to have the resolve to call it quits if that becomes necessary. You can avoid having to go to this extreme by holding a concession in reserve to be used as a last-ditch deal-maker. You have to let the other party know, however, that the concession is only being made in a final effort to reach an agreement. In fact, depending on the circumstances, you may not even want to offer it until after negotiations are suspended. Then, if you don't hear from the other negotiator in a couple of days, you can call and offer the concession. The other party will think you're doing this because they held your feet to the fire. You, of course, can rest secure in the knowledge that you had this planned all the way from the start. Even in a tense situation such as this, both parties will end up happy.

WHAT TO DO WHEN DISCUSSIONS KEEP DRAGGING ON

After what may seem like endless discussions, you may finally see some light at the end of the tunnel in terms of reaching an agreement. You may then, to your dismay, find the discussions continue to drag on as it becomes seemingly impossible to close the final gap separating the two positions. This shouldn't be surprising since by this point in the negotiations all the easy concessions have been made. Both parties face the equally difficult task of convincing the other party to accept their position or alternatively swallowing hard and accepting the other person's final offer.

Q: Why is it always so hard to compromise near the end of a negotiation, even when both parties have been reasonable throughout in finding a middle ground?

A: Aside from the fact that the easy compromises have already been made, both parties from the start have been forging ahead in an attempt to reach agreement without understandably thinking about a deadlock developing. This is a reasonable enough expectation because neither party has been negotiating with the objective of ending up in an impasse. For this reason, neither party has probably thought about what could be done to resolve the issue until it hits them head on. Therefore, neither party is likely to have a ready-made solution to offer. This points out the value of holding a concession in reserve for the purpose of breaking a last-minute stalemate. This, of course, was mentioned in the previous section.

Q: Most of the negotiation impasses I've had to deal with involved a difference in price, with neither party willing to accept the other's price, and one or both being unwilling to split the remaining difference as a compromise solution. Are there any effective ways to work around these price hang-ups at the end?

A: The primary focus for coming up with a solution should be on looking for a concession the other side can make that would compensate you for accepting the final price offer of your counterpart. Alternatively, you can think of concessions that would entice the other party to accept your price. It's generally easier, though, to concentrate on what benefit will satisfy you, since you can only speculate on what sort of concession you can make that would be acceptable to the other negotiator. In other words, since neither side is willing to budge on price, what you want to do is find a concession that can be offset against accepting the other person's final offer. The possibilities will vary with the subject matter being negotiated, but they could be something such as more favorable payment terms, the relaxation of product specifications, and so forth.

Q: I'm conducting an investigation that is going nowhere. The other negotiator keeps bringing up minor points whenever I try to bring things to a close. For some reason unknown to me, I think he's just stalling. Would it be feasible to go over his head to get someone to make a decision?

A: When you get to the end of the road in terms of what can be negotiated, there's not much to lose by trying anything possible to get an agreement. The negotiator could be dragging his feet for any number of reasons, some related to him, such as the inability to make a decision. If this is the case, going over his head will get the matter resolved. On the other hand, he may be deliberately stalling for a strategic reason. What that might be would be speculative. In any event, tell the negotiator if he can't make a decision, then you want to talk to someone who can. If he refuses, go over his head anyway.

Q: Our negotiation has reached an impasse. In looking for a way to resolve it, I gave some thought to changing the requirements to make the agreement more palatable for the supplier. The problem is that he won't accept the price we're offering because of the limited quantity we're buying. I'm thinking about offering an option for additional quantities, since this might overcome his objection. Does this sound viable?

A: Going beyond the present requirements that are being negotiated offers all kinds of opportunities for resolving a deadlock. In this instance adding an option for additional quantities should do the trick. Incentive provisions and price escalation clauses are just two of many possibilities that can be explored to work around last-minute hang-ups. In fact, the biggest drawback to finding a solution is a failure of the parties to look beyond the disagreement in terms of finding a solution.

CHAPTER 10

BRINGING NEGOTIATIONS TO A CLOSE

After a long and tough negotiation it's sometimes easier than expected to reach a final agreement. At other times, despite the relative ease of negotiating with the other party, it becomes a struggle to get the final parts of the deal done. Whatever the case may be, completing an agreement properly is crucial. Otherwise, you can easily give away all the terms and conditions that you fought so hard to win.

As a result, it's important to be certain that any written agreement properly reflects what was negotiated. If it doesn't, future misunderstandings will result. But to get to the point of writing the agreement you have to know how to bring negotiations to a close. This isn't always easy, especially if you're negotiating with someone who isn't very good about knowing when to call it quits.

Furthermore, although it may sound discouraging, there are times when you have to know when to walk away without reaching agreement. This isn't always easy to do, and more than one bad deal has been struck because of someone's reluctance to admit the negotiations were a failure. Last, but by no means least, there may come a time when changed conditions require you to renegotiate an existing agreement. These topics, and more, are covered in the discussions that follow.

TACTICS TO MAKE YOUR FINAL OFFER STICK

You may be the one to make a final offer to bring the negotiations to a close. No matter how attractive the offer, you may discover that some negotiators just don't know when to quit. There are people who will want to bargain back and forth right down to your last dime—and they will if you allow them to. This can be a time when things can get a little testy if you're not careful. After all, the negotiations may have been lengthy, and fatigue may be starting to set in. This sets the stage for things to get out of hand and a deal to fall through at the last minute if you're not careful. As a result, you have to persist in getting your offer accepted, while refusing to be annoyed by any last-minute stunts on the part of the other negotiator.

Q: **Having spent the better part of three days negotiating an agreement, the other negotiator and I have got things pretty much wrapped up, but I'm waiting for him to make a final offer. In the meantime we're essentially nit-picking at details in what has already been agreed to. I'm not impatient, but how can I get this deal finalized?**

A: This isn't an uncommon situation when negotiations are close to completion. Neither negotiator wants to be the one to make a final offer, so discussions drag on until one person or the other finally makes a move. What you want to do here is bite the bullet and make a final offer.

Q: **Wouldn't it be better for the other negotiator to be the one making the last offer?**

A: As a general rule, it's better for you to be the one making the final offer. If you make the offer, you have control of what the final price will be. Logically, your offer will be the best price you think you can get. If the other party makes the offer, they will be looking for the best deal from their perspective. Beyond controlling the offer, being the one to make the offer gives you control of the end game. If your offer is refused, you will be the one walking away with the suggestion that the other person contact you if they change their mind. Conversely, if your counterpart makes a final offer, you're on the defensive. Assuming you refuse it, you will be the one who will be invited to think it over.

Q: **I'm about to make a final offer to close a deal and want to do it in such a way that the person I'm negotiating with doesn't respond by saying something such as, "I can't do it for that amount of money." I know**

my offer is reasonable and every other possibility to close the gap in our positions has been explored, so it's essentially down to getting my offer accepted or nothing. How can I persuade the other party that this is it, so they are convinced that a refusal of my offer is the end of the road?

A: What it all boils down to is your ability to convey the fact that this is indeed your final offer. The closer it is to what your counterpart has offered to settle for, the greater the likelihood of it being accepted. It also depends to some extent on how willing the other party is to risk not making a deal by refusing your offer. If they don't have readily available alternatives, or badly want an agreement for some other reason, the odds of an acceptance are greater.

Nevertheless, you have to be ready for the expectation of a refusal. This means if you get a refusal, you have to be ready to walk away, but be able to do it in such a manner that it leaves the door ajar for the other party to contact you. As a result, you shouldn't express anger or issue any form of admonishment if your offer is turned down. This would only serve to discourage the person from contacting you later. Just say something such as, "You have my offer. If you change your mind in a day or two, give me a call."

Q: **Would it be a good idea to issue a deadline for acceptance of my offer, either when I make it or at the time it's refused?**

A: You don't want to include a deadline when you make your final offer, since it takes away from the finality of the offer. The signal you want to send is "It's now or not at all." If you say something such as "Here's my final offer. You have twenty-four hours to accept it," this removes the need for the person to accept or reject your offer then and there. It's an open invitation for the other party to call you on the phone the next day and make a counteroffer. The message you want to send is simple. You're through with negotiating, and you want a "Yes" or "No" right here and now. Anything that waters that message down is weakening the odds of your offer being accepted.

As far as issuing a deadline to call you if your offer is refused, this too gives the person an outer limit to play with. If you don't have a deadline, the person will be more anxious about you going on to explore other alternatives, while with a deadline, you essentially give them a guarantee that a deal can still be completed within that time period.

Q: If I give an "It's now or never" offer, what do I do when people say they need to get approval before they can accept my offer? As you know, in deals of any significance, the person negotiating doesn't always have the authority to make a commitment.

A: Ask them how much time they need. If it's a reasonable period, then establish that as the time you want an offer. Make it clear that all bets are off if the offer isn't accepted by that time. You have to be careful when someone asks for time to secure an approval when you make a final offer. It's a useful stalling tactic that a savvy negotiator will use to his or her advantage. This is one reason you should establish the negotiating authority of people at the beginning of negotiations.

Incidentally, it's important to distinguish between the need for approval to accept your offer and the routine approval cycle that completed agreements are subjected to before they are signed off. Generally, the person negotiating has the authority to make a deal, subject to higher approval. If this is the case, then don't let a negotiator off the hook with a plea for time to get higher-level approval. Just proceed as you would in a normal refusal of an offer and tell them to contact you.

Q: Is there any advantage to putting a final offer in writing?

A: You might want to try this if you think the situation warrants it. When something is in writing, it has an air of finality to it. Beyond that, it gives the other negotiator proof that this is your final offer. This could be helpful to that person in convincing higher-ups that it's decision time. On the other hand, final offers in writing may encourage the other side to respond in writing with a counteroffer, and what you have done is essentially traded face-to-face negotiations for back-and-forth bargaining in writing. Therefore, unless a special situation exists, such as complex terms and conditions that are better spelled out in writing, you're better off not even bothering with written offers.

HOW TO PROTECT YOUR INTERESTS IN THE WRITTEN AGREEMENT

It's a waste of effort to work hard at negotiating a good agreement only to have it diluted by not including provisions adequate to cover what was negotiated in the written document. Yet in the euphoria surrounding the end of hard bargaining, it isn't hard to get careless. Doing so, however, can undo everything you worked so hard to get. That alone is reason enough to exercise caution in terms of ensuring the document represents the intent of both parties to the negotiation. And if what was negotiated requires work to be performed over an extended period of time, a poorly written agreement can cause controversy for a long time to come. For these reasons, the minute an agreement is reached it's imperative to take the proper steps to implement it.

Q: **As if I didn't have enough problems during negotiations, the person I negotiated the deal with left for another job the day we completed negotiations. The person I'm dealing with now doesn't know what's going on, so I can pretty much put anything I want in the written agreement. How far should I go in slanting things in my favor?**

A: Stick to the facts, since trying to be cute can come back to haunt you. What makes you think the other negotiator didn't leave a detailed memorandum setting forth what was agreed to. Beyond that, and the questions of ethics, as you wrap up your agreement, it's good policy to be thinking ahead toward the prospect of future business. This is especially important if one of your goals is to establish a long-term business relationship with the other party. Even when future business doesn't appear to be likely at the present time, it pays to wrap things up amicably, since circumstances change rapidly in the business world. Last of all, if the agreement will require a working relationship in the weeks and months ahead, how well that will work can't be ignored when you're closing the deal. For these reasons, it's always wise to avoid putting the squeeze on the other party at the last minute if you're in a position to do so, since you may find it coming back to haunt you at a later date.

Q: **My counterpart and I just finished negotiations. I suggested we go over everything to be certain we were in total agreement. He wasn't too anxious to do that, and suggested we go over everything on the phone in a day or so. In looking my notes over, there are a couple of points where I'm not sure what we agreed to. Since he didn't even take any notes during the negotiation, I'm sure he probably is worse off than I am. How should I handle this?**

A: This situation looks like a disaster waiting to happen. First, your notes are incomplete, which means in the areas you have a question on, you might have to rely on the other negotiator's recollection of what was negotiated. Needless to say, he's not going to be looking at it with your best interests in mind, so your hard work in negotiating a good deal could be compromised by your negligence in keeping track of what was being agreed upon. This is one reason why it's so important to take notes of agreements reached as the negotiations are underway: it gives you a record to rely on when you get to the point where you are now.

The good news is that the other negotiator is just relying on memory, so to that extent you are in good shape. The bad news is that he has no written record at all, so if his memory is faulty, the two of you could end up doing some more negotiating to agree on any points that may end up in dispute.

To handle this situation, call him on the phone as previously planned and summarize everything that was agreed upon. In terms of the items you're not sure of, reconstruct the terms as best you can. If the phone conversation solves matters, you're all set. If not, schedule a meeting to sit down and iron things out—and be sure to take notes.

Q: Is there a preferred method for reviewing what was agreed to when negotiations conclude?

A: Go over all the points one by one to be certain you're both in agreement. It's preferable to do this as soon as the negotiations end for two reasons. One is that both your memories are fresh, so there's less chance of something being forgotten or misinterpreted than if you leave it for a later time. The second reason is that if there is a disagreement on anything, you and the other negotiator can iron it out then and there. This eliminates the need to try and work out an agreement on a disputed item over the phone or scheduling another meeting to do it. This approach is even more practical if the business locations of the two parties are in different geographic locations.

Q: The other negotiator has volunteered to write up the contract covering our recent negotiations. I agreed since it would save me some time. Besides that I know the other side won't have any reluctance to sign it since they wrote it up. My boss didn't think that was a good idea. She had been asking me for three days when I was going to be finished negotiating, and then she's critical of me for pawning the agreement off on someone else to write up so I can get back to work. Can you figure this out?

A: Sure, and so can your boss. You screwed up, she knows it, and you don't. Perhaps the agreement you negotiated is better than your judgment. Of course, the other side isn't going to object to a document they write up. It's going to contain the terms and conditions as they want them. Naturally, the contract will be reviewed by both parties before they sign, so if there were any changes in the terms and conditions that were negotiated, they can be corrected. What tends to get overlooked, however, is that many of the terms and conditions that appear in a contract weren't the subject of negotiations.

The major benefit of writing up the contract is that it gives you control of determining the details of how things are done in the performance of the work. Many of these minor items weren't significant enough to be separately negotiated. Taken together, however, they can substantially slant the benefits of the contract toward the party writing it. Even with terms that were negotiated and agreed upon, if there's any room for interpretation, the document can be focused to the liking of the party writing it.

None of this should matter, since the document will be subject to review. The problem is that unless something is of obvious importance, it's not likely to become an issue at this late stage in the process. For these reasons, along with the confidence you gain in knowing the contract is written the way you want it to be, it's far better to be the one who prepares the written document. Incidentally, other than the most routine transactions, it's important to have a legal review of any contract document before it's signed. This sometimes gets overlooked or ignored until it comes back to haunt someone when something goes wrong.

NOTE: In many business situations, who prepares the written document is pretty much determined by custom and standard business practice. However, whenever there's an option as to which party prepares the document, take advantage of the opportunity to protect your interests. This also applies to internal memorandums representing agreements you make with managers and others within your company. Here, there's wide latitude in how something is written up, which makes it even more important to handle the writing chore.

Q: Now that I've busted my back handling a negotiation that no other manager wanted to do, I'm getting criticized left and right about what I did wrong, and what I should have done that I didn't do. Where were all these so-called negotiation experts when I needed them?

A: They were probably ducking having to step up to the plate and show how little they really know. Don't let after-the-fact criticism bother you. Everyone likes to think they could have done better, but only the smart ones keep it to themselves. It's easy to criticize anything that's negotiated because there's generally no basis for direct comparison. Even when similar items are negotiated, different time periods, different negotiators, and different objectives can all result in agreements that vary widely. Some negotiations are criticized in the short term and turn out to be spectacular successes in the long run, while others win instant praise and prove over time to have been foolhardy agreements. Do the best you can and be done with it—and ignore the critics.

Q: An agreement I negotiated is now going through the review cycle. Arthur M., the manager of another department, is raising all kinds of objections to the agreement. This isn't surprising since he was opposed to having this work contracted out in the first place. That battle, however, was fought and lost a couple of months ago. My problem is that he refuses to sign off on the approval. Any suggestions on how to handle this?

A: It's assumed that you tried to answer his objections and were unsuccessful. That's not surprising, since he's just holding the agreement hostage because he opposes the project. If he won't give approval, then let him write a nonconcurrence citing his objections. Put your own rebuttal in the file and then continue on through the rest of the approval cycle. His original opposition to the project makes it apparent to anyone involved that he isn't being objective. If the sign-off procedure is such that this isn't feasible, then take the matter to the next management level for resolution.

WHAT GOES IN WRITING AND WHAT DOESN'T

The contents of the written document setting forth what was negotiated will vary widely to reflect the specifics of the particular negotiation. Some negotiations you have as a manager won't require any written memorandum, others will be covered by internal memos of a fairly informal nature, while agreements with other business entities will involve a formal document of some length. Whatever the situation may be, the important point is that whatever the document's format is, it should completely cover everything that was negotiated. A carelessly prepared document can undo all the effort involved in reaching a satisfactory agreement.

Q: I attended a meeting of several managers at which a number of agreements were reached on working relationships between different departments. Without too much debate, several operating procedures were agreed to. At the conclusion of the meeting I offered to write up a memo setting forth our understandings that was to be signed by every manager in attendance. I had good notes, so there was little problem in writing up the memo. It was when I sent it around to be signed that my problems started.

No two managers concurred with everything in the memo. It was almost as if we had all attended separate meetings. What a couple of managers thought we had agreed to wasn't even close to reality. I only wish the meeting had been taped so I would have a record of the proceedings. With one exception, all the complaining was done by phone or in person, since I didn't ask for any written response. I didn't see the need for it, since people were just going to be signing off on a memo that contained the contents of what they had already agreed with. At least that's what I thought at the time. In any event, I haven't gotten any signatures yet, and the general manager wants to know when we'll be finished working out an agreement. How can I get this matter resolved?

A: For starters, you had better get everyone together again to resolve the disagreements. Before you do that, however, you want to avoid a repetition of what happened in the last go-around. Send the memo you prepared listing the items requiring agreement to each of the managers involved. Ask for a reply in writing stating any objections they have to each operating procedure you have listed. This accomplishes two things. First, it requires each manager to put their objections in writing. This alone will cut down on the number of disagreements. For one thing, it's easy for someone to spout off if they aren't going to be held accountable. It's something else again when the complaint is in writing, since anything that's challenged can't be denied with a shrug of the shoulders and a comment such as, "That wasn't what I said." Beyond that, from a purely pragmatic standpoint, the written objections will be far fewer than you heard in person, since some people don't like to put anything in writing.

The second advantage of getting written comments is that it will allow you to prepare a compilation of the objections being made to take to the meeting. After you have done this, call a meeting of the managers so you can get everything ironed out. Use the memo you prepared as the basis for going over the items one by one. Hash everything out once and for all, until you appear to have either a consensus or else specific disagreements from one or two managers that apparently can't be resolved. Then, summarize the agreements reached on each operating procedure. Assuming you have dissenters on any of the procedures, state that you will prepare a memo setting forth the agreements reached, with an attachment containing individual objections identified by person. Then, prepare your memo and send it out. This time there should be no basis for any objections other than those contained in the attachment to your memo.

This example points out a couple of the difficulties associated with the informal negotiation meetings that managers frequently hold in performing their jobs. One is that the more people involved the harder it is to reach agreement. The second is that the person or persons you're trying to reach an accord with may have no interest in reaching agreement. In fact, for reasons of his or her own, a manager may have an agenda entirely different from yours.

Q: A lower-level manager who reports to me was discussing advancement opportunities the other day. The individual has promotion potential but could use some management training courses to improve his skills in a couple of areas. I told him this, and he interpreted it as a promise to promote him if he completed the courses. I emphasized that I wasn't making any commitment, but only suggesting what he could do to improve his chances. To say the least I was surprised to find him in my office the next morning with a memo prepared for my signature which listed two management courses being given at a local college. The memo was, in effect, a statement from me saying that the two courses were required as part of his job. I asked him what that was about and he mumbled something about needing the memo for tax deduction purposes.

I'm no tax expert, but he isn't required to take any courses as a condition of employment, and I'm not asking him to take any, so I don't think he has a valid tax deduction. In fact, what I think he's trying to do is get a written commitment from me so that after he takes the courses he can demand to be promoted. In any event, I refused to sign the memo, and I told him to check with his tax preparer about the tax deductibility before he took the courses. What do you think of this situation?

A: You certainly should admire the initiative of this employee. He's trying to get a tax deduction for which he's probably not entitled and a promotion commitment that wasn't made, with both wrapped up in one short memo. In any of the informal negotiating that takes place with employees, you should be cautious about what you put in writing. It's best to avoid any definite commitments on pay raises, promotions, job security, and similar issues. Events can intervene that are beyond the control of an individual manager that make it impossible or impractical to fulfill such commitments. So avoid making verbal commitments and by all means written ones, since they can come back to haunt you.

Q: Our company, a large manufacturer, recently signed a contract with a new supplier which is a small business. I'm the project manager for the group that uses the components the supplier is furnishing. The owner has been in to see me a couple of times already. On both occasions, he has pulled out his copy of the agreement and started asking me what this clause means and that provision requires. I didn't even negotiate the contract so I sent the person over to the purchasing department. This isn't the first time I've had smaller suppliers asking me about contract provisions. It seems to be that someone should be explaining these things before they're signed. Am I wrong about this?

A: This is an all-too-common problem, especially where large and midsized companies are negotiating with smaller organizations that may not have the administrative and legal expertise to sufficiently understand the terms and conditions they are agreeing to in a contractual document. It's relatively easy to say that it's their responsibility to know what they're signing—which it is. It's not always recognized, however, that it's to the advantage of a larger company to have these people understand the importance of the contract provisions.

If a small company signs an agreement they later find to be onerous, it can cause difficulties in performance, and perhaps even result in a failure to complete the work. This impacts upon the larger company that wrote the agreement as well as the supplier. Therefore, it's in the best interests of everyone to fully understand the ramifications of the contract provisions. As a result, if you're dealing with someone who may be naive in this area, it's important to go over the contract document very carefully.

In a related area, in negotiating with smaller suppliers it's in the self-interest of larger organizations to not take advantage of their negotiating strengths to impose burdensome and restrictive provisions on smaller companies. It does nothing to foster a good supplier relationship and may in fact endanger the supplier's ability to perform. A good negotiator knows when to call it quits rather than try to put the squeeze on a less savvy party, since short-term advantages such as these seldom result in long-term benefits.

Q: I'm the president of a small company with fewer than one-hundred employees. I put in a bid to do some work for a large company that would be an excellent market for our product. To my delight, I was selected to do some business with these people. Although I'd sure like to hook on with these people on a long-term basis, I'm not about to accept an unprofitable deal based on future expectations. I'm about to negotiate an agreement with this company, and I want to know how best to protect my interests in doing this. As of right now, I'm looking at a proposed agreement that contains a lot of head-scratching boilerplate that I don't understand. How should I handle this?

A: Most important, be certain you have an understanding of what you're agreeing to. Sit down with the person you're negotiating with and get any explanations you need to satisfy yourself. If there are terms you object to, bring them up and try to work out a reasonable compromise. Don't be intimidated by assuming you have to accept the document as it's written. Anything in an agreement is negotiable if you have the determination to argue your side of the issues. Don't be put off by someone telling you, "That's a standard provision that *can't be changed*." What they're really saying is, "That's a provision *we don't want to change*." Of course, after you argue the merits they may well change their position to, "That's a provision *we're not going to change*." Then and only then, you have to decide whether you will accept a deal containing the provision.

Naturally you have to be realistic in assessing what terms and provisions you can live with and those you can't. You also have to recognize that certain provisions may be generally accepted even though you don't particularly like them. It's not likely you will be able to get much—if anything—changed in the way of standard provisions. Nevertheless, you will at least gain an understanding of their potential impact, which will allow you to make an educated decision on whether or not to go ahead with the agreement. Your overall ability to negotiate a satisfactory agreement with a larger company is primarily determined by your ability to state your case and a willingness to walk away from a deal you can't live with.

Q: Are there any general guidelines as to what should be included in negotiated agreements?

A: The specifics of the subject matter, the nature of the agreement, whether it's a formal contract document or an internal memorandum, will all have a bearing on the terms and provisions that are necessary. But apart from this, and any legal or administrative provisions, most negotiated agreements should contain the following minimum provisions, although some of them won't be necessary in more informal transactions:

- A precise statement of what each party will do to meet the work or performance requirements of the agreement. The more clearly requirements are defined, the less likelihood of a future dispute.
- The dates for performance, including starting date, completion date, and any necessary schedules covering delivery or performance milestones.
- Any payment provisions, including precise definitions as to time of payment, method of payment, and any conditions covering requirements for withholding payment.
- Any specific provisions that were negotiated and agreed to by both parties.
- Any provisions for modifying or changing the agreement, including terminating it.
- Any provisions required to resolve any future disputes pertaining to the agreement.
- The signatures of the parties to the agreement.

SEVERAL WAYS TO AVOID FUTURE MISUNDERSTANDINGS

No matter how basic a specific negotiation may be, careless preparation of the written agreement can cause future controversy. Unfortunately, it's much harder to solve problems that come about after an agreement is made. It's not only inattention to the written document, however, that can cause problems. A cavalier point of view toward thinking about potential problems can also contribute to the sort of benign neglect that can sow the seeds of conflict at a later date. Let's look at some of the attitudes that can cause trouble, as well as some specific areas where a poorly prepared document can produce problems.

Q: I recently finished negotiating an agreement with a new customer of our company. They had a really extensive agreement that we reviewed, and some changes were made. In fact, the only thing brought up that we didn't discuss was a minor change in the technical specifications that the customer made. One of our engineers mentioned it wasn't that big a deal, but it could pose a problem if the provision was interpreted too strictly. My boss said not to worry about it, so I didn't raise it as an issue. Was it wrong to ignore the change after the engineer brought it up?

A: It would have been wise to address the issue rather than ignore it. It's usually the minor issues that don't seem significant enough to question that create difficulty later on. This isn't surprising since anything that's obviously important will be spotlighted and discussed. This leaves the secondary issues as the likely source of trouble. Sometimes this is due to oversight, while at other times they are recognized but not considered serious enough to argue about. Then there's the "I'll worry about that later" attitude that's sometimes adopted. Unfortunately, when this attitude prevails, the odds are there will be something to worry about later when the very problem that was anticipated and ignored rears its ugly head.

Q: I participated as a member of a negotiating team that was working on a substantial contract for new business. I know how important the contract was, and we were just notified we got the contract, so the champagne corks are popping around here. What bothers me is that our proposal was as tight as a drum in both the financial and technical areas with no leeway for anything at all going wrong. It seems to me we should have left some wiggle room for any contingencies that come up. When I tried to point this out at the time, I was abruptly told not to worry about what might happen. Was I wrong about this?

A: You were right to be concerned. It's always dangerous to assume everything will go exactly as planned. There's a reason for what is called Murphy's law, which says that anything that can go wrong will. It's because nothing seldom goes exactly as planned. Obviously, the desire to win the contract was why allowances weren't made for contingencies. Your thinking was right, but you were bucking the powers that be who wanted the contract and didn't want to hear anything that might interfere with that.

Q: Our office is in a state of panic right now, because our new computer system won't be arriving for another three months when it was due to be delivered this week. The problem arose because there were two conflicting delivery dates in the contract. One was in the contract, and the other was in the statement of work that contained the technical specifications and so forth. The statement of work was lengthy so it wasn't attached to the contract document itself. Instead it was incorporated by reference to it. Whereas we were going by the contract document, which required delivery this week, the supplier was going by the date in the statement of work, which is about three months from now. I suppose there will be a legal hassle over this, but that's not my concern, since we were counting on the system being up and running this month. How in the world could whoever negotiated this allow this to happen?

A: Carelessness obviously caused the problem. Whenever documents are incorporated by reference in another document, they should be cross-checked to be certain there are no conflicting provisions. Either that wasn't done in this case or the delivery provisions were overlooked. Because of their importance, however, it's more than likely the documents weren't reviewed for inconsistencies.

There are several other ways that problems of this nature can arise. Provisions that are too loosely written can be misinterpreted, resulting in a wide variety of disputes. On other occasions, necessary terms are left out of the contract, while at other times provisions are included that shouldn't have been. All these mistakes lead to misunderstandings and sometimes significant problems that could have been avoided with a little bit of care.

HOW PROPER TIMING CAN CLOSE DEALS QUICKLY

The proper use of timing can be an important key in different phases of negotiations and it's something that's often overlooked. It can be useful anywhere from the planning stages before negotiations even begin, all the way to getting your agreement through the approval cycle in your company. Let's look at a few ways that timing can be employed from start to finish.

Q: **I don't see where timing comes into play when you're planning your negotiation strategy. How does that work?**

A: It's of use in limited situations. For example, a supplier who needs the business is likely to give you a better price than one who has a heavy backlog of work. Therefore, knowing market conditions in general can be very helpful in timing purchases. This is especially true with commodities, or anything else where supply and demand fluctuate widely. Of course, this isn't necessarily the overriding factor in a buying decision, but it's one that can be taken advantage of if circumstances permit.

Timing can also be useful in the in-house negotiating that you do. For example, if you're looking to work out some type of agreement with another manager, it may help, and it certainly won't hurt, if you can do this when the person is in a good mood. Alternatively, it's wise to avoid negotiating situations when someone gives the appearance of not being in the best of spirits.

Q: **Where and how can timing be used during negotiations?**

A: There are two potential uses of timing during negotiations. The first use is as a tactic to bring the negotiations to a conclusion. If you know there is an issue of importance to the other side that you are willing to concede, don't say anything about it until negotiations are at the point where this is the last remaining major issue. If you then suggest you're willing to concede the issue in order to reach an agreement, this should bring negotiations to a close without a lot of the nickel-and-dime haggling that often takes place at the end of negotiations.

The other, and more prevalent, use of timing is when your counterpart is facing some form of deadline to conclude an agreement. This can take various forms, ranging from needing to get work under contract to meet a delivery schedule to having plane reservations for a return flight. The reason for the deadline is important, since the less likely the chance to work around the deadline, the better your chances of using it to your advantage. For example, needing items by a certain date may be crucial, while it's easy to cancel a plane reservation. So knowing the urgency of the deadline is imperative if you don't want it to backfire on you.

Q: I was negotiating with a guy last week who told me at the start that he had a deadline to meet. As it turned out, it came and went, and he didn't even bat an eye. When I asked about it, he said he had straightened it out. I'm wondering if he even had a deadline to begin with. If he did, what would the advantage be of telling me about it?

A: Perhaps the deadline was canceled as was stated. On the other hand, there's always the possibility there wasn't a deadline in the first place. Maybe the other negotiator just wanted to make sure the negotiations moved right along. Aside from the practical benefits of speeding things up, the reasoning could have been that by moving things along quickly, you would have a lesser opportunity to raise questions about their negotiation position. Unless it's obvious, the odds are that a negotiator may not tell you about a deadline for fear of having you use it to your advantage.

Q: I think I made a mistake recently in taking advantage of someone's need to meet a deadline. What happened was this. The person negotiating with me needed to get an agreement signed off with my company in order to meet commitments made to top management in his company. I held out right down to the wire, forcing him to offer a higher price than would have been necessary under normal circumstances. Even though I didn't say anything, he knew what I was doing, and he told me this was the last business they would do with us. Was I wrong in squeezing this deal the way I did?

A: There's certainly nothing wrong with using someone else's deadline pressures to obtain a good deal. Nevertheless, there's a fine line between that and forcing someone to accept an unreasonable deal. Doing that, of course, can cause irreparable damage to a business relationship. In addition, being too heartless about the sort of deal you will accept may force the other party to walk away without reaching agreement.

Having said that, it's the responsibility of the other party to determine whether or not they will accept the terms that are offered. It may be that the individual here is just blowing off steam because his deadline pressures forced him to pay more than he would if the timing had been different. Frankly, from a business standpoint, the other party put themselves in the position of having to make a quick deal. Anytime that happens, you're likely going to pay top dollar to get what you want.

Q: **I'm confused about the procedure to follow in order to take advantage of a deadline to obtain a favorable deal. Will you outline how this situation should be handled?**

A: In general, what you want to do is keep the negotiations going right down to the last minute whenever you know there is a deadline looming over the head of the person you're negotiating with. The reasoning is basic. The closer you get to the deadline, the more anxious they will be to reach agreement. This, in turn, should make them more flexible than they would otherwise be in accepting a final offer. The odds are they will make a final offer close to the deadline time in the hopes of wrapping the deal up. If it's reasonable, you can accept it if you choose to. Alternatively, you can refuse it and make a counteroffer that's even more advantageous to you. If it's not totally unreasonable, the odds are it will be accepted without debate since the deadline doesn't give the other party any option—other than no deal at all.

The flip side of the coin is that negotiations aren't conducted with both sides using the same script. You have your game plan, and they have theirs. For instance, you may reach the deadline and find your opponent continuing to negotiate with no sign of concern about a deadline. It could be, as mentioned before, that they don't even have a deadline, or perhaps they do, but it's not quite as soon as you think it is. If it's the latter, although they don't give in right away, they may within a short period of time. They may also decide to call it quits, and then call you in a day or two to accept your offer. There are a number of variables in any negotiation, so trying to predict what will happen beforehand is a little like forecasting where, when, or if a hurricane will make landfall.

Q: **Are there any timing techniques I can use to help me get negotiated agreements through the approval cycle in my company? It seems it takes longer to get approval than it did to do the negotiating.**

A: There are a couple of things that may help speed up the process. First, if there is internal opposition to the project, this may throw up additional roadblocks beyond those traditionally associated with getting the necessary administrative approvals. Any opposition will likely take one of two forms. The first is a honest difference of opinion over the viability of the project, while the second involves nothing more than the petty politics that exist in every workplace.

Try to neutralize any potential opposition to the agreement by garnering as much support as you can. It also helps to be able to raise potential objections—and answer them—before someone else does. This way, you are answering them on your terms, not someone else's. If it's feasible, it helps to show where some of the ideas and suggestions of anyone opposed have been included in the agreement. Conversely, you may be able to point out where their objections have been overcome in working out the agreement.

Beyond that, you may encounter some of the more routine bottlenecks that occur in a typical review cycle. For example, if you must deal with indecisive people, try to work around them, and if you face a mound of mindless details in getting approvals, leave as many of them as is possible to be completed at a later date.

HOW TO PROCEED AFTER AN AGREEMENT IS SIGNED

As hard as it might have been to negotiate an agreement, the road doesn't end there. Of even greater importance is ensuring that the performance of whatever is required by the agreement is completed both satisfactorily and on time. Otherwise, you may find yourself so immersed in trying to straighten out problems that you wish the agreement hadn't been negotiated in the first place. Naturally, with many of the informal internal negotiations you conduct, there isn't much in the way of follow-up involved. Yet even here, peers and others can cause you problems over relatively minor matters. So whether an agreement was simple or complex, within the company or with outsiders, whatever level of follow-up that's necessary is neglected at your peril.

Q: **Why should I have to do any follow-up work on an agreement negotiated with another firm? We have a written contract they have to comply with, and if they don't there are legal remedies.**

A: The most important reason is that you contracted for work to be performed, not for a lawsuit. Obviously the company you're doing business with has a responsibility to comply with the terms of the contract. Nevertheless, problems can arise and unless you're on top of the situation, they may get out of hand before you even know they exist. It's no secret that when little things start to go wrong, they escalate into major problems if they're not nipped in the bud.

Q: How do you determine how much follow-up is required in a given situation?

A: There are a number of factors involved in determining the degree of follow-up. The nature of the transaction, the company doing the work, and the degree of importance attached to the project are among the many determinants of the level of follow-up that's required. For example, routine jobs will require only minimal monitoring, while complex projects with a high priority will require a good deal of oversight. Furthermore, if you're dealing with a company that has a good track record in prior business dealings, you don't need to take the precautions you would take with someone unknown to you.

Q: My ears are still burning from a phone call I just received from the general manager of a company we have a contract with. They're all bent out of shape about the monitoring of the work that we're doing. He claims one of our technical people is over there trying to tell them how to do their jobs. He tried to tell me that if we left them alone, they might be able to get the work done. The fact is we're just trying to be helpful. Am I wrong, or is he out of line in getting angry about this.

A: That's impossible to say without full knowledge of all the facts in the situation. Incidentally, getting the facts is where you should start in sorting this problem out. In monitoring performance, it's imperative to do so without interfering in the internal operations of another company, or for that matter another department, if it's an internal agreement of some sort. There are times, however, when someone may be uncooperative in giving you information to which you're entitled. In these situations, you have to assert your rights.

Q: How useful is it to have reporting requirements in an agreement, and if you do, how does that affect any other form of follow-up?

A: Progress reports in general, and other reports warranted by the nature of the agreement, should be the cornerstone for monitoring performance. In fact, even in relatively informal in-house agreements with other departments and divisions of the company, progress reports are essential to ensure the work is progressing satisfactorily. In larger and more complex projects, other methods of follow-up should be used in conjunction with formal reporting requirements. These will vary with the project, but include financial reporting, on-site visits, and close contact with any employees who may be working with the contractor on this or other projects.

Incidentally, in many instances, you may not be doing the actual follow-up work yourself, but if it's delegated to someone else, make certain they provide you with periodic reports on the job's progress. Otherwise, you may find yourself getting stung by employees of your own company. For example, if a technical group is working on a project in conjunction with a contractor, they may be more interested in the technical aspects of the work rather than financial performance, meeting delivery dates, and the like. Therefore, if a problem crops up, they may try to resolve it with the contractor rather than advise you of its existence. Only when things get so far out of control that they are beyond redemption will you be brought on board.

WHEN TO QUIT WITHOUT REACHING AGREEMENT

As hard as it sometimes is to reach a negotiated settlement, it's difficult to think about quitting any negotiation without reaching agreement. This is especially true if a good deal of effort has been invested in trying to make a deal. Yet for a wide variety of reasons, there are times when it's necessary to call it quits. This can occur anytime during the negotiation process, starting with your planning before you even sit down to negotiate.

Q: I'm in charge of a team involved with seeking new sources of supply for some of the components our company uses in its products. We have identified one potential source, and the engineers on our team seem enamored with the technical performance of this company. It seems to be clouding their judgment on anything else, and they want to start working on an agreement with this company. In researching the matter, it turns out that this particular supplier produces top-quality components, but they have never done so in large quantities and have a dismal record for on-time deliveries. Our company has a just-in-time inventory management system, so we can't live with any supplier that can't meet rapid-response delivery dates. Furthermore, the quantities we're looking for would probably require the supplier to expand capabilities, which raises all sorts of different questions. I'm of the opinion that giving this supplier business is an accident waiting to happen. Despite the opposition I'm getting, I see no reason to go ahead and initiate any negotiations with this company. Is this being reasonable?

A: Sometimes the best deal you can get is the one you kill before it even gets off the ground. Whenever you are doing any prenegotiation planning, part of the process should be a determination as to whether or not negotiations should even begin. There are any number of reasons why it may be decided that it's better to forgo negotiations, or at least postpone them indefinitely. One of them is a situation such as here, where it's fairly obvious that it's unlikely this supplier could perform adequately. Another instance is where the other party may have such a preponderant edge at the bargaining table that it would be virtually impossible for you to get a fair deal. With the business risks involved with a contractor not being able to fulfill contractual commitments, it's wise to avoid situations where serious potential problems are uncovered in the initial planning stages.

Q: I'm the operations manager for a small company, and I was recently unable to complete a deal for a larger company to buy our products. They broke off negotiations at the last minute for no apparent reason and just said they were no longer interested. Did I do something wrong? If not, why would they do something such as this?

A: Negotiations are broken off for all kinds of reasons. In this instance, they may have just been evaluating your company as a potential source. Obviously, that's not an appropriate way to go about it, but things aren't always done the way they should be. Then again, perhaps there was another reason related to the negotiations themselves. Maybe there was something revealed during negotiations that gave them pause. What it could have been is purely speculative, and it doesn't imply there was anything inherently wrong with your product or the negotiations themselves. As you know, everyone has specific objectives when undertaking negotiations, and they may have discovered something that didn't make sense from their point of view. Finally, perhaps they were looking for someone they could dictate terms to and discovered that you weren't about to accept any old deal they decided to offer you.

It doesn't happen that often, but there are occasions when negotiations end up going nowhere. The possibility always exists that you may discover facts during the negotiation process that lead you to believe an agreement wouldn't be in your best interests. When this happens, break off the negotiations as diplomatically as you can, and try to give a believable explanation as to why you aren't going to go forward. After all, circumstances change, and you never know when you might want to do business with someone in the future.

Q: I was negotiating with a company to buy certain items, and out of the blue they told me the line was being discontinued, and they then proceeded to try and sell me an entirely different product that would only marginally meet our needs. To make matters worse, it was loaded with "bells" and "whistles" and was much more expensive. What do you make of that?

A: It's nothing more than a bait-and-switch tactic where you are planning on buying one thing and someone tries to sell you something different. Why they did this at the negotiation stage is problematic, but they probably figured they had a better chance of selling you in this manner. If they had told you up front, you probably would have just declined and gone about looking for your product elsewhere.

HOW AND WHEN TO RENEGOTIATE DONE DEALS

Whenever the economy stumbles, repaying bank loans becomes a problem for many a business. In addition, other types of negotiated agreements such as long-term contracts for the purchase or sale of goods may require adjustment because of declining demand. In fact, even in good times, changing circumstances may result in a business contract not being quite the good deal that was anticipated when it was signed. Often, unanticipated events beyond the control of a business can bring disaster near the door in terms of trying to meet existing business commitments.

No one likes to confront the reality that an existing agreement isn't working out as planned, especially with all the effort you put into negotiating it. Unfortunately, this can result in postponing dealing with the problem which only makes the situation worse. Actually, the sooner a deal that's going sour is renegotiated, the better it is for both parties to the agreement. Therefore, if you face a situation where an existing agreement is causing difficulty, it might be prudent to think about renegotiating the terms with the other party.

Q: **We're having trouble meeting the specifications on a contract for some work we're doing for another company. I'm concerned with having to tell my contact at the other company that we're having problems and would like some relief with the specifications. How should I approach this?**

A: One of the biggest stumbling blocks to renegotiating an agreement is a reluctance to admit that the deal can't be completed as originally negotiated. Naturally, every attempt should be made to live up to any contractual agreement. Nevertheless, it's equally important to recognize when that becomes impossible to do. You have to take the initiative to contact your counterpart and let him or her know about the problem. Renegotiating the specifications will minimize the damage for everyone involved.

Q: **I've just been told by my production manager that the delivery schedules in a contract we have can't be met. He claims they're unrealistic, and we shouldn't have accepted them in the first place. That may be true for all I know. The person who negotiated the deal for us is no longer with our company. I've never renegotiated anything before. How do I go about this?**

A: First, decide what delivery schedule you can live with. Then get the facts as to why the existing schedule can't be met. Then, get together with the representative of the company and see what you can work out in terms of a modification to the contract. They probably won't be happy, but if you can come up with a reasonable schedule that they can live with, the worst of the damage will have been overcome. Sometimes these situations can even surprise you. For one reason or another, the situation may have changed since the contract was negotiated, and perhaps the items aren't needed as quickly as was originally planned. If that is true, the other party may not even tell you this, even though they agree to revise the schedule. After all, even if you get lucky, that's not going to make them happy about what happened.

Q: **Are there any general guidelines for preparing to renegotiate an agreement?**

A: You essentially want to go through the same steps you would in negotiating anything from scratch, namely,

- Prepare your negotiation position before attempting to renegotiate. How do you want to modify the contract, and what is the reason for doing so?
- Try to anticipate the reaction of the other party. What terms will they want for agreeing to modify the contract?
- Gather all the information you can to show the advantages of negotiating new terms, as well as the problems if a new agreement can't be reached.
- Decide what concessions you can make in exchange for a renegotiated agreement.
- Carefully assess your alternatives and decide what you will do if the other party refuses to modify the contract.

Q: **If I attempt to renegotiate something, isn't the other party going to expect some form of consideration such as a price reduction or whatever? After all, I'm the one who wants to change the deal.**

A: It's entirely likely that you may have to make some form of concession. Then, again, it depends upon various factors such as the nature of the business relationship, the extent of the changes you want to make, and most of all, their impact upon the other party. Incidentally, it's entirely conceivable that you could have a situation where you want to renegotiate something and it would be beneficial to the other party; for example, some form of technical breakthrough that would improve a product you're manufacturing for someone.

APPENDIX

MANAGER'S CAREER NEGOTIATING GUIDE

INTRODUCTION

No matter how much, or how little, negotiating you do as a part of your job, there's one area where negotiation skills will always serve you well. That, of course, is in negotiating with prospective employers. Naturally, negotiating techniques can also be beneficial in negotiating career-related objectives with your present employer, but you're more limited in what you can achieve. For one thing, the existing salary structure limits salary increases, especially if you aren't changing positions. Furthermore, there are other subtle constraints on your ability to negotiate in your current job. For one thing, you don't want to run the risk of pushing too hard in negotiating with your own boss. Besides that, there's a natural pecking order internally that limits you to waiting your turn to move up the career ladder.

On the other hand, when you're talking to prospective employers, you have a clean slate to work with. Both pay and benefits are more open to negotiation. There are also other areas where a little bit of negotiating can yield big gains. If the job is at a distant location, there's room for bargaining over relocation costs. And if you have a trailing spouse, which is commonplace today, the opportunity presents itself to ask for assistance in finding a suitable job opening for your mate in the new location. In fact, when it comes to negotiating the terms of a new position, just about anything is open to negotiation. You may not get everything you ask for, but even if you don't, some savvy bargaining can get you a lot more than you expected before you sat down to bargain. And even when a prospective employer can't meet one or more of your terms, there's a good possibility the company may make it up in some other area. So all things considered, negotiating to advance your career can be the most rewarding negotiation you ever undertake. And what's even better about it, the benefits of career negotiating accrue directly to you. That alone is reason enough to know the ropes of negotiating for career success.

CAREER BARGAINING STARTS WITH PREPARATION

As with negotiating anything else, bargaining with a prospective employer starts with the proper preparation. How successful you are in negotiating your requirements in a new position ultimately rests upon the foundation you prepare before you even talk with a prospective employer.

Q: What sort of preparation is necessary before negotiating with a prospective employer?

A: Basically, you have to determine what your negotiation goals are. This includes factors such as the minimum salary you will accept, as well as the maximum salary you hope to get. However, your salary is only part of your total compensation package. You also have to consider the extent of the fringe benefit package being offered by a prospective employer. In general, the better the fringes, the lower the salary you may be willing to accept. You also should determine any specific benefits that will influence your acceptance or rejection of a job offer. For example, if the job is at a distant location, what is the relocation policy of the company you're talking with? Make up a list of all your requirements before you have your first interview. The important point is to set everything down in writing so you know exactly what you want before you start discussions. Otherwise, you may later discover yourself picking up the tab for expenses you didn't contemplate beforehand.

Q: Isn't it a waste of time to set down all your expectations in writing, since to a large degree the company's policy will dictate what you get, and there isn't that much you can negotiate?

A: To the contrary. First, unless you specifically determine your requirements, there's no way you will be able to meet your objectives. A prospective employer can't be expected to anticipate all your needs, especially if you have one or more unusual problems. Furthermore, although companies have policies on what they will reimburse new hires for, some flexibility is involved. So if you don't ask for something, it's unlikely it will be offered gratuitously by the company representative. Beyond anything else, the only way you will know if you can get something you want is to ask for it.

NOTE: In terms of preparation when job hunting, there are many considerations involved, such as resume preparation, researching potential employers, and other issues. Although these factors are an integral part of any job search, the focus of this appendix is on effectively negotiating the maximum employment package you can obtain. There are a wide variety of reference sources available that discuss these other issues in great detail. For this reason, this appendix assumes you're far enough along in your job hunt to be in the position of negotiating the terms and conditions of employment with a prospective employer. Any discussion of issues not specifically related to negotiating the best job package possible won't be repeated here.

Q: In preparing to negotiate salary, how should I go about establishing the salary I'm going to ask for?

A: Determining the minimum salary you're willing to accept involves many factors, some of which are general in nature, and others that are specific to your individual situation.

Q: What are the common considerations in establishing your minimum acceptable salary?

A: The common baseline is the salary of your current position. In most cases, you want to receive a premium over and above what you're making on your present job. You also have to take into account the duties of the new position. If you will be moving into a higher-level position with far greater responsibilities, then the increase in salary should be considerably more than what you're presently making.

The size of the company also has an influence on what sort of salary premium you can expect to command. Smaller companies tend to pay less than their larger counterparts. In fact, even companies of the same size have different salary scales, as some employers tend to be pay leaders, while others lag behind. The specific industry your prospective employer is in also has a bearing on salary scales. Therefore, if you're moving from a position in one company to an employer in a different field, you have to base your demands on the going rates in the latter industry.

Q: **What are some of the individual considerations involved in determining your salary requirements?**

A: Individual considerations can vary widely. For example, if you're switching careers, you may be willing to accept a salary well below what you're earning in your present position. Apart from that, you may be entertaining an offer from a small business that pays less for comparable positions than the company you now work for. However, for personal reasons, you may find the small company to offer advantages that will offset a lower salary. Finally, it's unfortunate but true that if you're unemployed—or about to be—the minimum salary you're willing to accept may be less than if you're looking for a new job to advance your career. It's easy enough to say, "Don't let that be a factor in determining the minimum salary you'll accept"; however, the reality of paying your mortgage comes before trying to maximize your earnings when times get tough. It's a lot easier to hold out for another 10% when you know where your next paycheck is coming from.

Q: **What sort of increase should you be looking for when you establish your salary requirements?**

A: This isn't cast in concrete since there are many other elements to a job offer that can influence what your salary demands will be. The fringe benefit package, and indirect compensation in the form of performance bonuses, stock options, and the like, will contribute to where you decide to set your minimum salary demands. Nevertheless, no matter how good these other forms of compensation may look, the basic priority should be salary, since that's all you're guaranteed to have to pay your bills. Furthermore, many performance incentives and stock options look better on paper than they turn out to be in reality.

As a general proposition a pay increase in the range of 20% isn't unreasonable when you're changing jobs. And even though your new employer may have a very generous benefit package, there are still risks involved in switching jobs. First, you have to consider any accrued benefits you will lose in your current position. And frequently there are expenses involved that aren't covered by any relocation package. For example, if you relocate some distance, you may face higher long-distance phone bills for those calls to chat with family and friends. Since there are so many variables involved in negotiating an employment package, it's helpful to look at tactics you can use in negotiating different elements of an employment offer. And there's no better place to start than negotiating your salary requirements.

SALARY NEGOTIATIONS

The first thing to recognize when it comes to negotiating salary requirements is that the company wants to get you cheap, while convincing you that you're getting a great deal. Even though job applicants know this, there's a reluctance to ask for a higher salary if an offer is made that is 10 or 15% higher than someone's current salary. And, in fact, there may be times when such a figure is acceptable. For example, if someone's present job is in jeopardy, a 10% increase looks great, particularly if no relocation is required and the responsibilities are similar. This is especially true if the benefit package is superior to that of your current employer.

On the other hand, a 15% raise can cost you money if you're relocating from an area where the cost of living is low to a high-cost region of the country. Even if that's not the case, there are risks involved in switching jobs, and just as with investments, the risk associated with changing jobs should be rewarded. Therefore, although individual circumstances will dictate what a reasonable salary is, make sure you make this determination honestly, and don't accept what's offered if you don't think it meets your needs. The flip side of the coin, of course, is to be realistic about your potential worth to prospective employers, since if your demands are out of line you will just be spinning your wheels.

Q: In a recent interview I was told that my salary request was too high since it would interfere with internal equity as I would be making more than other managers in the company with similar qualifications and experience. Whether or not this was true, the salary offered didn't meet my expectations so I turned the job down. However, in talking to people, I've learned others have run into this situation. Is there any way to work around this dilemma?

A: If you can make a good case for being worth what you're asking for, there are other alternatives for solving this problem. One way is for the company to give you a one-time signing bonus, which will compensate you for accepting a lower salary. Another option is to negotiate some other benefit that meets your needs, which you consider to be a satisfactory alternative to the higher salary you seek. Nevertheless, if you don't feel you're getting an initial salary that is reasonable, think twice about accepting an alternative. This is especially true if the company offers to raise your salary shortly after you come on board. If they're not willing to pay you what you think you're worth now, it's unlikely they will do so later. As a result, if a prospective employer pays less than comparable companies in the same industry, you'll always find yourself behind on the pay curve.

Q: I'm in middle management and may relocate since my spouse has received an attractive job offer. It would mean moving from the Northeast to the South. My problem is that in doing some research, although there are plenty of positions available within my field, the salaries are considerably lower than what I'm now earning. This doesn't bother me so much, since the cost of living in the new area is also lower. What I do wonder about is how to approach the subject of salary with a prospective employer under these circumstances. If I ask for the same or a higher salary than I'm presently making, I won't be competitive. Yet, I don't want to ask for too low a salary. From my research I know that salaries in the new area are about 20% lower. Is there a good way to handle this situation?

A: Actually, before you even get to sit down and talk about salary with a prospective employer, you should deal with this situation. One reason is that you can take yourself out of contention before you even get to have an interview. For instance, if a company asks for your salary requirements when you send in your resume and you're on the high side, you may not even be considered for the position. Alternatively, you may be asked to list your salary history. Naturally, this will show your current salary. However, this won't automatically eliminate you from contention, since employers will know salaries are higher in your part of the country. Nevertheless, they might prefer to hire a local candidate, on the assumption you might be unhappy at earning a lower salary.

A good way to attack this problem is to let prospective employers know you recognize salaries are lower in the geographic area where you are looking for employment. You can do this by stating in your application letter that you recognize salaries are lower in the area, and you could even go so far as to give a salary range that you would consider to be acceptable. Doing this tells prospective employers that you're aware of the salary differentials, and you prevent your resume from going in the rejected pile because someone sees your current salary is higher than their range for the position.

Q: I have plans to relocate to another part of the country. I've been told that salaries are lower than where I now live. Nevertheless, an acquaintance of mine moved there recently and was offered a job with a higher salary than she was making here. As a result, I'm in a quandary. I don't want to take myself out of consideration for positions by asking for too high a salary. On the other hand, I don't want to short change myself just because overall salaries are lower in the region. How should I deal with this?

A: As mentioned in the answer to the prior question, the key is to research the overall salary structure in the area you're moving too. However, even though you may learn, for example, that salaries are on average 20% lower, you shouldn't stop there. The important point is that these figures are averages. It may well be that the particular geographic area has an unusually high concentration of very small firms that pay lower salaries. Another possibility is that although overall salaries are lower, management salaries in your field of expertise are pretty much the same throughout the country. So for starters, you want to find out precisely what firms in the area pay for the type of position you're seeking. Although there are various ways to do this, such as published surveys, government statistics, or professional associations in your field, the quickest and most current information can be easily obtained by calling a few employment agencies in the geographic area. They can tell you right away the going rate for someone in your field with the level of experience you possess.

Beyond this, if the particular area where you want to move doesn't have a large talent pool of experienced managers to draw from in your field, they may be willing to pay much more for someone who is willing to relocate.

Therefore, even though you don't want to exclude yourself from consideration for positions by asking for a higher salary than appears to be justified by the local job market, you have to be careful if you decide to state you will accept a lower salary. Furthermore, you can't overlook the part that your personal circumstances play in the salary you're willing to accept. If you are moving no matter what the salary differential may be, and your financial situation is such that it isn't a major concern, then you might want to let prospective employers know you are willing to accept less. The flip side of the coin is that you may decide you're not willing to move unless your minimum salary equals or exceeds what you're presently making. Whichever way you play it, be sure to do your research and think your decision through before you act. That way, you won't be regretting it at a later date.

Q: A friend of mine interviewed for a job in another part of the country where salaries are lower. He didn't get the job, since he was told the salary range was much lower than what he was asking for. Nevertheless, five months later he accepted a job offer paying much more than the salary for the job he didn't get. Why the differential?

A: Although most companies try to be competitive with others in their industry, there are variances. Sometimes when you relocate to a new area that has significantly lower salaries, a company that wants to hire you will pay a premium to obtain your services. Although there are a number of reasons for salary differentials in different parts of the country, including living costs, supply and demand are also factors. If there aren't a lot of managerial jobs in your field in a particular part of the country, a firm seeking someone with specific qualifications may have to pay more to attract candidates from outside the area. This is especially true if the area isn't a particularly desirable one to live in. The flip side of the coin is that resort areas may offer lower than average salaries because of a surplus of candidates willing to work there. The bottom line is to get solid information on the salary possibilities if you're planning to relocate. You can't just go by generalities.

Q: A friend suggested that I boost my current salary 10% when I'm asked what my current salary is by prospective employers? She says it will allow me to get a higher pay offer without any hassles. Is this a proper way to achieve your salary goal?

A: This is, of course, dishonest, and it can cause plenty of problems if a prospective employer discovers you have done this. Besides being deceitful, it's an unnecessary risk that can damage your career. Even if it's not discovered initially, do you really want to have this worry hanging over your head for the foreseeable future? It's just as easy to negotiate the salary you want by asking for it. Assuming it's reasonable and within the employer's salary range for the job, the company should be willing to pay it if they really want your services.

Q: A small company has offered me a starting salary that is 5% less than I'm currently making in my present position. I really like the opportunity for growth that the job offers, but I'm concerned about taking a pay cut. The president of the company who offered me the job said they aren't yet in a position to compete with larger businesses on salary and benefits. Is it realistic from a career standpoint to take a pay cut?

A: As a general rule, smaller businesses lag behind their big business counterparts in terms of salaries. On the other hand, they often present greater opportunities for job growth, which means faster promotions and greater responsibilities a lot sooner than is possible in larger organizations. What you have to do is assess the risks and rewards over the long term and balance them against the lesser salary. If the future looks much brighter with the smaller organization, the pay differential shouldn't deter you from accepting such a position.

The bottom line, of course, is your financial situation. If you're struggling to make ends meet right now, even a 5% pay cut can be tough to handle. But if you're not living from paycheck to paycheck, then it may well be worth your while in the long run to seize such an opportunity. Nevertheless, be honest with yourself about your financial situation, since it's easy to say $300.00 or so less every month won't be a problem. If you're pushed to pay your bills right now, think about the impact of not having that extra money. Beyond that, you have to assess the relative job security. At one time, larger companies tended to offer better long-term job security. That isn't as true as it used to be, but it pays to do some checking on the financial viability of a smaller business before you sign on for the future. Some small companies are more financially secure than their big business brethren, while others are undercapitalized and struggling to meet their payroll. Knowing which are which before you accept a job offer can save you a lot of grief down the road.

Q: At what point in the interviewing process should I ask about salary?

A: You never want to be the one to raise this issue. You're far better off letting the company representative bring this up, and the later in the hiring process it is, the better off you are. The longer you're talking with a prospective employer, and the more interviews you have, the closer you become to being the candidate of their choice. And once the company decides you are the prime candidate, they become committed to obtaining your services. This gives you greater leverage when it's time to talk salary.

Q: What do I do if the company representative raises the salary issue early on in the discussions?

A: Be noncommittal and say something such as, "My salary is open to negotiation and depends upon the requirements of the position. I'll be better able to address salary matters after I learn more about the details of the open position." This should delay the matter temporarily, since it's quite logical for you to know the requirements of the position before committing yourself to a salary figure.

Q: When is the best time to discuss salary?

A: Salary issues are best discussed after you have essentially completed the interview process and have asked any and all questions to satisfy yourself as to the present requirements of the position, as well as the opportunity for future growth. But even when the company representative asks you what sort of salary you're looking for, try to parry the question with a question of your own. The point is that if you can get a feel for what the company is going to offer, you can use this to pinpoint your salary requirement. Let's look at an example of how this could be done.

Interviewer: "What sort of salary are you looking for?"

You: "My requirements are flexible. What is your salary range for the position?"

Interviewer: "We're competitive in our salaries. Now that we've discussed the position in detail, what do you think an acceptable range would be? We pride ourselves on employee input and would like to know what you think?"

NOTE: This sort of back-and-forth exchange can, of course, take a variety of forms, but there are several key points to keep in mind:

- It helps you to negotiate if you can pinpoint the company's salary range before you state your own position. Most of the time, the company negotiator will readily give you either a salary range or make an offer without too much prodding on your part.
- As long as you can logically toss the ball back in the court of the interviewer, try to do so until you are given a salary range. The best way to do this is to answer questions with questions as in the example. Don't overdo it in trying to string this out though, since it will only serve to aggravate the interviewer.
- If you run into an interviewer who is obviously going to hear your figure before making any offer, then give a figure on the high side of the salary range you developed before starting the interview process. Let's assume this happens and pick up the discussion at that point.

You: "I'm looking for something in the neighborhood of $150,000." (You will, in reality, accept a salary as low as $130,000.)

Interviewer: "Oh my! We were thinking more on the order of $130,000. That seems to be a very competitive salary for the position. What do you base your figure of $150,000 on?"

COMMENTS: This is a crucial juncture in salary negotiations, since what you say here can bolster your case for a higher salary. What you want to point out here is your value to the employer in terms of the contributions you can make to increase productivity, raise profits, cut costs, and whatever other specific angles pertaining to the position that represent value to the company. Don't overdo it though since exaggerated claims will be obvious.

Furthermore, you don't want to project as a know-it-all. Just be sincere and matter-of-fact in stating how you feel you are worth the money in terms of what you bring to the party.

Besides this angle, you also want to point out the costs to you in accepting the position. In fact, if you do this carefully, you may find the interviewer willing to offer one-time benefits of one form or another to meet your needs. In fact, although there is a later discussion on negotiating benefits, suffice it to say here that this is the point for raising questions in this area. It obviously implies that if the company can do something for you in some other area, then your salary requirement can be lowered.

After you make your arguments for a higher salary, it's likely you will be offered some figure above what the opening figure was. It's unwise to continue to try and nickel and dime a few more dollars if the figure is within your acceptable range. It won't be appreciated and can paint you as someone more interested in the money than the job. Maybe you are, but if so, it does not do your career any good to have someone thinking that. So if the figure is acceptable to you, and there are no other open issues, agree to it.

Q: I've been offered a salary figure that is acceptable and a pretty comprehensive benefits package. However, I need a little time to look it over before I make a commitment. How do I go about conveying this to the company representative?

A: This isn't a problem except in the minds of job candidates who worry they will lose the job if they don't accept it right away. As long as you only ask for a day or two to think it over, there should be no problem. In terms of how you suggest this, do so from a positive standpoint by emphasizing you are happy with the offer, but want to look the entire package over so there won't be any misunderstanding on your part. However, agree to respond by a certain date so nothing is left open-ended. Furthermore, don't worry about losing the job in the meantime. An employer who makes a job offer isn't going to go looking for someone else in the interim. If they preferred one of the other candidates, you wouldn't have been given the offer in the first place.

Q: I've been given a salary range for a position. Even the bottom figure is 10% higher than I'm presently making. What should I say my salary requirement is?

A: Some people would recommend that you ask for a salary somewhere in the top of the range. This isn't necessarily true, since in some situations it may be unrealistic. It certainly makes sense to shoot for as much as you can get, but the flip side of the coin is that you don't want to shoot yourself in the foot. For example, assume you're earning $80,000 a year in your current position, and the interviewer knows this. You've been given a range (or find it out independently) of $90,000 to $120,000. The interviewer then asks for what you're looking for in terms of salary. If you say something such as, "In the neighborhood of $120,000," you have lost your credibility. It's far fetched to assume you will be given a 50% pay increase, and if challenged, you would be hard pressed to justify it. Incidentally, this also applies to being cute and saying something such as, "A salary of $117,000 would be acceptable." Staying just under the maximum wouldn't impress anyone as anything other than a gimmick, and savvy interviewers might conclude you were implying they were dumb enough to be fooled.

What you want to do in such a situation is aim for the middle ground such as $110,000. It may be high in the eyes of the interviewer, but at least it's within the range of credibility. By doing this the interviewer may feel compelled to offer you something more than the low point of the range, even though that figure of $100,000 would give you a 25% raise.

Of course, in a situation such as this, a sharp interviewer might preempt any opportunity for you to take advantage of a situation such as this. For example, the interviewer might say, "Since the beginning salary in our range is $100,000, we will start you off there even though that represents a 25% raise over your present salary of $80,000. Is that acceptable to you?" Here, you can argue the case, if there are relevant factors that justify it, but don't make waves unless you have a valid argument. Generally, situations such as this are most likely to occur if you're moving from a position with a nonprofit or government entity, which has a salary structure significantly lower than the business world in general.

Q: **When asked for my salary requirement, am I better off giving a salary range or a specific figure?**

A: For the most part, a range is preferable. The logic is simple. If you give a range there's an implication that you expect an offer that exceeds the lowest point in the range. Incidentally, don't make the range too broad in hopes of falling somewhere within what you perceive to be the salary range for the job. A broad range implies that you're on a fishing expedition. Make your range narrow, with the low end at or slightly above the minimum salary you would accept. Putting the figure slightly above gives you a little flexibility in the event the company doesn't pay quite as well as you anticipate. If that's the case, they may offer you the minimum or slightly below it. If you had set your range slightly above your minimum target salary, then you will more likely get your minimum salary if they make an offer below the bottom of your range. For example, you want $100,000 and give a range of $105,000 to $120,000. They counter with $100,000, which is lower than your range but equal to your unrevealed acceptance figure.

Q: I've accepted a job offer elsewhere and gave my notice to my present employer two days ago. Yesterday, my boss told me how much the company wanted to retain me and offered to raise my salary 10% over what I was offered on the new job if I stayed put. Admittedly this is attractive, since it eliminates the uncertainties associated with starting a new job, along with the hassles of moving, since the new position is 300 miles from where I now live. Should I accept this offer, or go ahead and take the other job?

A: There's both a general answer and a specific answer to this question. In broad terms, it's not usually a wise move to accept a counteroffer from your present employer. In the first place, why are they willing to pay you now what they weren't willing to do before you received another job offer? If they had, you probably wouldn't have been job hunting in the first place. Who's to say that your pay raises won't be few and far between once you commit yourself to staying? In that fashion, your present employer will recoup the immediate cost of giving you more money by holding down your future raises. Sure, you can always look for a job later, but if that happens then you have essentially put your career on hold for a while by postponing the inevitable for a short-term financial gain.

Beyond the salary issue, the counteroffer may be based on keeping you onboard for the short term because your experience is needed at this time. If the situation changes, however, you might be more vulnerable to the job ax, since you aren't perceived to be a loyal company employee. Furthermore, the working relationships that previously existed might be altered. Your boss might expect considerably more from you because of the pay increase. Other relationships can also change. For example, anyone who viewed themselves in line to move up when you left, may be unhappy at your change of heart. This certainly isn't likely to promote a high degree of cooperation if you have to deal with someone with such an attitude.

All in all, from a general standpoint, the negatives tend to outweigh the positives in agreeing to accept more money and/or a promotion from your present employer in response to your notification of accepting a job elsewhere. Furthermore, you have to factor in the specifics of your own situation. Why were you looking for another job in the first place? If it's because of your dissatisfaction over future career possibilities, then they aren't going to get any better. Maybe you were unhappy with your boss, or some of your peers. Those people will still be there for you to contend with. Then, again, maybe you had concluded that the company's future didn't look too bright, so you decided to look elsewhere. That too hasn't changed. In essence, a pay raise alone won't change any of the other reasons you were looking for a job. And even if you try to rationalize that the pay increase will make the other problems easier to deal with, it won't be long before you realize the fallacy of your reasoning. Therefore, for the most part, once you have committed to moving on to another job, you're better off taking the plunge rather than postponing a move because of money alone.

Q: **I've been offered a middle management job that I really want to take. It's in an industry that has strong growth prospects; unlike the company I work for now. The problem is that the salary is 20% less than I'm now making. That, in itself, doesn't bother me, since I know I'll be better off over the long haul. The trouble is that I don't know if I can meet my financial obligations if I accept the position. Should I mention my personal financial problems as a means of prompting the prospective employer to offer me a higher starting salary?**

A: Your skills and experience are what a prospective employer is willing to pay for, not the expense of your personal life-style. In fact, even mentioning this as a justification for a higher salary won't be seen in a favorable light. For example, an interviewer might wonder how someone who can't manage their own finances can be expected to manage a department budget.

It's common in situations such as switching careers or moving from a large employer to a small business to encounter the reality of accepting a lower salary. This really leaves you only two choices, which are to reject the job offer or to take a hard look at adjusting your personal finances to live on lower earnings. In fact, anytime you're contemplating a change in jobs that may result in a lower salary, you should analyze your personal financial situation beforehand to get a handle on the minimum salary you need to earn.

Q: I'm going for my third and final job interview with a company tomorrow. It's scheduled with the division general manager I will be working for. Salary hasn't been mentioned yet in the two prior interviews, so it's likely to be raised tomorrow. If the salary issue hasn't been addressed as the interview starts to wind down, should I bring it up? I know it's smart to let the employer make the opening move, but I'm concerned that perhaps the personnel office and the operating department both assume salary has been discussed with me by the other group.

A: The situation will vary from company to company as well as with the level of the position you are filling, but in many situations the human resources people will be the ones who discuss salary and benefits with you. This, in fact, is probably why the issue hasn't been brought up yet. Once you have been selected as the candidate the company wants, the salary issue will be raised. One good reason for it being handled by human resources is that it removes the possibility of spoiling your relationship with a new boss before you even start the job. Therefore, keep your powder dry and don't raise the salary issue yourself. One of the keys to successful negotiating is the ability to be patient.

NEGOTIATING BENEFITS AND PERKS

Naturally, every company will offer you their standard benefit package, which covers all employees. Beyond this, however, are any number of perks and benefits that you may be eligible for according to how senior a management position you are eligible for. But even if you're in a first-level or middle management position, there are a number of benefits you can negotiate for when you're starting a new job. For one thing, employers recognize the costs involved with changing jobs. This is especially true when you're relocating to a different part of the country. An employer may also be willing to provide additional benefits when a salary scale, or some other impediment, prevents them from giving you the salary you're asking for. The bottom line is that your ability to obtain additional benefits depends to a large degree on your willingness to raise the issue with a prospective employer, along with the ability to furnish convincing reasons to justify what you're asking for.

Q: In my job I'm required to do a lot of travel by automobile to manage project teams doing on-site work. In my present position I use a company car. I'm considering a position with another company that requires the use of your own automobile with reimbursement at a mileage rate for company business. In doing some figuring, I find it will cost me money on this basis. In fact, up front it will cost me a lot of money, since I'm driving an old clunker, and with the amount of miles I will have to travel on business, I need to buy a new car for reliable transportation. Furthermore, I'll be putting miles on the new car quickly, which means I will be replacing it a lot sooner than I ordinarily would. For this reason, even though the salary the company is offering is satisfactory, this situation diminishes its worth. How should I deal with this issue in negotiating the terms of my employment?

A: This situation shows how you have to weigh the total compensation package you're offered and not make a decision just on the basis of salary. An otherwise attractive salary quickly becomes unappealing if the benefits or conditions of employment cost you money out of pocket. Here, you should raise this issue directly. It will help if you can show what the company policy will cost you in monetary terms. Since the company has a policy in place, it's unlikely they will change it to provide you with a vehicle. On the other hand, it's reasonable to assume they would be willing to adjust your salary accordingly to compensate for your financial loss. As another alternative, they may be willing to give you a monthly car allowance. Naturally, if you're unsuccessful in obtaining any form of concession on the matter, you have to reassess your willingness to accept the position after factoring in the additional costs you will incur.

Q: I've got a great job offer in Utah, which means my spouse and I will be relocating from Virginia. The only hitch is that this move will require my husband to job hunt in the Salt Lake City area. Aside from being potentially unemployed for a while, neither of us is familiar with the area, so we don't know where to start in terms of his searching for a comparable position to the one he now has. Would it be feasible to raise this problem with my prospective employer, and if so, when's the proper time to mention this?

A: It's not only feasible but proper to raise this issue. Two-career households are commonplace and employers recognize this. And while some companies only sympathize with the problem, others have formal spousal assistance programs and will aggressively assist in helping a trailing spouse to land a job. As for the proper time to raise the issue, you're better off doing so before you accept the job offer. Once you become the job candidate of choice for the company, your negotiating position is at its high point. And although the company may still be willing to provide assistance after you accept the position, there's less of an urgency on their part to help solve your problem.

Q: **I'm considering accepting a job offer with a start-up company. The salary isn't great and the fringe benefits are minimal, but I've been offered a pretty substantial stock option package that could yield significant sums in the future. Furthermore, if the company grows rapidly, I'll be in senior management within a short period of time. How do I go about determining whether or not to accept the risks involved for the prospect of substantial financial gain in the future?**

A: With any new job there are risks; in some jobs more than others. On the other hand, there are risks in trying to hang on to your present job if the future of the company isn't too bright. The first thing you have to determine is the amount of risk you are willing to accept. It's rather like making the same determination you would concerning your investment strategy. In fact, this sort of situation is a career investment, which can soar or go sour much like any other investment.

If the salary is one you can live with, then the next step is to determine the odds of the company succeeding so you can reap your rewards. If it's financially feasible for you to do so, you might want to secure the services of a financial analyst to investigate the prospects of the new enterprise. Otherwise, do all the research you can on your own. Is the firm sufficiently capitalized? What business experience and expertise do the founders have? Does the product or service being offered by the new company have competition, and if not, why not?

By looking into the matter as much as you can, you will get a better picture of the potential risks involved. Incidentally, don't be shy about raising your questions with the person who is offering you the position. If the answers to your questions aren't forthcoming, or are vague, it should give you pause about accepting the job. Finally, if you do decide to go ahead and accept the job offer, make sure you get some form of employment contract in writing. It, of course, should contain the terms of any stock options or equity provisions to safeguard yourself. It is also advisable to have your attorney review the document before you sign it.

Although you can't guard against the potential failure of the new enterprise in the future, you can certainly take steps to minimize your career risks. Don't be shy in this sort of situation, since a new enterprise needs your management expertise a lot more than you need the risks involved. For this reason, you are in a solid negotiating position.

Q: How can I distinguish between benefits that are negotiable and those that aren't? After all, I don't want to overdo it in asking for too much.

A: Obviously everything a company offers in the way of benefits isn't negotiable. Those that are pretty much set are the standard benefit package offered to all employees such as medical benefits, vacations, employee assistance programs, and so forth. Other benefits will vary with the level of the job you're seeking. Top executives generally have stock option and bonus provisions not available in lower-level management positions. What you want to do is review the benefit package being offered and then raise the issue of any benefits you may be looking for. However, always have a justifiable reason to support your request.

For example, say something such as, "I'll be losing a $10,000 performance bonus I would have earned on my present job. I obviously have to consider that in terms of any salary and benefit offer I receive. What sort of bonus program will be available to me here?" This tells the interviewer that you're looking for some form of compensation for the bonus you will lose on your current job. Undoubtedly, this will lead to a discussion of whatever bonus programs will be available to you. It may also inspire some form of signing bonus being offered to you as partial compensation for the loss of your other bonus. This is especially true if the employer doesn't want to distort internal pay scales by paying you a salary that is beyond the range for the position. Of course, it's also financially advantageous to give you a one-time bonus rather than increase your salary significantly.

Certainly you should raise issues such as this, but it doesn't mean you will be totally successful—or even partially so—in getting what you want. After all, the prospective employer's negotiator may decide that the company isn't going to compensate you for a lost performance bonus as a result of you leaving another job. On the other hand, it depends upon your bargaining power. If they want you badly enough, they will go to some length to be creative in terms of how they can entice you to accept the position. Just be sure you are realistic in terms of assessing your worth to prospective employers. Nevertheless, if you're going to err, do so on the side of being aggressive in asking for an employment package that meets your needs. Otherwise, you may accept a position only to find out later that you shortchanged yourself. That, of course, isn't good for either you or your employer, so companies expect job candidates to be forthright about the employment package they're looking for before being hired, rather than complaining about it later.

HOW TO BARGAIN IN JOB INTERVIEWS

The bottom line in negotiating the best possible employment package ultimately rests on your skill in presenting your position during the interview process. Obtaining the best salary and benefit package requires the ability to project confidence in presenting yourself as a job candidate who is well worth the compensation you seek. Nevertheless, self-confidence alone won't carry the day. You also have to be able to convince those interviewing you of the benefits to be gained by securing your services. Doing this successfully isn't difficult if you're prepared, but it's a hopeless task if you're not. So let's look at some of the hurdles you may face, and how you can easily overcome them.

Q: I had an interview not too long ago where the interviewer mentioned my current boss, said he knew him, and that he was a tough person to work for. I agreed, and the discussion never went any further than that. I'm wondering if I gave an appropriate response since I didn't get the job. Should I have said something different?

A: Interviewers will sometimes ask vague questions designed to elicit a different response than you would give if you recognized the true intent of the question. You may think you're responding to what was being asked when the interviewer's question had an entirely different intent. At other times, interviewers may make a statement to see if—and how—you respond to it.

On the surface agreeing with the interviewer's question that your boss was tough to work for can be interpreted a couple of ways. It could simply mean he's a hard taskmaster who expects things to get done. That's certainly not a bad trait. It could, however, have a negative implication that he's a difficult boss or perhaps even an out-and-out S.O.B. If that's what the interviewer was implying then it didn't serve your cause to agree with him, even if the statement was true.

This sort of response can leave the impression that you're not very loyal to your boss. And no one is going to hire someone whom they view as being potentially disloyal. One of the cardinal rules for job interviews is to refrain from any criticism of any present or former employer. Furthermore, interviewers aren't interested in any blow-by-blow details that you could furnish to prove your case. From where they sit, anything said is self-serving, since they can't confirm it. Therefore, always be positive in any statements made on this subject. For instance, when the interviewer made the statement about your boss being tough, you could have responded by saying something such as, "I've always found him to be fair, and I've never experienced any difficulty with him." This statement can't be misconstrued.

Whenever an interviewer asks you leading questions, vague questions, or those that can result in misleading answers, always seek clarification of the question before you respond. For example, when the interviewer remarked about your boss being tough you could have responded by saying, "I didn't realize you worked for him. Why did you find him to be tough?" Not only does this require the interviewer to define what he means, but it also gives you information as to how the interviewer knows anything about your boss. It may even be that this information is based on something another applicant told the interviewer.

Q: At a recent interview I had a very unpleasant experience. I was hardly seated when the person interviewing me started making references to how much money I was making in my present job, and even went so far as to ask if I had a mentor pushing me along since I had progressed so fast. I simply answered that my progress was based on hard work and ability. The interviewer then said he couldn't hire me since I was already making more money than he was. I then asked why I was called for an interview, and was told the person wanted to see who I was. I then replied that there was no point in continuing the interview. Frankly, I was pretty miffed and wouldn't have gone to work for this person no matter what. I then said I'll check out through personnel as they told me to stop back after the inter-

view. The person who interviewed me said that wasn't necessary and directed me to the exit. To be honest, if I had gone to personnel on the way out, I would have told them how unhappy I was about being called for an interview when there was no intent to hire me in the first place. Can you make anything of what happened here?

A: There are instances where a potential boss won't hire anyone whom he or she perceives to be a career threat. These people are very insecure and prefer to hire those who aren't quite as competent. You're always better off not getting these jobs since you would only be stymied every step of the way in terms of career advancement. You apparently ran into such a situation here, although it's an extreme example. Usually, in these situations, the person is at least smart enough and subtle enough to go through the motions. Here you had the misfortune to run into someone who really should be worried about the person he hires, since anyone with any ability will easily outshine him if given the opportunity.

Q: **I've been offered a pretty good package of salary and benefits and have a final meeting with my new employer scheduled to iron out the details. I'm in a bit of a quandary, since I don't want to do anything to lose this job. On the other hand, if I work seven more weeks in my present position, I'll be eligible for about $7,000 in profit sharing. I remember it being mentioned that the new company wanted me to start work in four weeks. Should I just forget about the money or try to work something out with my new employer?**

A: You're only talking three weeks, so I wouldn't casually throw $7,000 away. Unfortunately, this is an issue that you should have raised the minute the interviewer asked when you would be available, assuming that was done. If that subject hasn't been raised yet, it's even less of a problem. In any event, just tell the interviewer your dilemma when you meet tomorrow. Phrase it in such a way that you'll start in four weeks if it's absolutely necessary, but would prefer to start in seven weeks if it's at all possible. It's highly unlikely the company will let another three weeks stand in the way of hiring their preferred candidate.

Frankly, starting dates aren't generally a major issue in negotiations, except in rare situations where an employer has an urgent need to fill a position. Nevertheless, they can arise, such as when someone is trying to fill a vacancy before a hiring freeze takes effect. However, even here there are ways to finagle the deal if the people doing the hiring are creative at working around bureaucratic procedures.

Q: What should I get in writing when I receive an offer of employment?

A: Get everything you can in writing. Naturally, companies are reluctant to put too much in writing since they don't want to commit themselves to anything that can come back to haunt them in the form of a lawsuit if things don't work out. Nevertheless. as a minimum you should receive an offer letter setting forth the starting date, salary, position, and other basic details. If you have negotiated anything out of the ordinary, this also should be included in the written agreement so there's no misunderstanding. It's also useful to get any termination provisions spelled out including the amount of severance pay to which you will be entitled. Of course, the higher the management position you are occupying, the more complex any written agreement should be. At higher levels, you would obviously expect an employment contract covering the terms of employment and what happens upon termination. These extensive agreements should not be undertaken without securing legal advice. You can bet that the company has used their legal counsel in drawing up the document, so you certainly should insist on having your attorney review it before it's signed.

Q: I'm about to accept an offer of employment for a senior management position. The headhunter who initially contacted me about the position says the employment contract looks great and I should just go ahead and sign it without having my attorney review it. Is this wise?

A: No. The contract may be perfect in the eyes of the headhunter since he or she has probably seen thousands of them. You, at best, have probably only seen a handful during your career. Even though the headhunter may be expressing an honest opinion, you're the one signing the contract. Furthermore, the headhunter has a vested interest in completing a successful search, since his or her compensation may be based upon that. Naturally, over the long term any recruiter's reputation depends in part on the future success of the person he or she placed in the position. However, first and foremost you want to be reassured that the document passes legal muster in protecting your interests. Therefore, no matter what advice you're given, or however well-intentioned it may appear, take the time to have your own lawyer look the document over.

Q: How do I handle the standard question of why I'm leaving my current position?

A: With an answer that implies you're bottlenecked in advancing your career in your present job and are looking for challenging opportunities and greater responsibilities that you feel the company you're interviewing with can provide. Be matter of fact about it, without reflecting negatively on your present employer. And even though you want to project self-confidence, don't go overboard to the extent of implying you're too good to be true. No one appreciates someone with a big ego, and when you're being interviewed the power to deflate an ego rests with the people doing the hiring.

Q: I'm looking for a job since my company is downsizing. My position isn't in danger yet, but it may be in the future, and I don't want to start looking for a job from the unemployment line. Should I tell prospective employers that I'm looking for another position because my company is cutting back?

A: If it's common knowledge and the interviewer asks about it, you can acknowledge it as one of the reasons. If you do this, though, emphasize that you don't think your job is at risk. If your position is safe despite cutbacks, it conveys the impression that you're relatively indispensable even when times are tough. This creates a favorable impression of your capabilities.

On the other hand, if an interviewer senses you're desperate to obtain employment, then it weakens your negotiation position. You're in a much better position to be offered a better deal if there's no apparent urgency attached to obtaining another job. Therefore, if it's feasible, don't let prospective employers know you're looking for a job because of pending cutbacks where you work.

Incidentally, if your job has been cut, let the interviewer know the details if it shows your job loss was in no way a reflection of your capabilities. For example, if you can assert something such as, "The entire marketing department here in Albuquerque was eliminated, and all of the functions will now be handled from headquarters in Minneapolis," this will readily explain why you're looking for work.

Q: I've been out of work for three months after being fired. A new division vice-president was appointed and he wanted to put his own people in key slots, so I was told my position was being abolished. I don't know how to explain this in interviews so I tend to gloss over it. I think interviewers may think I'm trying to hide something. Is there a better way to handle this situation when I'm asked why I left my last job?

A: Be both factual and brief in your answer. Say something such as, "A new executive came on board and wanted to fill key positions with his own people." People lose jobs left and right for all sorts of reasons, so there's nothing to be ashamed of. The danger is in lying or being hesitant to the degree that the interviewer thinks you're trying to hide something.

Q: Is there a particularly good point in the interview process to raise questions about salary or fringes?

A: Raise issues on anything that you want to negotiate at the point that the interviewer brings the matter up. Don't leave everything until the very end and then ask if it's possible to do this or that. All this will serve to do is aggravate the interviewer. Even worse, from your standpoint, there's a much greater likelihood that the interviewer will be more inclined to try and brush off any of your requests. Just as with any other negotiation, interviewers don't like to be confronted with last-minute roadblocks just when they think everything is pretty well wrapped up.

Q: Won't trying to bargain for a higher salary tend to be viewed negatively by an interviewer?

A: To the contrary. Someone who is assertive is sought after, while someone who is passive tends to be viewed as indecisive. Companies are looking for managers who can get the job done, not people who shirk from confronting difficult issues. Therefore, your willingness to look out for your best interests is expected by interviewers, and is far preferable to creating an image of someone who isn't assertive. Nevertheless, don't carry your desire to get the best deal you can to the extreme. If you go over the line by trying to nickel and dime for more after you have been offered an acceptable salary, it can have negative connotations. For one thing, it can create the impression that all you care about is money rather than the job. If an interviewer senses this, it's logical to conclude that if you're hired you may quickly jump ship the next time a few more dollars are dangled in front of you.

Q: **What's the best way to support arguments for a higher salary, or unusual perks or benefits?**

A: Naturally, it's to prove your worth in terms of what you're asking for. Therefore, you want to be as convincing as possible in making your case. The better you're able to show your potential value to prospective employers, the greater your chances for getting what you want. A great way to support your claims is with written documentation or third-party testimonials. After all, no matter how eloquent you may be at presenting your achievements, there's always the unavoidable fact that you're touting your own wares so to speak. Therefore, interviewers are prone to downgrade anything you say in making their assessment of your value. However, it can create a significant impact if you are able to reach in your briefcase and pull out documentation where others have commended you for precisely what you're talking about. Needless to say, don't be shy about touting your abilities, and if you can produce paperwork to prove it, so much the better.

Q: **I've received a job offer but have decided to stay put with my present employer for another year until my youngest daughter finishes high school. What's the best way to turn this offer down without eliminating myself from future possibilities with this employer?**

A: Be forthright about it and say, "I really like the position you have offered me and thoroughly enjoyed meeting with you. However, my daughter has one year left in school, and after much thought I've decided it would be better not to relocate until she finishes." This is a valid reason anyone can understand, so it leaves the door open for the future. Any sound reason won't lead to bad feelings, but if you use excuses that are critical of the job or company who made you the offer, they won't be happy about it. Another thing that won't sit well is telling someone you accepted a counteroffer from your present employer. In this regard, it doesn't pay to have an attitude of not caring since you won't ever be working for that company. You never know where in the future you may cross paths with someone who interviewed you, so being diplomatic protects your future interests.

Aside from giving a good reason for rejecting an offer, you should also write a brief "thank you" note to everyone who interviewed you. This is such a small thing to do, but it's so often neglected that it sets you apart in people's minds. Therefore, if someone has a future opening, they may well remember you and give you a call.

Q: I recently had the experience of enduring a group interview that I found to be very difficult. For one thing, I didn't have much time to think since the minute I answered someone's question, someone else was asking me something. Furthermore, it wasn't very structured, and it kept jumping from topic to topic, including some questions that didn't have much relevance to the job. How can I be better prepared for group interviews in the future?

A: First, always be consistent with your answers. Nothing will make you look worse than giving different responses to similar questions. This may seem like a no-brainer, but when questions are coming at you left and right from several sources, it's easy to get confused. For this reason, in group interviews strive to make your answers short and direct. In addition, don't fall into the trap of directing most of your answers to one person. You may notice one dominant personality in a group interview and wrongly assume that's the person who will make the hiring decision, when it may be someone else, or even a committee decision. So if you inadvertently ignore people, they might not like it, which won't bode well for your chances of being hired.

If it's possible, try to learn something beforehand about the people who will be interviewing you. If you're working with a recruiter, he or she may be able to brief you on the personalities involved, or you may be able to get information from contacts who are familiar with the company you're interviewing with. Above all, keep your cool and remain calm. Take your time answering questions, since your composure alone will be a plus in your behalf.

NEGOTIATING RELOCATION BENEFITS

If you accept a position that will require you to relocate, there will be additional items to be negotiated in your employment package. First and foremost will be the relocation costs to be paid by your new employer. It does not stop there, though, since any relocation requires a more in-depth analysis on your part of what sort of offer you will consider to be acceptable. And in doing this, there are many elements you will have to take into consideration, some of which will be obvious and others less so. Let's look at some of these factors and how best to handle them when you're discussing an employment offer.

Q: I certainly understand the financial considerations involved in moving from one part of the country to another, but what about some of the intangible benefits? How do I factor these into what I consider to be an acceptable job offer? What I'm referring to are such things as moving away from family and friends and things of this nature. They obviously can't be quantified in dollars and cents. Nevertheless, it's worth something additional to me to have to pull up roots and move. Therefore, I would expect to be compensated better than I would if I was changing jobs locally.

A: You can't put a number on the many intangibles involved in relocating from one geographic area to another, but even though you can't quantify them, you may want to estimate their value to you. This is a very personal matter. Some managers are very reluctant to relocate for a job no matter how good the career opportunity may be. For these folks, an outstanding compensation package will never completely substitute for the loss of geographic proximity to family and friends. Then, there are those who welcome periodic moves to a different locale. For this group, the question of placing a premium on what would be a sufficient job offer to entice them to move isn't necessary. In fact, there are people who would be willing to accept a lesser compensation package for the opportunity to relocate to a desirable area.

If you do decide that you will relocate only if the career opportunity and compensation package are sufficient to overcome the negative aspects of relocation, then you should be as practical as possible in establishing your requirements. Admittedly, this isn't easy to do, since in large part these are emotional factors, especially if you're distancing yourself from close family ties. Nevertheless, don't exaggerate on either the positive or negative side. For example, communicating with your family and friends long distance may not be as difficult as you perceive it to be. And from the flip side, the dream resort area you always vacation in may not be quite as desirable a place to reside permanently, if you evaluate the community closely.

The bottom line in all this is that you have to carefully assess your willingness to relocate. When you do, you may decide relocation isn't an option for you. On the other hand, you may decide it's not your first choice, but if a good enough opportunity comes along, you'll make the move. What will be a good enough offer to entice you is a subjective judgment, but if you would change jobs locally for a 20% increase in salary, you may decide 30% is necessary to make a long-distance move.

Q: When I'm negotiating with a possible employer, how do I go about presenting a case for a higher salary because I will have to relocate?

A: First, diplomatically. You obviously can't infer you need more money to relocate to a city that records an average annual snowfall of fifty inches if you hate cold weather. After all, the people you're interviewing with may be natives who think it's the greatest locale in the world. But beyond the need to exercise diplomacy, you don't want to imply you're less than enthusiastic about relocating. Otherwise, you won't even be offered a position. Savvy interviewers look for clues from job candidates that indicate a reluctance to relocate. No company wants to go through the expense of hiring people and paying relocation expenses, only to have them quit in six months because they aren't happy living in the new community.

For this reason, concentrate on justifying your salary demands based upon your value to the company. However, it's certainly justifiable to say something such as, "Although I'm really excited about the job, and even though your relocation package is excellent, there are still both hidden expenses and disruptive influences involved in moving from one location to another." This statement is both factual and serves as justification for a higher salary.

Q: Why would a company be willing to pay more to someone who is relocating than someone from the local area?

A: One simple reason. You're the best candidate for the job. Never forget that when you're negotiating with a prospective employer. A company isn't going to pay thousands of dollars to relocate someone if they have as good a candidate locally. There's a caution to be noted here, though. If you're moving from a high-cost area to a lower-cost one, the compensation package offered could conceivably be less than you were making—relocation or no relocation. As a result, you have to factor in living costs in formulating your salary demands when you are contemplating a move from high-cost to low-cost areas, as well as the reverse.

Q: I presently reside in a midsize Midwestern city, and I'm contemplating moving to a large East Coast city. Before I do any serious job hunting, I want to know what salary range I should be looking for. I know it's more expensive to live in the city I'll be moving too, but I don't have any particular details to go by. What types of data should I be looking for and where will I find them?

A: Statistics are published by the federal government as well as private organizations, and local cost-of-living indexes are available from different sources. The problem isn't so much finding data as it is finding useful data. For one thing, comparing average salaries between two distant locales doesn't tell you much, since the cost of living may vary significantly in the two areas. Even regional price indexes can be deceptive. Take housing costs, for example. The price of essentially the same house can vary significantly in two adjacent suburbs. This can be accounted for by factors such as better schools, higher or lower property taxes, the proximity to shopping, and any number of other factors. Even something as intangible as people's perception that one community is a cut above another as the place to live can translate into paying more for the same house.

For this reason, the preferred way to get a handle on cost differences is to spend some time in the community in which you'll be relocating. Find out in person what the cost of housing is in the particular area of a new community where you will be buying a house. If this isn't feasible, get several back issues of the local paper from the city to which you will be relocating. Not only will you pick up a great deal of information on schools, shopping, crime, and so forth, but the real estate section will give you good clues as to what comparable housing will cost you.

Q: I live in a state where state and local taxes are high and I'm considering relocating to an area where taxes are lower. Is this wise?

A: State and local tax considerations should be at best only a secondary consideration in any career move. Where taxes are low today, they may be higher tomorrow, so basing job decisions on such factors is a dicey move.

Q: I recently had a job interview in a distant city, and while I was there I checked out the local housing market. What surprised me was that the average selling price of houses was about the same as where I now live, but for the average price I'd be getting a much better house. How come, since the average price is the same?

A: Average housing prices are deceptive when it comes to making comparisons. The quality of house you buy in two different communities can differ markedly even though the average selling price is the same. A major reason is the makeup of the housing that goes into the averages. Let's look at a simple example:

City A and City B both have a recent average selling price of $250,000 for homes in their respective areas. Since you happen to be looking for a home in that price range, you anticipate no problems. However, it turns out that the makeup of the homes for sale in both communities differs so that only City A offers any significant number of homes in your price range of $250,000. To illustrate this, let's look at a price breakdown of five homes in each city which is representative of the overall sales pattern.

House Selling Price	City A	City B
1	$300,000	$350,000
2	250,000	400,000
3	200,000	150,000
4	240,000	180,000
5	260,000	170,000
Average selling price	$250,000	$250,000

From looking at the figures it's easy to see that City A had three sales right around the $250,000 you want to pay for a house, while in City B all the sales were for more or less expensive homes than you want. Obviously the example is simplified to demonstrate the point and any sizable city will have housing stock in all price ranges. Nevertheless, there are substantive differences in what you get for your housing money from one area to another. For this reason, average price figures are only a very rough guideline. You have to know the makeup of the housing stock in the area you're moving to, and even more important the price of homes in the neighborhoods you want to live in.

Q: I recently suffered housing cost sticker shock. For the most part, housing prices in the city where I'm relocating are comparable to where I now live. The problem is that in the area that has the best schools, the housing is considerably higher than what I expected to pay. Is this typical?

A: You can find considerable differences in house prices from one area to the next in a community. People with children are usually willing to pay a premium for housing to live in what is at least perceived to be a better school district. As a result, if you have school-age children, it's important to determine housing costs in the area where the best schools are located. Otherwise, you may find yourself getting hit with the hidden expense of private schooling if you're not satisfied with the quality of the local schools. You have to investigate all these factors when you're making relocation decisions. Otherwise, that great salary package you've been offered will be quickly eaten up by added expenses you did not anticipate.

Q: How do I bring up the subject of housing costs or other expenses I anticipate incurring when I'm negotiating a compensation package with a prospective employer?

A: The bottom line is you have to tell it like it is. If you find the expense of relocating will cost you out of pocket, raise the issue when you're discussing salary and benefits. What, if any, your costs will be will vary, both due to your own circumstances, as well as the relocation assistance package offered by your prospective employer. Even if the employer's relocation package won't cover a particular expense, such as housing, an employer who recognizes a valid obstacle may try to come up with an alternative to solve the problem. For instance, if the employer's relocation expense policy won't allow you to buy a comparable house because of higher housing costs, the employer may be willing to give you a signing bonus or a low-interest loan. The possibilities are varied, but when you're dealing with these issues, you have to be informed and willing to lay the problems on the table. Otherwise, your options will be limited to turning down an offer because you don't feel you can afford the move financially or else making the move and living to regret it at a later date.

Q: I was talking to a friend who told me that I shouldn't worry too much about the cost of living when I relocate, since salaries tend to be competitive with the cost of living in different areas. In other words, where salaries are higher, costs are also higher, so they tend to balance out, with the same being true with lower salaries and costs. Is this true?

A: They equate only in a very broad way, and you can run into serious problems if you rely on generalized data rather than working out the specifics of your own situation. For example, both salaries and living costs are higher in the metropolitan areas of the northeastern United States, than in, for example, rural areas of the South. But look at one problem you could run into if you moved from a small southern town to New York City. Sure, you will probably get a substantial boost in pay. But let's assume you owned a home in the southern town that you can sell for $80,000. Let's say to buy a comparable house in the New York metropolitan area would cost you $240,000. All things being equal, you will get the additional cost of the new home back when you sell it. However, the immediate problem is that you have to come up with the financing to pay for a much more expensive house. Sure, your salary is now higher, but it will be a long time before you recoup the additional housing expense from your monthly paycheck. In the meantime, unless you have a lot of equity built up in the home you're going to sell, you're faced with stiff mortgage payments, and perhaps have to come up with a chunk of cash for a down payment. So much for that great pay package you've been offered. To answer the question specifically, salaries and living expenses don't precisely parallel each other. But of even greater importance is your personal situation. Everything from school-age children, to a working spouse, to commuting distances can influence your income and expenses. Therefore, you have to work out the details of your own situation and not rely on generalized figures.

Q: I've wanted to relocate to a particular area for a number of years, but I've always hesitated in even looking for a job because everyone tells me salaries are lower where I want to go. Even though I've heard that the cost of living is also lower, I can't put a precise handle on how that would work out in terms of making less money. What I fear is accepting a salary 10 or 20% lower and then discovering it's costing just as much to live there as in my present location. Is there a way to work this out so I know where I stand?

A: This is a situation that requires careful analysis and knowing what to look at and what to ignore in terms of various cost-of-living factors. It's further complicated by word-of-mouth assertions by acquaintances and others who frequently have little on which to base their statements. The biggest hurdle of all is money. When people think salary, they neglect to consider purchasing power or what that salary will buy. For this reason, a lower salary is equated with having to make do with a lower standard of living. That simply isn't the case, since in some areas you can live a lot better on what you earn than in other areas. Incidentally, this concentration on salary to the exclusion of living costs can cause problems, not only when you consider moving from a high- to a low-cost area, but equally so when the reverse holds true. Someone who receives a significantly higher salary offer to move to a high-cost area of the country is inclined to jump at the opportunity without considering the higher costs involved in maintaining their standard of living. As a result, when a job offer is forthcoming, candidates don't always relate the salary to the expenses of living in the new area.

In fact, even within the same state, the difference in living costs in different areas can be substantial, so this isn't just a problem involving long-distance relocation. For example, housing costs alone, can vary widely over a very short distance. Since housing is generally the major component of your living costs, this alone can make the same salary go a lot further if you live in an area where housing is less expensive.

In any analysis, of course, you can't ignore trade-offs. For example, if housing is cheaper, but you'll have a much longer commute to work, then what you save on housing may be eaten up on transportation. There are all sorts of variables that can make your situation different from someone else. For example, take two couples who move to an area where housing is less expensive. The public schools in this area, however, are perceived to be of relatively low quality. As a result, one couple with school-age children has to spend thousands of dollars to send their children to private school, while the other couple without school-age children reap the savings from the lower-cost housing.

In general there are two important things to be said about the importance of living costs when you're job hunting. First, unless the cost-of-living differential is significant, ignore it, since your personal spending habits will outweigh any minor difference in costs. This is simply to say that unless you're one of those rare people who are truly disciplined in your personal financial planning, saving a few dollars on living costs won't show up in your bank account. Second, if the cost of living is substantially different from one area to another—either higher or lower—take it into account in negotiating your employment package, but, unless it's absolutely justified, don't let it override making a sound move that will advance your career.

Q: This whole area of cost of living and salary is confusing. Could you give me an example for comparative purposes?

A: Let's assume that someone named John G. who lives in the Northeast has been offered a management position with a company in the Sun Belt. His current salary is $100,000, and he has been offered a comparable job that pays $90,000. Let's look at some of the considerations John takes into account in figuring whether it's worthwhile to accept the lower salary.

Housing

After considerable research, John, who has been renting, is planning to buy a house. He knows he can buy a comparable house in the new community for $50,000 less than where he presently lives. So for starters, John's mortgage will be $50,000 less if he decides to relocate. Assuming principal and interest payments of $10 per month per $1,000 on the mortgage, John will pay $500 per month less on his mortgage. His property taxes in the Sun Belt location will also be $50 per month less, for total out-of-pocket savings of $550 per month on housing costs.

Taxes

Based on lower state and local income and sales taxes in the state where John has been offered a job, he calculates he will save another $50 per month, which brings his total savings to $600 a month.

Summary

Let's look at a rough salary comparison of the two jobs with the facts we know.

	Current Salary	*Job Offer*
	100,000	90,000
Federal taxes (assume 20%)	20,000	18,000
Net income after federal taxes	80,000	72,000
First-year mortgage payments	17,400	10,800

	Current Salary	*Job Offer*
(Assume $1,450 mortgage at current location, which will drop to $900 per month at new location, which represents $500 in principal and interest and $50 in property taxes per month)		
Net income after federal taxes and mortgage	$62,600	$61,200
First-year payments on state and local sales and income taxes (assume John pays $2,600 at current location and estimates his first-year taxes at $2,000 if he relocates)	2,600	2,000
Disposable income after taxes and mortgage	$60,000	$59,200

Based on this example even though John will be making $10,000 less in salary in the new job, he is losing only $800 out of pocket in his first year after relocating. All other things being equal, he probably wouldn't take the job unless he could get more money.

On the other hand, if John has strong personal reasons for wanting to move to the new area (perhaps it offers life-style advantages), then going through the calculations lets John realize that he really isn't giving up $10,000 in purchasing power by accepting the lower salary.

Caution

This example is obviously oversimplified, and changing the assumptions, naturally, will change the result. However, the example does show that the cost of living can have an impact from one area to another. What it is for any particular individual will depend on the financial situation of that person, as well as their mode of living.

Comments

This example is, of course, basic, and there are any number of other factors to consider such as commuting costs in both locations. For example, John might have used public transportation to get to his current job, but because of a lack of public transportation, he may have to purchase another car if he accepts the job offer. This would, in turn, lower or completely negate any savings from relocating. The important point is that you have to evaluate all the factors surrounding a move to ascertain how good the salary being offered is in terms of your actual purchasing power in the new location as opposed to your current place of residence.

Q: I'm looking to change careers since even though I know I will have to take a cut in pay, it's what I want to do at this stage of my life. I am further thinking of moving to an area where the cost of living is much higher than where I presently live. I know this is a foolish question, but is this a smart move?

A: No matter how much you analyze the situation and how hard you work to negotiate the best deal you can when you're looking for a job, the final determination on what you decide doesn't depend upon logic, mathematical analysis, or negotiation skills. It comes down to what you want to do with the rest of your life. You're far better off sacrificing money for happiness. Otherwise, years later you may be financially successful, but regret not doing what you know you would have enjoyed doing. For this reason alone, pursue your goals first. You can always go back to your former career, but if you don't give yourself the chance to try something different, you may never know what you missed.

INDEX

S

T